DATE DUE

SEP 30 Ret	OCT 24	Ret JUN.08.1988	RET
APR 2 8 Ret	SEP 1 6	Ret NOV.28.1990	RET
JUL Ret		APR 1 8 1997	
NOV 1 3 Ret		OCT 0 4 2004	
NOV 2 6 Ret Ret			
FEB 2 1 Ret			
FEB 2 7 Ret			
APR 2 4 Ret			
Ret			
FEB 2 7 Ret			

*Philosophical
Theology*

IN TWO VOLUMES

VOLUME II

Philosophical Theology

by

F. R. TENNANT,

D.D. (Camb.), B.Sc. (Lond.), Hon. D.D. (Oxon.)

*Fellow of Trinity College & Lecturer
in the University of
Cambridge*

VOLUME II

THE WORLD, THE SOUL,
AND GOD

CAMBRIDGE

AT THE UNIVERSITY PRESS

1930

REPRINTED

1968

Published by the Syndics of the Cambridge University Press
Bentley House, 200 Euston Road, London, N.W. 1
American Branch: 32 East 57th Street, New York, N.Y. 10022

PUBLISHER'S NOTE

Cambridge University Press Library Editions are re-issues of out-of-print standard works from the Cambridge catalogue. The texts are unrevised and, apart from minor corrections, reproduce the latest published edition.

Standard Book Number: 521 07434 7
Library of Congress Catalogue Card Number: 29-3316

First published 1930
Reprinted 1968

First printed in Great Britain at the University Press, Cambridge
Reprinted in Great Britain by John Dickens & Co. Ltd, Northampton

PREFACE

This volume is continuous with the first. But while its opening chapters still carry on the inquiry, begun in the preceding volume, into the scope and nature of science of the physical world, they also contain the first stages of an argument for theism, and so effect the transition from philosophical prolegomena to natural theology.

Professor E. W. Hobson has been so kind as to read this part of my work while it was in manuscript, and I am gratefully indebted to him for comments and suggestions of which I have made use.

I would also express my thanks to the Syndics of the Cambridge University Press for their permission to reproduce some of the substance of essays which I had previously contributed to a volume entitled *The Elements of Pain and Conflict in Human Life*, etc., and to Messrs Hodder and Stoughton for allowing me to reprint passages from articles of mine which had appeared in *The Expositor*.

F. R. TENNANT

1929

CONTENTS

CONTENTS ix

pages

CONTENTS ix

CONTENTS ix

pages

CHAPTER I

The Conformity of the World to Law

INTRODUCTION.

In the first volume of this work, entitled *The Soul and its Faculties*, the several mental processes and products comprised by the name 'knowledge' were examined, and kinds of cognition were distinguished in which private percepts, common Objects, pure ideas, and ontal entities co-operating with subjects to produce phenomena, are respectively said to be known, or known about. The only ontal thing, as to whose essence even a pittance of 'knowledge' of any kind was there claimed to have been found, is the soul itself.

In the present volume, in which transition from propaedeutic studies to theological issues will before long be made, the possibility of passing from phenomenal knowledge of the external world to knowledge as to its ontal nature is one of the first problems to be investigated. Our attention will therefore move from science, considered as knowledge-process, in which aspect alone it has thus far been treated, to science as also a knowledge-product. The structure, as well as the constructing of the architecture, of theoretical physics, as distinguished from the lower storey of empirical fact and observable law from which this superstructure rises, will likewise call for examination. For it is this part of what is elastically covered by the name 'science' that has suggested a world-theory in which science has been alleged to issue. Some study of this field is indispensable to the philosophical theologian for several reasons. Firstly, the world-view which has issued from theoretical physics takes the physical world to be the primary existent, the soul to be subsidiary or derivative, and God to be a precarious, if not a superfluous, supposition. Thus an alternative to the theistic view of the world is offered, of which the theist must take account. Further, if, as was maintained in the preceding volume, there be no special faculty of the soul, supplying (ps)[1] immediate knowledge of God or even of other souls, natural

---

[1] The letters (ps) and (ψ) are abbreviations for 'psychological' and 'psychic', as technically used to designate two different standpoints of an experient: see vol. 1, p. 46.

theology must be an outgrowth from discursive thought on the world, man, and man's experience. Physical science is thus one source of data for the natural theologian who would forswear the *a priori*, and follow the empirical, approach to cosmology and theology. Such will none the less be the case if he should come to find that other categories than those used in physical theory, and concepts derived from what, for philosophy, is a more fundamental science, are requisite for metaphysical translation of physical facts.

The natural theologian does not need to study in detail any branch of physical science; but he should acquire the ability to judge whether theoretical physics is a means for understanding, in a special sense, the phenomenal, or is a revelation of the ontal that underlies the phenomenal. He must enable himself to weigh such reasoned views as that physics is reducible to mechanics, and that mechanics is expansible into a mechanical cosmology: views from which it would follow that the world is a closed system, under a reign of law that "binds all things fast in fate", admitting of no influence from without and allowing no spontaneity within. With materialism or mechanical naturalism, purporting to be grounded on the deliverances of science, the theologian needs to reckon. And this will involve some consideration of the classic mechanical physics, which, if now largely obsolescent, will remain historically important.[1] Whether or not this kind of science was fashioned in order to explain observable conformity to law, it contains the inter- pretation of Nature's law-abidingness that physics for a long time suggested: an interpretation which has been carried into fields other than the purely physical, though it accounts for law wholly in terms of matter, as conceived in the traditional mechanics. The theory which provides this interpretation demands consideration independently of its bearing on the question of law; but the regularity of Nature, of which it offers explanation, may be dealt with first.

---

[1] In view of the trend which physical science has taken since the late Prof. J. Ward wrote his *Naturalism and Agnosticism*, rendering some of its controversial and illus- trative matter obsolete but not affecting the value of its general epistemology, the im- portant question is no longer whether or not the world is wholly representable by a mechanical system, in the older sense, but whether it can be regarded as a rigidly determined 'closed system' of *any* kind. This more general aspect of the theological issue, it is hoped, is sufficiently dealt with, directly if incidentally, in passages of vol. I, and both directly and indirectly in the earlier chapters of this book.

I.   DOES MAN LEGISLATE FOR NATURE?

The plain matter of fact that has been spoken of as Nature's
conformity to law is the regularity of sequence and concomitance
between certain events and certain others. Cases of such regularity
must have been thrust upon human minds, and have shaped some
measure of human prudence, before men betook themselves to
social legislation and formed the forensic notion expressed by the
word 'law'. And this regularity of succession or concomitance,
apart from its causal construing as constant connexion, of other
than spatio-temporal kind, is as purely Objective and devoid of
anthropic analogising as fact can be. Analogising entered when
the idea and the name of law were borrowed from jurisprudence
for use in science. Transplanted from its original sphere, this word
'law' has carried with it associations incongruous with the altered
signification given to it in its new home; and misconceptions have
thus arisen. There is really very little likeness between civic and
natural laws. Civic enactments are imperatives of the 'thou shalt
not' kind; laws of Nature are not prescriptions to things, but
descriptions of how things have behaved and may be expected to
behave—according to one acceptation of 'law'. If natural laws are
imperatives in any sense, it is in that—according to another
acceptation, presently to be discussed—they describe invariable,
as distinct from hitherto unvarying, connexions, and so demand
recognition from all who would think truly about facts. But if
natural laws bespeak such necessitation, civic laws hint at none:
they can be, and are, broken. And civil laws do not describe unvarying sequences, etc., which is the essential function of laws in
science. Perhaps the only point in common between law proper
and law so-called is that both are man-made. Yet in this statement,
unless it be interpreted with discretion, it may be argued that there
is as much error as truth. For while civic laws are made, both as
to their content and as to their verbal form, by man, the laws of
natural phenomena are inventions only in respect of their formulation in terms of humanly devised symbols or concepts, and
apparently not at all in respect of their perceptual matter: unless,
indeed, the dismembering of the world into the more or less isolated systems that we name 'things' be but a teleological device
in all cases save when we refer to psychical organisms. But if we

find ourselves disposed to think that the bodies, between every pair of which the law of gravitation asserts the relation expressed by mm'/r^2, are only fictitious entities summoned from the deeps of creative imagination, and having no counterpart in Reality, so that the law of universal gravitation is a truth about fictions, explanation is due from us why this fancy tallies with the Actual that is appearance of the Real.[1] That in some such thoroughgoing way the human mind imposes law on Nature, and that the only order or rationality in our world is what is put there by us, has been upheld on various grounds; and these must be examined because the issue is important for ontology and theology. The view involves much more than that every law of Nature originates as a hypothesis in some mind and remains merely an invention until verification, finding it valid, proves it to be also a discovery; more than that laws, as formulated formulae, generally contain conceptual symbolism, sometimes undergo amendment or replacement, and do not exist as symbolic formulae before they are formulated. So much can be allowed without implying that, in a more ultimate sense, man gives law to Nature, even to Nature as known. It can still be held that, just as we do not set up the sequences, etc., which our science tentatively describes, so we do not read into them a regularity that they do not possess: as if the heavens first became a cosmos when Newton hit upon his law of them. Nevertheless, some philosophers have argued that the source of the conformity of the phenomenal world to law lies not at all in things *per se*, but in the *a priori* machinery, so to speak, of our understandings, or else in our selective attention guided by interest.

Historically the most important argument belonging to the former of these types is that of Kant, who taught that man legislates for Nature in prescribing the general or universal, though not the special and empirical, laws of physics. Kant's own utterances, however, with their concessions and qualifications, suggest that cross-examination would have wrung from him an admission that the universal laws are actually reached by way of abstraction from the empirical rules, there being continuity between the two, and not disparateness, in respect of origination; that these rules are

---

[1] The ambiguous, but scarcely avoidable, word 'Real' throughout the present context means ontal, or non-phenomenal.

dictated to us by Nature; and that they, in turn, as well as the forthcomingness of the sensa which they relate, must be determined by the activities of the ontal world. But, what is more important, these conclusions seem inevitable for us, once Kant's unhistorical procedure is superseded and his oversights are corrected. His 'Copernican revolution' in epistemology, and his doctrine that "the understanding is itself the source of the laws of Nature", are bound up with the *a priori* elements that dominate his theory of knowledge; and these have been rendered superfluous by the genetic psychology of common, as distinguished from individual, experience, which he so largely refrained from investigating though he was the first to descry it.

Of the other type of argument, which appeals to the selectiveness, rather than to the supposed constitutive machinery, of the mind, as sufficient for imposing order on what would otherwise be chaos, the most unequivocal instance is that presented in *The Grammar of Science* by Prof. Karl Pearson. This writer suggests that order in the co-existences and sequences of impressions is found by our minds because they are sorting-machines which, in the course of evolution, have become capable of receiving only some kinds of sensa and rejecting others; much in the same way that automatic deliverers of certain commodities will accept pence alone and refuse other coins. But, even supposing this analogy were psychologically correct, it does not help to account for regularity of connexion within the kinds of sense-data selected, such as makes formulation of law possible. The fact that in a rainbow we discern but seven out of an indefinite number of colours will not suffice to explain the unvarying order of the seven colours in the rainbow. Attention to what interests, and ignoring of the indifferent and unpleasant, would indeed carry us some way toward instituting regularity of *experience* in a world presenting recurrences, yet without law unto itself; but even this would not take us far towards imposing on our world the many laws found by science, which is ever on the look-out for facts of every sort, whether practically interesting or not.

That all these laws, with the exception of those of atomicity, 'action', and *quanta*, and all the *Gesetzmässigkeit* of molar and phenomenal Nature, as set forth by physicists, are of human prescription has, however, recently been submitted afresh by

Prof. Eddington.[1] His theory has points in common with both of the views already commented upon. But it differs in other respects from either, and it is not at once plain with which of them it should be classed. Prof. Eddington attributes almost all the laws of physics to the selectiveness of the human mind, as directed not to sensa but to what presumably are their ontal sources. If selection out of what is, as distinct from reading-in of what is not, were all that he would assert, as when he says "What we have called building is rather a selection from the patterns that weave themselves",[2] he might be ranged with those phenomenalists who hold that, while to every detail in the structure of the phenomenal there must be corresponding detail in the Real, the Real may also contain much that is not phenomenally manifested. But from this position Prof. Eddington, if I rightly understand him, generally dissociates himself. For instance, he expresses doubt whether [ontal] Nature deserves *any* credit for furnishing material with properties lending themselves to mechanical and physical description. Such doubt associates him rather with Kant, in implying belief that our minds foist into the phenomenal world, or superimpose upon the ontal world, a conformity to law that belongs not to the ontal itself. "So far as I can see", he writes, "all that Nature was required to furnish is a four-dimensional aggregate of point-events; and since these and their relations...may be of any character whatever, it should in any case be possible to pick out a set of entities which would serve as point-events, however badly Nature had managed things in the external world. For the use made of the point-events mind alone is responsible." We are not told what is the status of the "entities", a set of which might be picked out to "serve as" point-events. If they were no other than point-events, the equivalents, in Prof. Eddington's theory, of the things *per se* of Kant—in which case "pick out" would be an appropriate phrase—these entities, in spite of being but a selected portion of the whole, might still be credited with the conformity to law that their phenomena display; and it would be

---

[1] See his essay on *The Domain of Physical Science* in the volume entitled *Science, Religion and Reality*, and more especially his Art. in *Mind*, N.S. No. 114, whence is taken the quotation occurring further on in this paragraph: also his Gifford Lectures, *The Nature of the Physical World*.

[2] *The Nature of the Physical World*, p. 241.

a further question whether for 'might' we should not substitute 'must'. But presumably this is not the meaning intended, as the words "serve as" seem to indicate. The entities in question can then only be either pure fictions or else appearances of point-events; and before they can be picked out they must be *made* either out of point-events or else out of nothing. The former of these alternatives, as involving term-to-term correspondence between the phenomenal and the Real, Prof. Eddington seems to repudiate. Hence his theory, though purporting to appeal only to our selectiveness, appears rather to imply or assert our creativeness of phenomenal relations out of nothing, or without co-operation on the part of the ontal, *i.e.* point-events. The difficulty is then courted of accounting for the rise, out of unprovoked and externally or ontally non-controlled subjective states and acts (which psychology, by the way, disallows), of Objective science, possessing pragmatically verified validity as to the phenomenal, and therefore ultimately as to the ontal; not to speak of the further difficulty of assigning a reason why Reality does not resent and avenge the enormous liberty we take with it.

Obviously, if room is to be made for this extensive reading-in of law-relations, Reality must be emptied of much with which phenomenalism, of any kind more practicable than Kant's, would credit it. And inasmuch as the question of natural law is here being investigated mainly with a view to ascertaining what is its ontological and theological significance, it will repay us to examine the conception of the Real world, and of its things *per se*, which is presupposed in, and determinative of, the theory of physical law that is now under consideration.

The things *per se* with which we are to be confronted are the point-events that have figured in the preceding paragraph. They differ markedly from the mass-points provided by the classic mechanical physics to philosophers who would take theoretical science for ontology. Indeed they are the outcome of a special metaphysic that has grown up with the general theory of relativity. This theory is of interest in connexion with the realistic, and the so-called idealistic, interpretations of science, which will need to be discussed later; there is, therefore, the more call not to refrain from undertaking here and now such study of its epistemological bearings as is requisite for weighing a particular argument, for the subjectivity of most of our physical laws, that has been based upon it.

In so far as Einstein's theory consists in an application of a kind of pure geometry, itself a science of ideal objects and their postulated relations of order, etc., for the purpose of abstractly describing or representing measurable spatio-temporal relations between phenomenal Objects, it is a scientific theory or device, which explicitly has no more of metaphysical significance than has, *e.g.* the Newtonian system, of which it is an emendation. It is concerned to give expression to the inter-dependence of spatial and temporal measurements, indicated in the adoption of the concept of space-time instead of the supposedly independent concepts of absolute time and absolute space. It also expresses the fact that the numerical values to be assigned to the spatial and temporal distances or intervals, as measured from some material body (*e.g.* a place on the earth), in terms of reference to some spatial axes or frame (*e.g.* the fixed stars) and to some chronometer (*e.g.* a pendulum), will vary according to the relative motion of the observer and his apparatus. The relativity contemplated in the theory is physical. The nature of the theory has, therefore, been misconstrued when it has been taken, as by some recent philosophical writers, to be intrinsically a theory of relativity to our minds instead of to our bodies, our standing-ground and instruments; or, in other words, when it has been supposed to have any immediate bearing, not possessed by previous theory of like function, on the epistemological question of the relativity of knowledge in general. But the theory has sometimes been expounded, by its founder as well as by those who have developed it, with admixture of explicit metaphysics. The relativist takes his departure from the Newtonian and traditional concepts of absolute space and time, without caring how these concepts, more abstract than those of physical time and space used in measurement of phenomena, and vastly more abstract than the private spaces and times of individual perception, were genetically reached. This is no source of harm so long as nothing more than scientific description or abstract representation is contemplated; although in these concepts no perceptual element remains save that of order, and though dates and time-intervals are reduced to numbers. But if ontology, rather than conceptual systematisation of the phenomenal, be the relativist's goal, he does but follow the time-honoured but misleading tendency to take the most abstract for the metaphysically fundamental.

By revision of the Newtonian conceptions of space and time the equally empty concept of space-time, variously resolvable into purely spatial and purely temporal relations, is obtained. But the ideal Objects of so pure a science as chrono-geometry are no more ontal than they are perceptual; and the only relation that such a science can have to phenomenal Actuality is that of applicability. From a manifold of points to a space of any kind that is of use to science, and of which there is to be a particular geometry, there is no way save that of imposing, with some arbitrariness, what mathematicians call a metric, or a metric system, on the ideal entities which, without it, are an aggregate ordered only by corre-lation of its elements with values in the ordered arithmetical continuum. And from such a geometry to ontology there is no way save that of hypostatising the purely ideal. Both these ways are adopted, and the nature of the former of them seems to be misread, by realistic interpreters of Einstein's 'theory'. The metric imposed on the space-time continuum and manifold is selected, under the guidance of the calculus of tensors, to yield a geometry such as is applicable to the most comprehensive field of phenomena, while most economical of physical concepts. But, instead of being regarded as brought to the manifold and imposed on it by human postulation, the metric seems to be looked upon by realistic or metaphysical exponents as if originally and neces-sarily intrinsic to it; so that the manifold is called "the world", is spoken of as having "structure", and is even taken to be the ontal or the absolute. So, again, the fact that, by change or manipulation of metric, local gravitation-phenomena can be represented in the conceptual scheme without resort to the notion of gravitational force is construed in such terms as that, in some regions, space is puckered or crumpled. This, of course, is literalisation of a metonymy. Expressions such as 'curvature of space', which figure in non-Euclidean geometry, do not mean that space, as if substantial or quasi-material, is curved, but indicate a characteristic of the metric that is arbitrarily introduced into the ideal manifold. Similarly, the fact that the general theory of relativity, which more obviously than most theories is "a policy

rather than a creed", requires that its space-time be of different
structure in different regions, and so involves obliteration of the
distinction between it and the matter or the events that occupy it,
is of no metaphysical import: alteration *ad hoc* of metric, and
postulation *in loco* of field of force, are but alternative *conventions*.
If the former of them had monopoly of metaphysical import, the
ontology indicated would be comparable to Pythagoreanism.
Space, time, and space-time are neither phenomenal nor ontal
things. They are, rather, names for systems of postulated relations
between ideal entities, which abstractly represent, like a diagram
or a map, measurable relations between phenomenal and largely
conceptual things and events. Whether ontology be an attainable
kind of knowledge or not, it certainly is not to be attained by
reifying our most abstract ideal constructions. Thus, if space-time
remained the formal concept of a pure mathematics, the point-
events, into which it is said to be "analysed", should be instants
at points, unextended bodies at instants of time, or entities non-
existent save as ideas presented by an abstracting subject to himself. However, the point-event of geo-chronometry has been
reified into an ontal something, described as "indefinable", which
here does not mean familiar yet ultimate, but ineffable. Among
the relations, inclusive of others than those imposed by a defined
metric on the original and purely ideal point-events, that are
posited as subsisting between these now ontal and monadic point-
events, is one called 'interval'. This, again, is ineffable. What it
is in itself, that is to say, cannot be imagined or conceived, still less
specified; but it reveals itself to minds, and is measurable, in the
forms of space and time.

Presented in such metaphysical guise, the theory of relativity
becomes a synthetic philosophy. It is no longer economically
descriptive conceptual apparatus, such as Newton took much of
his own dynamics to be, but rather ontologised geometry. And
it is upon such metaphysical presuppositions as have been indicated, that Prof. Eddington has based his suggestion concerning
Nature's conformity to law. He apparently regards matter not as
expressing, among other relations between point-events, one upon
which the mind concentrates attention and which it selects out,
but, rather, as expressive of a relation that is wholly read in. Such
selectiveness is really creativeness. However, it is attributed to

human predilection for the permanent: a permanent body in motion is said to be the outcome of our preference for one particular way of partitioning and measuring space-time. The transient, it is observed, does not interest us: the Real or substantial, for us, is the permanent, because that alone is amenable to human understanding.

As an account of the scientific selectiveness involved in advancing from sense-knowledge to theoretical physics with its conservation-principles, these representations might readily be accepted. But it should not be overlooked that the permanent must be Actual, and be recognised as permanent, before we can be interested in permanence. And man does not enter into this life, and into selective *commercium* with the external world, possessing the tastes, preferences, and intellectual dexterities of the rational physicist. Historically the substantial, for us, is at first the solid or the resistent. We do not seem to be impelled, by an innate propensity toward the unapprehended permanent, to create matter *ex nihilo*; but from sensa provoked by the ontal we construct bodies, and eventually arrive at the notion of their permanence. If matter be made by our reading of relations into point-events rather than by sense and understanding selecting such relations as they can grasp, the laws of mechanics and physics following as a matter of course, then indeed the discovery of these laws is but the fashioning of a science of our own footprints on the shore of the unknown. But if the physicist's concept of matter has been reached from the individual perception that is the foundation, *in ordine cognoscendi*, of all knowledge whatsoever, in a way essentially analogous to that in which the concepts of space, time, and space-time have been obtained, there is no *prima facie*, and no *a priori*, reason for selecting any one of these concepts as metaphysically more ultimate than another. And if things *per se* of some kind must be invoked to account for the emergence of perceptual objects, it seems arbitrary to deny the need to invoke them for explaining the equally objective relations that subsist between percepts, and to refuse to things *per se* the conformity to law that our conceptualised percepts evince. If regularity in the phenomenal have no counterpart in the ontal, it must be assigned not to the selectiveness, but to externally uncaused creativeness, of our minds; and in that supposition all the difficulties that are taken so lightly by many idealists are shouldered.

The phenomenal world is, as a matter of fact, largely ordered by measure, number, and law. It cannot *be* numbers and abstract laws; for they contain no alogical and perceptual element whereby phenomenality is constituted. Nor can number, etc., constitute the ontal world, of which the perceptual realm is appearance: the alogical cannot be extracted from what contains no Real counterpart to it. Plato, building on Pythagoreanism, made it plain at the beginning of philosophy that metaphysics, proceeding along such lines as he pursued, comes at once to an absolute *impasse*. It seems, from the history of philosophy, equally plain that human souls do not elicit the perceptual variety of phenomenal Nature from their subjective acts and immanently caused states alone, uncontrolled by Reality external to them. This way also leads to an *impasse*, revealed, in spite of themselves, by Berkeley and Leibniz. Lastly, if the only remaining line to take be that of inferring from phenomena to things *per se* that are not abstract ideas such as numbers, etc., but agents with which our minds are in *rapport*, and which furnish the objective factor of our subjective-objective experience, it must be submitted that impenetrable mystery will still confront us unless we postulate, not things *per se* that merely evoke orderless sensatio, but ontal agents, of whose regular interactions physical law-relations are the manifestations to our minds. That we can create order out of nothing is as much a mystery as the creation of orderless objects out of nothing; that ontal Nature, imperious enough in dictating our brute sense-*fundamenta*, tolerates our imposition upon them of an order that exists but in our fancy is yet another mystery: and one that is quite superfluous, in that some relations, at the perceptual level, are as objective, as willy-nilly, as independent of subjective interest, as the terms between which they are read off. Both mysteries, however, are resolved if we but bear in mind that, in order that the phenomenal—whether *fundamentum* or relation—be forthcoming, it must be appearance *of* something as well as appearance *to* somebody.

The truth, then, would seem to be that laws of Nature are Subjective or anthropic in so far as their imagery and their conceptual formulation are concerned, but no further. Our time-span and *tempo*, the range of our senses, our choice of space-metric, our 'real' categories and stock of previous ideas, are involved in all such formulation; intelligibility is conditioned by human mentality as well as by ontal behaviour. Doubtless Maxwell's demon would give to some laws an expression different from that which we have devised. He would, perhaps, formulate some laws to which we have no equivalents, and have no need of others that to us are indispensable. Moreover, within the sphere of science the metaphorical term 'law' must be understood to mean no more than 'formula'. Our laws of Nature are in some measure laws as to our thinking, as well as laws as to the ontal; that is partly why similarities exist between equations belonging to different departments of physics, in spite of profound difference between the phenomena of which they obtain. Laws contain elements that are needful for our minds, in order that they may trace order or reason in our perceptions; and they can never be independent of the processes by which they have been established, nor be other than laws as to what our minds *make* of the ontal. Nevertheless, phenomenal Nature is so constituted as to admit of routine-formulae and physical constants being applied to some of her processes; and that fact, it has here been argued, could not be forthcoming if in the ontal realm there were not at least as much of regularity-nexus as science will ever discover in the phenomenal world. Too much, as well as too little, can be ascribed to the faculties of the soul when, disdaining to take measure of them by psychological examination, philosophy would proceed to interpret a world that is knowable only to an extent dependent on their range, and only in a sense that is conditioned by their nature.

2. THE MEANINGS OF 'LAW'.

When we inquire more closely into the connotation of 'law', as a technical term of science and philosophy, we at once discern that it has borne two very different meanings. In the one of these the idea of necessity, of one or more kinds, is essential and of paramount importance; from the other it is altogether absent. The latter of these conceptions of law is the one that prevails in current science such as avoids metaphysical insinuation, and, chary as to *a priori* principles and methods, proceeds empirically and inductively. Scientific writers now commonly insist that laws, such as that of gravitation, are brief descriptions of observed similarities.

They are known to be valid of certain things or phenomena up to date. They are not known to possess universality, *i.e.* applicability to the as yet unobserved, or to possible experience: that is matter of conditional certainty or probability. Laws state what has been, and what may be expected to be; not what always will be, or what must be. Of "laws that never shall be broken" science knows nothing: a broken law would be but a descriptive formula at length found to be inadequate or false. Indeed laws are provisional generalisations that may be revised or superseded as knowledge advances. When a law refers to uniformities of co-existence and to static similarities, or is classificatory, it is no more than a docket into which we collect phenomena having features in common. When laws refer to change, they are generic concepts for the changes of Nature; and a law also asserts *how* a phenomenon changes in time. 'How' may mean 'like what'; also, 'in what manner'—when it is often expressible quantitatively: but the word is intended to point antithesis to 'why'. Hence laws are said to be descriptive, not explanatory: they do not explicitly assert causal connexion or Actual necessitation, but involve only what philosophers call 'occasional' causes.

Laws, in empirical science, originate as generalisations and refinements of what Kant would distinguish as empiric rules. They are not to be included in the primary data, the facts or instances, with which scientific or common-sense knowledge begins. Even the simplest and most easily read-off relations, such as similarity and succession, are objects of higher order than the *fundamenta* between which they subsist, and are apprehended in a different way. And the crudest of laws are not simple relations, such as that expressed in the words 'this body, rubbed on that, grows warm'; but generalisations of them, such as the rough induction 'friction produces heat'. At a more advanced stage of science, relatively brute facts are themselves resolved into co-existences and sequences; and the relations expressed by the relatively brute or empiric law are transformed into more complex relations between more simple, but purely conceptual, bodies. As the Nature, of which science tells, becomes more conceptual and less perceptual, symbols, as distinct from percepts, enter into laws or formulae; and eventually symbols such as involve complicated theories.

Actuality or existent things. The necessary is the logically or implicationally necessitated; and as there is no necessity *per se*, so to say, none that is intrinsic or self-subsistent, unmediated or non-necessit*ated*, there can be no necessarily true premisses, even in the realm of ideas or of the pure sciences. In geometry and dynamics, *e.g.*, we must conventionally or volitionally posit our points, mass-particles, and number of space-dimensions: none of such things being immediately thrust upon us from without, as are sensa. Having created such entities by selective imagination or otherwise, we can establish propositions about them, connected by logical necessity; and if we please to call such pure science 'necessary truth', we use 'truth' in a distinct and technical sense that sharply differentiates it from 'knowledge', when that word refers to the Actual or the existent. Bearing in mind these distinctions and cautions when we use phrases such as 'pure *sciences*' and 'necessary *truths*', we can recognise that pure sciences—the realm of *ordo ac connexio idearum*—and mechanical laws express necessary truth about an ideal world, and calculabilities as to number, measure, etc. In this realm laws characterised by *logical* necessity undoubtedly subsist: but they are not necessarily laws of Nature.

In order that laws of this kind may be also laws of Nature, *i.e.* laws valid of our Actual world, obviously further conditions must obtain. For the *fundamenta* from which knowledge of this world sets out, whatever it may end with, are not the imaginal or ideal entities of pure science, such as the point-events of the theory of relativity, but sensa thrust upon us in our commerce with existents other than our souls. Here we have a realm of *ordo ac connexio rerum*; facts in place of thoughts, substances in place of ideal forms; *rapport* or interaction instead of logical and static relation; nexus that is not compacted dialectically, but so that the effect of a cause can only be known by observation. There is no *a priori* ground, in the ideal realm, decreeing that Actual or ontal things shall conform to its necessary laws. Whether there is any such conformity, and, if so, how much, are therefore further questions, entirely alien to the sciences of logic and mathematics.

Rationalism, in its various forms, virtually denies that there is any such further ·question. Spinoza did so by dogmatically assuming the two orders and connexions to be the same; Kant, by teaching that the mind superimposes its thought-order on the data supplied chaotically by the thing-order, thus constituting a pheno-menal system, of which there cannot but be *a priori* and necessary knowledge. Here is the ultimate source of Kant's belief in the forthcomingness of natural science that is scientific in so far as it is mathematical. These and equivalent doctrines have previously been examined and rejected; in this place there is but need to indicate the truth after which rationalists, from Descartes to Kant, were groping, but which they may be said to have mis-stated. This is that *if* there be natural science characterised by the logical necessity that finds place in the deductive processes of mathematics; *if* there be a knowable universal reign of law: then there must be some kind of correspondence, other than identity, between *causa* and *ratio*; and some sort of determination of the behaviour of things, corresponding to the logical necessity of implication sub-sisting between propositions, whose terms are pure ideas. In other words, if there is to be conformity of the Actual world to law, there must be Actual determination or necessitation in things or existents, as well as logical necessitation between propositions involving number, measure, etc. Neither of these kinds of deter-mination logically implies the other; there is no *a priori* necessity that the Actual shall conform, or that the ideal shall apply. But that there shall be both kinds of necessitation, and that they shall, so to speak, march together, is the logical precondition of the *a priori* science of Nature that Kant conceived. It is only the necessarily connected that logical thought can penetrate, that knowledge (in the rationalist's sense) can know, and that science can 'understand' and unconditionally predict. The conceptions of law and conformity to law with which we are at present concerned may then be said to be logically necessary preconditions of necessary knowledge of the world: and if laws are to apply, things must conform.

Whether things do rigidly and wholly conform; whether uni-versal laws apply; whether there is, or can be, any such science of Nature as Newton hoped for and Kant thought Newton had furnished in his dynamics: these, once more, are further questions. And they were not silenced by the rationalistic school which too hastily assumed science, such as Kant would deem alone worthy of the name, to be forthcoming. Nowadays there is scarcely a philosopher, logician, or physicist but thinks otherwise. Much relevant knowledge, hidden from the eyes of Spinoza and even of Kant, has been acquired which inhibits confidence such as they enjoyed. As to the attitude which the modern physicist has been led by such knowledge to adopt something has already been said; as to that of the recent logician a few words shall presently be added: as to that of the philosopher, if such there yet be, who would construct cosmology in general, and a conception of natural law in particular, in aloofness from data afforded by physicist and logician alike, nothing need be said.

Meanwhile there is one element in what has been called the rationalistic idea of law that remains to be considered. The formulae that were once commonly regarded as fixed laws of Nature were supposed to govern the universe: with or without the aid of God, as the case might be. Not only physicists and philosophers but theologians also, of past generations, entertained and applied this belief: indeed, it would seem that to-day it is considered in some quarters to be a mark of theological modernity. Baden Powell, one of the contributors to *Essays and Reviews*, and apparently a disciple of Mill, invoked it in order to reform or demolish belief in miracle; and Tindal, the typical representative of English deism on its philosophical side, practically based his natural theology upon it. This writer evinced a horror, equal to that of Spinoza, of any attribution of arbitrariness to the Deity, and sometimes spoke of laws which it "was fitting" for God to observe: a phrase suggestive of yet another sense of 'necessity', sometimes credited to natural laws, viz. that of self-subsistence. When the deist supposed a scheme of laws to subsist independently either of God or of the Actual world, he was not merely using a conception such as might be called a survival of a bygone notion of the scope and nature of physical science; for this system included ethical laws also. He rather took over from philosophy the rationalistic doctrine that laws constitute an eternal *prius*: a form or mould into which being had to fit, in order to be; or into which it behoved God to fit it. This is to construe 'validity of' as 'existence before, or independently of', the Actual. It involves a form of the ontological fallacy or of the doctrine of the *universale ante rem*, attributed in earlier chapters to a misreading of the relation of thoughts to things, and of the relation of words to thoughts. Happenings, even orderly happenings, do not pre-suppose laws; laws describe the happenings, or the behaviour of agents of some kind. As Boutroux has happily expressed it, "laws are the channel along which rushes the stream of facts: these latter have hollowed it out, though they follow its track". In the case of the existent and what is valid of it there is no before or after other, whether in logical or in temporal order. We can indeed no more say that relations presuppose things than that things pre-suppose relations: 'co-suppose', if there were such a word, would better meet the case. Laws, apart from things figuratively said to obey them, are, like all form apart from matter, nonentities or non-Actualities. The idealist who pleads for them that they 'exist' in the mind of God—*i.e.* exist in another sense, which is not relevant—can offer no ground for the difference between laws valid of Actuality and laws contradicted by the behaviour of things: the law of the inverse cube presumably having 'existence', in his sense of the word, equally with that of the inverse square. This appeal, of Berkeleian type, to the Divine or Absolute Mind effects nothing towards abolishing the distinction between the valid and the Real, or towards grounding the distinction between the Actual and the possible. The only significant sense, then, in which law may be said to 'exist', is that of Actual subsistence as a relation between Actual things, or between their activities and states. Things, by their behaviour, make their laws, and "obey" them by making them with persistent regularity.

This being so, further investigation of the regularity of Nature, as expressed in physical laws, must wait on inquiry as to what the ontal things which underlie phenomena may be. Indeed, inductive logic has of late made it plain that assertions of nomic necessity presuppose ontological dogma as to substances and causes. The gist of Mr Johnson's observations in this connexion may be briefly set forth once again. The 'universal of law', he says, is wider than the 'universal of fact', as established by simple enu-meration, or as made probable by problematic induction. The inductively obtained universal of fact is of the nature of an assertion that *every* substantive, characterisable as pq, is q if it is p. The universal of law asserts that *any* pq would be q, if it were p: it thus extends beyond the sphere of Actual experience to all possible experience; a fact, while describable only as, say, 'a pqr

which is an x', may be a contingency, in the sense that a pqr which is not an x may yet appear; but when adequately described, as 'a $pqruvw$ that is necessarily an x'', it no longer has contingency but nomic necessity. Such adequate description, however, would involve knowledge that the character x is dependent on there being a finite and enumerable set of properties, p—w: and this never admits of scientific demonstration. It rather belongs to the ontological and causal principles which must be true, *if* induction or law-making is to yield universal and necessary knowledge.

We have seen that the same conclusion emerges from the recent re-examination of the basal principles underlying induction. Those principles are both ontological and indemonstrable. And here we come upon the answer that is to be given to our question as to the epistemological status of the proposition that physical Nature is a realm of universal law. It asserts what is neither empirically knowable fact, nor *a priori* truth, nor self-evident axiom, nor essential precondition either of experience or of such science as we have, nor inference logically derivable from anything certain: it is a postulate, embodying the particular kind of 'hope for the best' in which the faith of science consists.

The conception of law, in so far as it transcends actual experience, being neither *a priori* nor *a posteriori*, represents a character that we must read into the world, or into things, if we would make them expressible by mathematical and mechanical symbols. Like the categories of substance and cause, it is a teleological device, adopted in order to make us wise, in a narrower sense than that in which those categories make us wise. Within limits the device has been highly successful; but there is no *a priori* necessity that it should be. The only necessity that empirical science and inductive logic allow to be associated with the conception of universal reign of invariable law is its needfulness for the persistent—and quixotic—endeavour of theoretical science to rationalise completely a world that obviously and admittedly is irrational enough to reveal its secrets only to experimental, as contrasted with synthetic and deductive, inquiry. The logically and scientifically unwarrantable assertion of immutable and all-pervading law, dictated by things whose very nature constitutes them a closed system within which every change is fated, has been found to be a useful instrument for exploring a largely alogical world; it becomes absurd when taken for adequate description of a whole, to but a part of which it is known to have but approximate application.

When the travesties of such reign of law as science may legitimately assert, made by philosophy that would scorn empirical evidence and control, are set aside, there remains the fact that laws have obtained and do obtain, whatever the future may bring forth. And this fact must have a sufficient reason, though neither science nor certain kinds of philosophy may concern themselves to look for it. Unvarying concomitance or sequence is, indeed, logically distinct from necessary connexion; but it points to Actual connexion and necessitation. All laws concerning Actuality, even if merely spatio-temporal descriptions for science, must be causal laws, in the broad sense that fuses substance and cause into one category and takes account of immanent as well as of transeunt causation. If we rule out the *prius* of necessary law we must also rule out ungrounded coincidence, as no satisfactory explanation of Nature's conformity to law: not taking it as the final word of philosophy on the matter before the attempt to elicit a further word has proved futile. It must be admitted, to the logician, the neo-realist, and the philosophical agnostic, that no conclusion can rationally be reached; but it may prove possible to be reasonable where rationality is precluded.

It is only in the form of what one has ventured to call travesties of the known reign of law that this conception has put difficulties in the way of belief that the world is a realm of ends under a rule of God. If law bespoke fate, if the world were a closed system, if instead of being in part and with approximation mechanically describable it were a mechanism and no more, there would indeed be no need of the hypothesis that there is a God. But these are not conclusions to which science, as a whole, points; certainly they are not items of scientifically acquired knowledge. Save as methodological postulates, comparable to the rules of a game, they have no place in science such as knows its own nature and minds its own business. They are ghosts which empiricism has laid; they no longer haunt science and scare theology. On the other hand, it is upon such conformity to law, more correctly called regularity evocative of law, as the world evinces—and must intrinsically possess in order phenomenally to manifest it—that theistic argument is ultimately to be based. In the relatively settled order of Nature we may see the first link of the chain of facts which, while they do not logically demand, nevertheless cumulatively suggest as reasonable, the teleological interpretation in which theism essentially consists, in so far as its intellectual aspect is concerned.

CHAPTER II

Law and Mechanism

The conception of law with which science works has been found to be that of constant, but otherwise undefined, relation between past and future phenomena; and a law, in science that has become quantitative, is generally expressible by differential equations or other formulae involving the use of the differential and the integral calculus. When science has proceeded to interpret in its own way the regularity of Nature which laws express, and to determine more definitely the causal relation involved in law, it has done so by using the concept of the mechanical. What different meanings 'mechanical' may bear will be inquired later. For the present the word may be taken to signify that the ultimate constituents of the physical order are invariable and inert; that their interactions are unguided by mind, the changes due to their movements giving no hint of progress, meaning, or purpose; and that causal determination is by a *vis a tergo*, whatever the figurative term *vis* may mean. It has been held that science, in describing and explaining the observable, *i.e.* the molar or macroscopic, in terms of conceived microscopic constituents, achieves pure knowledge of the ontal behind the phenomenal: the phenomenal, or the sensible, being then regarded as but subjective symbolism. Further, the ultimate microscopic constituents have been credited with none but purely mechanical properties; and it has been represented that only when the sense-symbolism admits of translation into mechanical equivalents, involving nothing but mass, space, and time, is scientific knowledge *par excellence* attained, and the Real—which, for such science, is the quantitative—revealed. Macroscopic laws may obtain and be known without knowledge as to either the microscopic or the ontal structure of Nature; but some physicists have asserted the possibility of translating these laws in terms of what is sensibly inapprehensible, but scientifically and noümenally knowable. Thus it has been claimed that mechanistic physics yields metaphysical interpretation of the law-abidingness which reveals itself superficially or phenomenally to inductive research. Whether science has thus succeeded is bound up with the wider question whether the method of theoretical physics, pursued with the strict exclusiveness that is essential for science, is capable of leading to ontology of any kind: and this issue is now to be discussed.

We may first recall the few conclusions of ontological rank that have already been elicited from the same sphere of fact that compels invocation of an ontal realm at all. Two of these conclusions are of general nature, and therefore have relevance to the cosmological department of metaphysics as much as to any other. Firstly, the phenomenon being appearance *of* the ontal, as well as appearance *to* knowing subjects, and the phenomenal being characterised by change, it follows that the ontal is responsible, so to say, for phenomenal change: at least, for all in it that psychology is forbidden by fact to assign to subjective causation. The ontal, then, cannot be dogmatically asserted to be immutable. The great *a priori* philosophers who have assumed ultimate Reality to be changeless, while omitting to account for mutability in its Actual appearances, have ignored the implications of those deliverances of fact, of which metaphysics, relevant to the Actual world, should be an explication and a translation. They have rather been seers in an ideational realm than solvers of actual problems: for they have set out, not to interpret what is given to us, but to construct a rational dream-world out of concepts devised to satisfy predilections, of aesthetic and such-like nature. The empiricist, on the other hand, can submit reasons in place of motivations, and reasons open to inspection, for believing that the ontal, as much as the phenomenal, is a world of becoming, so that "naught may endure but mutability". Secondly, objectively determined relations subsisting between perceptual objects, and also relations between the phenomenal Objects (which are facts, as distinguished from mere thoughts, in virtue of their objective or perceptual kernels) must, equally with the terms between which they subsist, have some noümenal counterpart. In particular, phenomenal regularity, such as finds expression in natural laws, bespeaks regularity of ontal activities, which, as was argued in the last chapter, cannot be explained away into subjectivity. And now it may be remarked that nothing further can be ascertained about the ultimate nature and cause of this regularity unless the nature of the *onta* be ascertainable. Thirdly, the only ontal existents, as to whose essence there has as yet been occasion to assert that we possess knowledge, are souls and their acts, etc. This claim is made on the strength of the consideration that, though soul-activities might conceivably be appearances *of* something metaphysically still more ultimate, they cannot conceivably be appearances *to* any beings whatsoever: and both of these relations, denoted by 'of' and 'to', are essential to constitute a phenomenon. Souls and soul-activities are not directly apprehensible, phenomenally or otherwise, by other subjects. It would be playing fast and loose with the word 'appearance', and at the same time be leaving the ontal status of the soul unquestioned, to say that its activities are appearances of itself to itself; while, to say that the soul and its acts are appearances of an underlying noümenal non-soul, or of The Absolute, as do some absolute idealists, seems but to use words with a similar disregard of their meanings, as well as to create new, gratuitous, and unsolvable puzzles as to The Absolute's works of supererogation. Moreover the word 'phenomenality' loses its distinctive signification when it does not bespeak the particular kind of immediate apprehension called sensibility. It is not self-evidently applicable to the knowledge yielded by introspection, or so-called inner sense. Introspection, indeed, may 'make a difference to' Real psychical happenings, owing to the subject's limitations in respect of discrimination, *tempo*, and so forth: its vision may be telescopic; but it may still be achromatic, so to say, or non-phenomenalising. The soul or active subject, then, is the one kind of thing *per se* that we have as yet been enabled to assert to be knowable. And, previously to inquiry, the ontal that lies behind or beyond physical bodies and phenomenal events may be supposed to consist of soul-like monads, or to be of essentially different nature. Science is sometimes thought to point to the latter kind of theory, or to imply a dualistic or a materialistic metaphysic of Nature. And this brings us back to the question of science's capacity to prescribe metaphysic of any one type rather than of another, and to its conception of mechanism, as determinative of Nature's regularity.

The mechanical theory, or world-view, is what in this connexion is of direct import for philosophers and natural theologians. And this theory needs to be distinguished from the science of mechanics, whether pure or applied, and also from the mechanistic method that has been largely adopted in physics. But, inasmuch as the relation in which the theory stands to mechanical science and to mechanistic method is the point on which the philosophical issue turns, these departments of science proper must to some extent be surveyed before the situation can be grasped.

Though the mechanical theory, that all change in matter is but change of the motions of its parts, is older than Newton, having been stated by Descartes and Hobbes in its *a priori* form, the foundations of the modern science of mechanics, and the source of the mechanistic trend of physics, are the Newtonian laws of motion. These laws are the essence of the generalised science, of the motion of material bodies, which Newton established, and which, since his day, has been but supplemented, revised, and refined. Descartes had professed to admit into physics no principles that are not admitted in mathematics. He defined matter as extension, so that 'bodies' should, for him, be but geometrical figures. He thus pretended, after the rationalistic fashion, to absorb mechanics and physics into the pure sciences. Newton, on the other hand, generalised the empirical laws of Kepler and the observations of Galileo. He invoked the 'real' category of cause or force as well as the sensibly given property of inertia, thus replacing the Cartesian pure kinematics by applied dynamics. It was these empirical elements in Newton's science that made his system fruitful, and that provided a host on which Cartesianism, with its shew of deductiveness, parasitically maintained itself.

At the same time the Newtonian mechanics itself transcends empirical knowledge. By this statement is not merely meant that Newton assumed Nature's uniformity without limit, and so forth; but rather that his method consisted in arguing, firstly, from particular observable effects to their particular causes, then from the particular cases to generality or universality, and thence back, deductively, not only to all particular cases but to the ultimate, pure, and exact laws by which the original approximate formulae could be replaced. Newtonian science is both analytic and synthetic, both inductive and deductive. The laws of motion, in particular, have been compared with the laws of thought in logic. The laws of logic guarantee the truth of no premises, and therefore of no conclusions; though they shew that some conclusions do, and others do not, follow from given premises. Similarly the laws of motion do not tell us that bodies will move, nor state the particular way in which one part of the world will set up motion in other parts; but, if true, they confine possible movements within certain limits. Thus they underlie, but do not embrace, physics; just as logic underlies, yet does not include, historical and other sciences.

The particular form given by Newton to the fundamental laws of motion is determinative of the somewhat vague sense of the word 'mechanical', as used in scientific literature. Confining ourselves for the present to this determinate, though—for certain specific questions—relatively unprecise, meaning, we may proceed to extract it from the laws, at the same time ascertaining their epistemological status.

The first law is that every body remains at rest or in uniform motion (velocity) in a straight line, unless it be compelled by impressed force to change its state of rest or of motion. Two essential factors of the Newtonian notion of the mechanical are here indicated: inertia and impressed force, or *vis a tergo*. To every material body is ascribed the property of inertia, or of mass, in the qualitative sense of the latter word. This is persistence, in respect of motion, *in statu quo*; or incapacity of the body to initiate of itself, or from within, any change in its velocity and direction. From the point of view of empirical science, inertia is an ultimate or inexplicable sense-given quality. And, in so far as the science of motion is concerned, it (apart from movability) is the sole quality of matter: whatever other qualities this or that body may possess, they are irrelevant to the determination of its motion, and therefore to molar mechanics. 'Mass' is more commonly used in its quantitative sense; but if this name be also given to the quality called inertia, we cannot say that matter is mass, but that a material body has mass, or is massive. When inertia is attributed not only to visible and tangible bodies, all of which have it in so far as approximate observation can go, but also to all bodies whatsoever, microscopic as well as molar, it becomes a postulate, and a postulate that is fundamental both for the mechanical theory and for mechanistic method. For it is in virtue of this inertia of matter that motions are calculable. Hylozoism, or the doctrine of non-inertial matter, is "the death-blow" to what Kant would fain call science: *i.e.* knowledge in which there is so much science as there is mathematics.

The other essential concept contained in this law is that of impressed force. By 'force' Newton here meant, simply, efficient cause of motion; and when force is called 'impressed' nothing is added but what is already involved in the notion of inertia: viz. that force is always *ab extra*, or that there is no *vis insita*. If forces were restricted to moving bodies or to impacts, it would follow that there is none but transmitted motion. But the first law does not prescribe such restriction. So long as 'force' denotes whatever causes change in velocity, room is left for more than one kind of it. All that has been laid down is that force is impressed from without. That mind or spirit can cause phenomenal matter to move is not denied: the question is not contemplated.

Newton's first law, it has been said, is empirically derived in so far as it was suggested by observations on molar bodies, and is established in so far as such mass-aggregates are found approximately to conform to it. But it goes beyond empirical facts, as indeed must any universal statement about Actuality. We can never isolate a material body from all others or from all forces. We can observe, as in the case of a smooth ball rolling on smooth ice, that the less there be of friction the nearer we approach to perpetual uniform velocity in a straight line. But that the weight of the ball and the pressure of the ice do not affect the horizontal motion "can only be inferred when other parts of the dynamical scheme are taken into account".[1] And it is neither self-evident nor *a priori* necessary that, in the absence of all force, uniform velocity should be self-maintaining. Whether, if we could realise the condition of 'no force', we should find constancy in the rest, the velocity, or the acceleration, of the body is an unanswerable question. On which answer we assume depends the order of the differential equations to be applied; and Newton's assumption involves that they be of the second order. Thus the law is a carrying to the limit, on the assumption of continuity and by extrapolation, of what is vouched for approximately by observed facts. When extended to bodies of all magnitude, or universalised, it expresses a further assumption or convention.

The second law of Newton states that change of motion (motion now meaning not velocity but quantity of motion, or momentum, mv) is proportional to the impressed force, and takes place in the

[1] Prof. E. W. Hobson, *The Domain of Nat. Science*, p. 187.

direction of the straight line in which such force is impressed.
Here again we are presented with two conceptions of first
importance in connexion with the remoter developements of
Newtonian mechanics: force, apart from its specific characteristic
indicated by 'impressed'; and rectilinear direction of force-action,
which is involved in the doctrine of central forces.

With regard to the former conception, it is certain that Newton
here uses it in the sense that is wont to be called realistic or metaphysical: *i.e.* as a 'real' category. More recent physicists, who
would purge mechanics of 'real' categories as tainted with
metaphysics, interpret this second law of motion to be a definition
of force as rate of change of momentum. The force (p) varies as
the product of the mass (m) of the body in which it causes change
of velocity, and the acceleration (f) that is effected: $p \propto mf$, or is
$d(mv)/dt$. Some philosophers consider force, equally with shape,
etc., to be sense-given. Pressure or strain, they say, is a sensum,
not a sensatio, and can well exist in material bodies that have no
sensatio of it. Thus they would attribute the descriptionist's
suspicion as to the reality of force to his arbitrary preference for
the deliverances of some human senses rather than for those of
another. But, as against this view, it may be remarked that, in our
experience called exertion of force, our activity is not presentational but is rather thought-explicated *erleben*; while our experience
of force exerted on us by other bodies is presentational, and can
scarcely be immediate apprehension of their causal activity or
efficiency, which we do not *erleben*: yet this is the only kind of
causality here in question. Such causation is always read in, not
read off; it is a 'real' category, not a sensum. Again, it is affirmed
that force, as to which Newton's second law is said to present a
substantial statement, rather than a definition, can be measured
otherwise than as this law indicates: viz. statically. Poincaré,
however, denies that such is the case, on the ground that Newton's
third law, asserting the equality of action and reaction, is then
involved, which in turn presupposes the dynamical measurement
of force and mass. But, however these matters be decided, there
can be no doubt that Newton himself was no descriptionist in the
formulating of his second law of motion. His descriptionism
rather emerges when, as in his science of gravitation, he speaks of
force of attraction while demurring to action at a distance and at

the same time repudiating occult or metaphysical hypotheses. His preference for impact-action, due to nothing more profound than inherited common sense and custom, led to his type of mechanics or dynamics being called 'mechanical' in a narrower and more specialised sense, contrasted with a similarly specialised sense of 'dynamical': these words then respectively indicating mechanics based on contact-action and mechanics based on action at a distance.

Whether the second law of motion be construed as a definition of force or as a statement as to how the effects of an agency are to be measured, its usefulness and importance, in rendering generalisation possible, are obvious. This law is also important in that it supplies a quantitative meaning for inertial mass. From mass, as a quality intrinsic to bodies, we can now pass to *the* mass of a body, *i.e.* to the measure of its inertial tendency. At the same time we find this measure to be relative. The mass of a body can be measured only in relation to that of some other moving body, and in terms of some standard; the mass now becomes a number, and the concept of mass is devised for the facilitation of calculating. If the forces p and p', applied to the same body, respectively produce in it accelerations f and f', then $p/p' = f/f' =$ a constant, which is m, the mass of the body. The only actually measurable thing, here, is acceleration: m is a coefficient, *apparently* corresponding to 'quantity of matter'. This phrase is a merely verbal definition of mass, and one which only acquires definiteness when it means the number of mass-points in the body: then, however, mass becomes purely conceptual. And unless force be definable otherwise than in terms of mass and acceleration, and rate of change of momentum be not the definition of force but the expression of the measure of its effect, 'force' becomes a figure of speech in the science of mechanics. This is what the nominalist or the descriptionist asserts to be the case; and if the realist's alternative is to be maintained, it would seem that a 'real' category of interpretative understanding, rather than a datum of sense, needs to be invoked.

The other fundamental statement contained in the second law of motion is that which refers to the direction of force-action. Taking force to be action of body on body, this action is asserted to be in the direction of the straight line joining them. The law of central forces, into which this assertion enters, is of the greatest importance for classical mechanics. For it is in virtue of it that the principles of conservation of energy and of least action are deducible from Newton's laws. By means of these principles problems can be solved without knowledge as to the details of the structure of physical systems, such as might require impracticable analyses, or as to anything more than the initial and final whole-states of the systems. But this law of right-line action cannot be significantly stated without reference to some physical frame, in relation to which straightness is determined; it cannot be stated significantly, without further presuppositions, save as to mass-points, when it becomes purely ideal; and, so far from being a necessary or universal law of Nature when these conditions of its applicability to Actual bodies have been fulfilled, it does not seem to be valid of so-called phenomena of the subatomic order.

The second law, as applied to mass-particles rather than to molar bodies, may be interpreted thus: in an isolated system of particles, each particle can be assigned a coefficient denoting its mass; the mass-acceleration (ma) is a function of the masses, relative positions, and velocities, of the particles at the moment; and this function is constant for all times—whence the 'timeless-ness' of the laws of abstract mechanics. The function in question, however, involves other coefficients besides masses, viz. those which are marks of the physical properties, gravitation, elasticity, etc. From these physical properties, as we have seen, molar mechanics makes abstraction, because for that science they are irrelevant. But if the mechanical theory of Nature is to be scientifically established, it becomes necessary to replace all physical properties by their mechanical equivalents, *i.e.* by masses, velocities, and geometrical configurations. That this should eventually be achieved was Newton's hope. Physics would then be absorbed into mechanics, and a thoroughgoing mechanical explanation of the physical world would be provided. Here we meet with the most rigorous sense that the word 'mechanical' can bear. The mechanical theory, according to this meaning, asserts that the world is not only a closed system but a mechanism and no more. There is no change in it save change of motion or con-figuration. There are no agents, and no actions save impacts or attractions of moving bodies, qualitatively identical, whose sole property is inertia. The only 'causes' are motional causes, acting from outside the body moved. Every effect persists, is equal to its cause, and is in turn a cause. Efficiency being discarded, causes become constant relations between configurations in time, such that, two configurations at times t_1 and t_2—which constitute a cause—being known, any other configuration at t_3—which will be the effect—is theoretically calculable. The goal of science, accordingly, is to find the world-formula or world-equation. Laplace's notion of a wholly predictable world was based on the assumption that Newton's laws apply to all bodies and velocities, of whatever order of magnitude. That belief is no longer entertained; it is now known that Newtonianism needs to be revised and supplemented. But this is not of first importance for the mechanical philosophy which first based itself on the all-sufficiency of Newton's principles. If *any* such laws apply universally, it is enough for mechanism of the Laplacean type. At the same time, any laws that will serve the same purpose as that which mechanists hoped for of Newton's laws must be of similar nature and epistemological origination. And what that is, the foregoing intrusion into the domain of mechanics was intended to make plain. Suggested and, within certain ranges, verified by approximate observation, Newton's laws soar on wings of extrapolation and idealisation far above our empirical ken, within which they originated. They are not inductive laws of Nature merely, but also postulates and definitions. In so far as they set forth eternal verities or universal truth, they belong to the realm of pure sciences such as arithmetic. They then treat directly not of perceptual or of physical bodies, space, and time but of conceptual and fictional bodies, space, and time, such as have instrumental and limited use in so far as they are approximately applicable to Actuality. Newton's laws define a certain kind of matter, characterised by inertia. But whether there exists any such matter is another question: and one with which, as pure science, they are not concerned. For then facts do not enter into the premises, and consequently are not contained in the conclusions. These laws, again, contemplate only isolated and closed systems; and such systems, for all we know, are not the only kind, if indeed any such are actually forthcoming. It may be that, while lifeless bodies form practically closed systems, organisms and their parts do not.

Mechanics, as based on these laws, can indeed recognise none but transmitted motions; but as to whether a good deal of observable motion in our world is not of that sort they can say nothing. The undefinedness of the agency which Newton called 'force', allows of no possible breakdown; but, if there be any action other than that of inert matter on inert matter, his first two laws, which are really one—the first being included in the second—can have but limited applicability. Further, once mechanical explanation or description resorts to the conceptual and microscopic in order to mechanicise the perceptual and molar, it may continue indefinitely. Such description is ever possible if at every *impasse* further hypothetical mechanisms are devised to help us over. But if Nature were amenable to description of this kind it would not necessarily follow that Nature is a lifeless machine, or that physical bodies are inert, and so on. Lifelessness might be simulated by what was not inert, but conative; routine might be settled habit; mechanicalness might be a statistical emergent of random events. And such suppositions might none the less be true for being superfluous for the purpose of physics based on mechanical presuppositions.

These, however, are remoter problems. At present we are concerned with the question whether the fundamental principles of mechanics, Newtonian or other, are of such a nature as to rule out the possibility of the alternative suppositions just indicated, however plausible these may otherwise be made to appear. And the answer to which we have thus far been led is that in themselves these principles dictate no conclusion, because in themselves they are principles not concerned directly with Actuality but with conceptual definitions and postulates that may or may not prove applicable. If 'mechanics' mean pure or abstract mechanics, it has no necessary relevance to a mechanical philosophy of this particular world, which is not purely conceptual; and it cannot absorb physics into itself.

The next question, therefore, is as to the applicability of pure dynamics to the Actual world: what 'application' means, within what range it obtains, and what are the possible philosophical consequences of such application as has been found to subsist. We pass, then, to the consideration of applied mechanics, or the mechanistic method in physics, having already found that the application of pure dynamics to physical Objects is at best a tentative pursuit: a method of studying motions rather than a science of motion. It now needs to be inquired whether, if mechanistic physics be taken realistically, or as metaphysical and explanatory, it does not over-reach itself by issuing in kinematics; and whether, if taken as conceptual and economical 'description', it does not prove to be vain in proportion to the purity of its mechanicalness, because involving itself in ever-increasing complexity of hypothetical supposition. It may turn out, from further investigation of the method in question, that Nature does not admit of being comprehended by the theoretical framework; or, in other words, that rigorously mechanical principles cannot apply to physical phenomena, in the sense of describing or accounting for them without remainder. These are debatable issues; and they can only be decided, in the one or the other way, after further incursions have been made into the province of physical science.

Pure or abstract mechanics, such as Newton's system becomes when purged of the 'perceptual' elements that are not assimilable with its vastly larger conceptual ingredient, has already been shewn to be no such thing as might be called undenominational physics: it is not physics at all. When universalised, Newton's laws are foundations of a science of motions and configurations of ideal bodies, such as mass-points. Whether or not those principles might subsume all physical laws, once these have been discovered, or be a blank form capable of embracing all physical phenomena and processes, it is plain that physical laws and constants cannot be deduced or extracted from a blank form that does not contain them. Physics cannot be a deductive scheme such as Descartes and several French physicists, on whom his rationalistic mantle fell, misconceived it to be. Pure mechanics must be replaced by applied mechanics for the physicist's use. And the latter science can at best be wise after the event: that is to say, it may conceivably subsume, describe, and predict, after, but not before, brute facts, phenomenal qualities, and physical constants, have been empirically, or 'perceptually', ascertained.

The classical mechanico-physics has been found to consist in such doctrines as that there is but one kind of matter, with the sole property of inertia, and but one kind of change—of motion or configuration; also in a few such laws as those of central forces, inverse squares, and the parallelogram-law. And it now may be remarked that the mechanical method, which should consist in immediate application of these definitions, postulates, and laws, is impracticable. Theoretically, by compounding for every pair of mass-particles in a system we could ascertain the configuration of the system at any instant, if we knew the masses and the velocities of the particles at two other instants. But the complexity of the calculations, not to speak of the analysis of a molar body into Actual particles equivalent to ideal mass-points, would surpass human powers. We cannot proceed synthetically, by compounding the motions of microscopic elements, to physics of molar phenomena. Hence other methods, dispensing with impossible 'last analyses', have of necessity been adopted in mathematical physics or applied mathematics. Molar bodies can be treated as continuous, instead of as particle-aggregates, by resort to principles which may be called developements of Newtonian dynamics, provided that 'developement' connotes somewhat of epigenesis and not merely deductive self-unfolding. Thus d'Alembert postulated spatial connexions, called rigid constraints, between constituent elements of a system, such as limit the number of possible modes of motion. For these connexions Newtonianism furnishes no general expression. They are not deducible, without further assumptions, from Newton's principles. Indeed, in any particular case, they are only prescribed by sensible experience of the molar. Here is a rift in what purported to be deductive physics, and a fresh indication that there is no universal mechanics into which physics can straightway be absorbed. Observation, not deduction, decides what particular integration of the microscopic particulars must be adopted. Instead of yielding a synthetic or deductive dynamics, d'Alembert's principle rather pointed to the necessity of the analytical method, which sets out from empirical data to discover their analytical conditions. And, in fact, the most important step in the advance of classical dynamics is represented by the analytical mechanics of Lagrange. Using the principle of d'Alembert as the foundation of his dynamics, and the principle of virtual displacements as his basis in statics, Lagrange attained to a more general principle, and found equations of motion such as involved measurable quantities (his generalised co-ordinates), wherewith invocation of fictional or microscopic particles was made dispensable. Yet more highly generalised is the scheme of Hamilton, within whose principles of least action and of varying action the whole of dynamics is comprised. Here, again, deduction from Newton's laws is not forthcoming, save on an assumption which is not adequate to the complexity of Actual systems, and which only holds of such systems as are conservative or reversible. Moreover, Hertz has adduced a particular phenomenon (rolling without slipping) to which the Hamiltonian scheme does not apply; and he observes that the scheme provides for motions that do not occur in Nature. Thus the theory is wider than the facts; while a perfected dynamics should supply reasons why some, and not all, of its possibilities are realised.

The Lagrangean or Hamiltonian principles are the basis of all current dynamical explanations of physical processes, so long as Newtonian frames of spatio-temporal reference are retained. Briefly summed up, they prescribe that every material body or particle moves just as if it were assigned the problem of attaining given positions in given times, in such a manner that, throughout the time, the mean difference between its kinetic and potential energies shall be a minimum. They do not subsume the whole of physics, however. For it appears that neither temperature-properties nor the non-reversibility of macroscopic processes have as yet been satisfactorily deduced from them. They require that the transference of energy from one form to another shall be continuous in amount: an assumption jeopardised by the quantum-theory. Further, they have the disadvantage that their results find expression in terms of dynamical quantities, such as energy, so that empirical knowledge is required before they can be translated into terms of physical quantities, such as temperature or intensity of electric current. Lagrange's differential equations, derivable from Hamilton's principle of varying action, express all that can be known as to the course of Nature on the macroscopic scale, or without ascertaining the details of the microscopic structure of a mechanical system, and in so far as physical knowledge can be learned from our perception of the effects of Newtonian force. And Dr Broad has shewn how great is the latitude with which 'mechanically explicable' can be interpreted, when it means obeying the Lagrangean equations or others that, employing different frames of reference, are practically equivalent to them.[1] Some of his observations may be here reproduced, as they are relevant to the subject-matter of this chapter, and enable mechanical explanation to be discussed with clarity and precision.

In the set of simultaneous equations with which Lagrange describes the changes of a physical system, the left-hand side is subsumptive of the general laws of mechanics, and implies that all motions, however caused in any system whatsoever, are subject to certain formal conditions. This side contains only dynamical terms: viz. a function (energy), the variables in which are the spatio-temporal magnitudes fixing the position and configuration of the system. The right-hand side, however, consists of functions involving variables that belong to other systems, and whose forms depend on physical constants and relations, peculiar to the particular system considered and to such parts of the rest of the world as mechanically affect it. On these functions no limits are imposed in respect either of their form or of the number and kind of their independent variables; these variables are not confined to geometrical and temporal magnitudes; and such of them as are geometrical may be differential coefficients of *any* order that the physical facts demand. The generalised co-ordinates of the left-hand side can be further generalised, as, on occasion, by Maxwell, Sir J. J. Thomson, etc., so as to include other than geometrical magnitudes; while different degrees of restriction can be imposed as to the form and nature of the functions, and as to the variables, which figure on the right-hand side. Dr Broad finds that then at least five different meanings emerge for the word 'mechanical'. Thus, such a statement as that everything physical can be explained mechanically, or that a certain department of phenomena does not admit of mechanical explanation, is too indefinite to be accepted or rejected until indication has been given as to which, among some half-dozen propositions, it is intended to assert or to deny.

Of the three types of mechanism which are yielded by the several possible interpretations of the left-hand side of Lagrange's equations, but one calls for notice here. Its conditions are the following. First, the 'co-ordinates' are generalised so as to include physical magnitudes, such as temperature, current, or charge. Secondly, the measuring-instruments are included within the

---

[1] *Proceedings of the Aristotelian Society*, N.S., vol. xix, pp. 86 ff. This masterly article is indispensable for the study of mechanical theory.

system, and these physical magnitudes are replaced by the pointer-readings in terms of which they are measured (so that a current, *e.g.*, becomes a deflection of a galvanometer-needle). Thus transition is made back from the physical to the geometrical and temporal. A kind of mechanical explanation is then obtained which is not merely descriptive, in the ordinary or non-technical sense of that word, because it is also metrical, and which is macroscopic in that it invokes no microscopic and theoretical transactions. This type of mechanism is important because it is the only one that is a *conditio sine qua non* of scientific explanation, or of quantitative, and so-called exact, science. It is, however, not a sufficing condition, because it takes no account of the special laws of Nature, one or more of which must always be embodied in the right-hand side of the Lagrangean equations: a fact from which it follows that mechanical explanation, of any type, can never mean explanation in terms of the laws of motion alone. If scientific explanation be taken but to involve obedience to laws of *some* kind, its possibility will depend on the epistemic consideration that these laws are not so complex as to be undiscoverable. It is a fortunate fact, considering the limitations of our senses (preventing accuracy of measurement save of spatial magnitudes) and the limitations of our understandings (preventing us from dealing with laws of indefinite complexity), and considering also that the forthcomingness of macroscopic and metrical mechanism is no logical necessity, that mechanism of this kind nevertheless prevails very widely, at least. And, to pass from this particular form of mechanism to mechanical explicability in the general sense of obedience to Lagrange's equations, it may be observed that, as Dr Broad points out, satisfaction of these equations is neither a sufficient nor a necessary condition of scientific explanation. It is not sufficient, because the physical laws involved in the functions which appear in the equations might be of opaque or unanalysable complexity. And it is not a necessary condition, because the general laws of motion that must be knowable, if scientific explanation is to be possible, need not for that purpose be of the particular form embodied in the equations of Lagrange.

Two further types of mechanism emerge when restrictions are imposed on the interpretation of the right-hand side of the equations, both of which are more rigid than the type that has previously been mentioned. If the functions be assigned no constant, other than mass, save the universal constant in gravitation-theory, or other than electric charge and the velocity of light in electron-theory, we get a "homogeneous microscopic mechanism", in which macroscopic diversity of matter is resolved into microscopic identity. And if the form of the functions be restricted, so that the variables are of the same kind as those of the left-hand side (time, geometrical co-ordinates and their first differential coefficients), we obtain "pure mechanism", exemplified in the theory that all action is by impact, or in the yet more strictly mechanical theory of central forces. It is probably a combination of these two types of mechanism that is commonly in mind when 'mechanical' is used with rigorous intent. And both types, in order to be valid at all, must be true of microscopic entities and their transactions, since neither is true of Nature on the macroscopic scale.

The relation in which microscopic explanation stands to mechanical theory is a matter of importance, and one that is liable to be misunderstood. Rigid mechanism, *i.e.* mechanism of either or both of the kinds that respectively have been called by Dr Broad homogeneous and pure, *must* hold of the hypothetical atomic and sub-atomic entities of which theoretical physics treats, *if* molar physics is to be reduced to mechanics, or if Nature, in spite of appearance to the contrary at the molar level, is to admit of rigorously mechanical explanation. And, doubtless, desire to realise Newton's hope has largely constituted the motivation of microscopic theorising. If physical phenomena such as those of light are to become wholly describable in dynamical terms, ether is a requisite. But the Actuality of a microscopic realm, such as phenomenal facts indicate, does not of itself suffice to render Nature either 'homogeneously' or 'purely' mechanical. Mere smallness, exceeding our powers of observation, does not imply such mechanicalness: movements might be microscopic and yet not obey Lagrange's equations. In fact the atomic theory, as used in Chemistry, is microscopic but is not rigidly mechanical. Its particles are not homogeneous; and it needs no assumption that the laws of atomic interaction are those of 'pure' mechanism. The success of this theory affords pragmatic justification of the belief that matter has a grained structure, but no justification of either type of rigid mechanism. Again, if the electron-theory could be believed to possess the abiding successfulness enjoyed by the atomic theory, it also would reflect no credit on rigid mechanism: in positing both the proton and the electron it is not perfectly 'homogeneous'; and, in that its fundamental laws are other than those of central forces, it renounces 'pure' mechanism. Lastly, the successful dynamic theory of gases is an application of 'pure', but not of 'homogeneous' mechanism. Thus, the scientific explanation of particular departments of phenomena does not involve knowledge that the more rigid types of mechanism either must, or do, prevail within the microscopic realm. And when we proceed from particular fields to their interconnexion, and inquire as to the scientific contemplation of the world as a unified whole, we again find rigid mechanism to be dispensable. It would doubtless supply a neat unitary explanation; qualitative identity and dynamically analysable laws certainly possess aesthetic seductiveness for lovers of the simple, the clear and distinct. But whether Nature, blushing unseen as to her microscopic structure, is as logically beautiful as we can imagine she might be, cannot be inferred from the portraits of her that science possesses. Perhaps to assume that logical beauty is her supreme charm, as if she were hard-featured and expressionless, is to pay her a compliment that is doubtful in more senses than one.

If scientific explicability consist essentially in satisfaction of the Lagrangean equations in any form, it has been shewn that these equations can hold without being interpreted in their more rigid senses. We should then be presented, as Dr Broad has shewn, with a hierarchy of laws instead of with the minimum required by pure and homogeneous mechanism. Things might obey laws that are none the less laws for not being deducible from dynamics, or for dynamics having no reason to suspect their existence. The dynamical laws apply only to isolated systems. But science may be, and in the case of organisms and their parts seems to be, confronted with Actual systems that are not isolated, and which, though not without law, are not subject to laws of the purely dynamical kind. Science can and does proceed and succeed without invoking or requiring rigid mechanism: no physicist works with it. Metrical science implies neither the necessity nor the possibility of a microscopic realm subject to rigid mechanism. That which does imply such things is the ideal science of which the physicist can only dream. And not only is rigid mechanism scientifically dispensable; "no one", says Boltzmann, "maintains that we have obtained proof that the whole of natural phenomena can certainly be explained mechanically". It may be added that there are no strong reasons for believing rigid mechanism to be true. For such reasons we must wait until electron-like entities have been devised and found negotiable, that are of one kind only, and obey one simple law of central forces. Further, if science were dependent on pure and homogeneous mechanism, it would not follow, or be logically certified, that those theories are true. Lastly, if they were true, such mechanism could not possibly be the whole truth about the material world. For any interaction between matter and spirit would be beyond its range: yet, without some interaction between spirit and matter—or rather, between spirit and the ontal counterpart to phenomenal and conceptual matter—perception, etc., become unthinkable.

The nature of mechanics and of the mechanical method in physics have now been sufficiently examined to provide the knowledge that is requisite for understanding the relation in which the mechanical world-view stands to science. In the Preface to his *Principia* Newton expressed the hope that the laws there formulated would afford some light either as to the mechanical derivation of physical phenomena in general, similar to that by which he accounted for the motions of the planets, etc., or as to "some more perfect method of philosophy". The latter alternative, however, was discarded by many investigators. Thus Huyghens spoke of the *true philosophy*, in which the causes of all natural effects are conceived as mechanical grounds (*raisons*), and asserted that, in his judgement, they must be so conceived, else all hope of ever understanding physics must be renounced.[1] And physicists have often regarded the bounds of the applicability of rigid mechanism as constituted by the limitations of our understanding, not by the limits of the mechanical method. Huyghens' "true philosophy", or pure and homogeneous mechanism, has already been shewn to be no requisite, and no implication, of quantitative physics. But, lest to fall back at once on Newton's second hope seem premature, we may consider such approximations as science has made towards

---

[1] *Traité de la lumière*, 1690, p. 2, cited by Mach.

rigid mechanical theory, in order to estimate the likelihood of his first hope being ever fulfilled.

It is partly with a view to reducing physics to some kind of rigidly mechanistic theory that science has increasingly speculated about a microscopic realm. There alone can mechanical explanation of macroscopic phenomena be sought. And when we turn to the method of investigation pursued, we observe the necessary difference between it and that of molar mechanics. Molar mechanics is abstract or partial, but also direct or perceptual. Microscopic physics is not abstract, for it deals with the properties which molar mechanics sets aside; but it is indirect, in that its *mikra* are imperceptible and can be dealt with only in crowds or as averages rather than as individuals, in so far as hypothesis can be tested in respect of compatibility with observable facts. These *mikra* must be of finite magnitude, else physics lapses into a pure science of mass-points. Yet they must not be endowed with any of the qualities which, as belonging to molar bodies, they are invoked to explain mechanically. As they are non-impressional, there is no direct vouch for their Actuality. As Objects of cognition, in the most non-committing sense of 'cognition', they are forthcoming in virtue of conception or constructive imagination. They are ideal; and if they have Real or ontal counterparts, that can only be ascertained reflectively or indirectly, as in the case of the soul. Imperceptibleness does not preclude such Reality; it only precludes direct knowledge thereof. But whereas the ontal existence of the soul seems to be an indispensable condition of the explicability of a multitude of empirical facts, the Reality of the physicist's *mikra* is not: it is not a condition of the forthcomingness, or even of the explicability, of the facts, but only a condition of their *mechanical* explicability. And intelligibility of that particular sort is no precondition of science; it is but a human desideratum or an aesthetic luxury.

The indirectness of the method of microscopic science raises further questions. Firstly, we need to inquire as to the nature of the 'verification' on which the realist relies, who would take any of the *mikra* of theoretical physics to be ontal existents, or Objects of possible or conceivable, if contingently precluded, experience. This question is readily answered. Since molar phenomena afford the sole external control by which microscopic theories can be tested, it follows that 'verification' must consist in shewing that the theories are compatible with the molar facts. Such pragmatic verification, we have already seen, is disparate from logical certi-fication. It may shew that Nature behaves *as if* its structure were what microscopic theory represents it to be; but that is far from proving that Nature *is* what it is thus represented to be. A hypothesis may fit the facts without being the only one that fits them: it may be sufficient without being necessary, or exclusive, or final, or true. Pragmatic verification may inspire the maximum of mental certitude, though establishing no logical certainty. As motivations to belief, these epistemologically disparate things are equivalent; they are commonly referred to by the same name: hence they are very often confounded or falsely identified. And this is the case when the physicist regards his conceptual entities as ontal. The history of science testifies that the certitude of one generation as to the Reality of particular *mikra*, such as the hard atom, the vortex-atom, or the quasi-material ether, is wont to give place to the scepticism of another generation. The probability, in fact, of microscopic theories, is of the alogical kind; and the realist's sanguine confidence is rather a matter of more or less reasonable belief than of rational knowledge. In this connexion it is but fair to mention that convincedness, as to the Reality of the *mikra* that are adopted in any given age, is not due so much to the satisfactori-ness of a particular *mikron* for explanation of a particular restricted sphere of phenomena, as to the inter-relatedness and inter-dependence of several hypotheses which conspire to furnish a coherent science. The sub-atomic physics that has of late grown up commands respect in this way, and compels belief that it sets forth some version of the truth, if not the ultimate and literal truth, as to the constitution of matter. That crystals can be used as diffraction-gratings to analyse recently discovered radiations, while, inversely, the radiations confirm the atomistic hypothesis as to crystal-structure; that sub-atomic particles can be turned to account to solve long-standing puzzles concerning the atomic weights of certain elements, and to explain irregularities connected with the periodic law: these and similar instances of one micro-scopic hypothesis playing into the hand of another certainly justify, as reasonable, the conviction that such scientific theory is in touch with Reality. The realist's *apologia* is akin to that of the theist who relies on the interconnexion and cumulativeness of the facts which suggest cosmic design. Neither the sub-atomic hypotheses nor the belief in a Designer possesses what some would call *a priori* or antecedent probability; both are entertained because of the agreement of some of their consequences with observable facts. But we may accord to fruitful theory as to hypothetical *mikra* the appreciation that is due to it without identifying what may be a figurative version with literal truth, and while recognising that the pragmatic method of verification can never yield knowledge other than that of the 'as if' kind. It suffices to affirm that the relations, expressed in the equations of science, subsist between the unknown *onta* of Nature as they do between our imaged or conceived *mikra*, and that electronic charges and masses, quanta, etc., represent something significant of the physical world; but it is gratuitous to cherish the further belief that the *mikra* are identical with the *onta*. The ether, the electron, the nucleus, the revolutions round the nucleus, the electronic leaps from one orbit to another, the quantum-change, and all such microscopic machinery, are neither observed nor inferred: they are conjectures which, within limits that are elastic with regard to time, fit with marvellous accuracy, if with some internal inconsistency, a vast collection of molar facts. That they alone fit is unknowable; that they all will continue to fit facts yet to be discovered is historically improbable. That they largely represent Nature's constitution to the human mind, are 'true' in the pragmatic sense, and are related to ultimate reality and verity, is all that we are entitled to assert, and all that science need demand. That they mediate metaphysical knowledge, pure and phenomenally undefiled, or the whole truth and nothing but the truth, is a belief that is as precarious as it is superfluous.

Indeed the microscopic theories of physicists may be accepted as revelations of Objects of possible phenomenal experience without our being brought any the nearer to an identification of physics either with ontology or with rigid mechanism. The *mikra* that have successively proved serviceable to science have often been the macroscopic over again, merely reduced to Liliputian stature. The rigid atom, the elastic atom, the various models conceived in order to make the structure and strains of the ether imaginable, have all retained physical properties which it is incumbent on rigorous mechanism to eliminate from molar bodies: all have been but non-mechanical reduplications of the non-mechanical. The electron-theory is the nearest approach that has as yet been made towards fulfilment of the demands of homogeneous and pure mechanism; but it has already been observed that it falls short of satisfying either kind. It would appear, then, that microscopic physics reduces, more or less, the manifold qualitativeness of molar phenomena, but does not eliminate it. The approach to the limit of homogeneity or identity is asymptotic.

Moreover, if science could realise its hope of reducing physics to pure and homogeneous mechanics, it would *ipso facto* cease to be science. In coming to perfection it would perish. Instead of issuing in ontology, *i.e.* instead of discovering what goes on behind the phenomenal scene, or even of revealing (to the eye of the understanding) Objects of possible experience, it would lapse into pure kinematics, and so over-reach itself. This is best illustrated by a particular microscopic theory which has not proved permanently serviceable to physics, but which in its brief day inspired confident belief that at last the ontal had been disclosed: Lord Kelvin's kinetic theory of matter. Matter, with its Newtonian massiveness that is empirically manifested and mechanically effective, was conceived by Lord Kelvin as a mode of motion of a perfect fluid, or as non-matter in motion. Its massiveness needed to be regarded as a semblance of some ultra-physical 'mass', or of a property of modes of motion, instead of as a property of matter itself; and such *quasi*-mass proved a very complicated and obscure conception. But more important is the fact that the non-material plenum, endowed only with negative attributes, is an indeterminate abstraction, and therefore nothing ontal or substantial. Thus homogeneity was secured at the expense of Actuality. And apart from this particular attempt, it is plain that the abstractions space, time, and mass, with which alone rigid mechanism should work, cannot yield the Actual, the ontal, or the substantial. Mass either is a property intrinsic to some *thing*, or else is a number: it is no more a substantival entity than 5 per cent. is a sum of money. Without the substantial we may have rigid mechanism and kinematics; with it we may have physics that is not mechanics, and metaphysics that is not physics. The inherent trend of physics, in so far as its abstract theories are construed as ontology,

> is like a circle in the water,
> Which never ceaseth to enlarge itself,
> Till, by broad spreading, it disperse to nought.

In conclusion, it may be observed that the endeavour to explain matter and its properties in terms of the dynamical alone, though achieving much in the unification of separate fields of phenomena, has led neither to simplicity, or economy in respect of hypothetical existents, nor to exhaustiveness, nor to finality, nor to consistency.

Instead of the simplifications that were desired and sought, science presents an unwieldy and ever increasing collection of hypothetical models. Atoms have been conceived as vortices, knots of strain, points of emergence from a fourth dimension, solid spheres separated by gaps, and so on. Instead of observable physical qualities, we have been offered quasi-mass, quasi-elasticity, quasi-impacts, and quasi-matter. Every attempt thoroughly to mechanicise Nature has involved resort to the mysterious and unknowable. If Hertz's system be the climax of the classical dynamics, it presents us with an indefinite number of "hidden" masses and motions for the explanation of those we observe; if Helmholtz's device for reducing Nature's irreversibility to an outcome of the purely mechanical and reversible be the most considerable attempt to mechanicise the statistical second law of thermodynamics, it also resorts to concealed masses and motions, which, in the opinion of Poincaré and other critics, are as insufficient for their purpose as they are purely hypothetical. Reduction of bodies, properties, and changes, to only one kind of each has been attended by enormous complications in the realm of the non-observable. And, notwithstanding the inordinate complexity of the highly suspicious mechanisms required, whole tracts of phenomena, such as gravitation, chemical affinity, temperature, not to speak of life and mind, remain unaccounted for by any rigidly mechanical system that has developed out of Newtonian or Lagrangean dynamics. Neither the impact-theory of motion, which is based on the concepts of inertia and impressed force, nor the theory of central forces and of action at a distance, allows of the deduction of the empirical second law of thermodynamics, the significance of which is not abolished when one points out that it is a statistical law. According to that principle, the capacity of a given quantity of heat to do work is greater when a higher temperature is in question than when a lower temperature is concerned. Thus temperature, or something qualitative, over and above equivalence in respect of energy, enters into the determination of Actual process. Carnot's principle, in fact, gives the lie to a purely dynamical theory involving reversibility. Here is a hint, supplied by physics itself, that in the course of Nature ἐνέργεια rather than Newtonian δύναμις, creative evolution or emergence rather than change of configuration of identicals, occurs: that *causa aequat effectum*, and the 'timelessness' of abstract science, are not metaphysically true. As yet there is no purely dynamical explanation forthcoming of the fact that filled time flows but one way which passes as satisfactory. Hence rigid mechanism may be said to be inexhaustive. Newton's first law, ruling out all *vis insita*, has been found to be not universally applicable. Where there is change, there also, it would seem, is diversity, not identity in a new configuration. Newton's second law does not hold when mass is dependent on velocity, nor therefore if the now ruling sub-atomic theory is to be accepted. It is not valid if electrons are non-material, in the old sense, nor of atoms if they are wholly composed of electrons. Newton's third law is incompatible with prevailing theory and with the particular phenomenon known as the pressure of light. Lastly, the quantum-theory implies that Nature is discontinuous, or that *per saltum* is her method; whereas Newtonian, Lagrangean, and Einsteinian forms of mechanism bespeak continuity. In the case of radiation, the tendency of the energy of a system, moving in a medium, to be transferred to the medium in the shortest vibrations of which the medium is capable—a tendency that is a direct consequence of Newton's laws—does not appear to exist; and Planck's law of phenomena due to isochronous vibrations involves the leaps, or the atomicity in what is technically called 'action', asserted by the quantum-theory. This theory seems to many physicists to be required by various molar phenomena, such as line-spectra, photo-electric effects, and deviation of specific heats from older law; though a few think that a truer theory of the electron would make the quantum-dynamics superfluous. If the action-leap should come, as seems overwhelmingly probable, to be unanimously accepted as a new universal constant of Nature, another piece of evidence will have been supplied by physics that macroscopic phenomena cannot be construed as crowd-effects or appearances of microscopic *onta* obeying the principles of pure and homogeneous mechanism. Moreover, no laws are as yet indicated to prescribe when, or why at any given moment, or in any given atom, the quantum-change should occur. The quantum is another alogicality in Nature; and it is unintelligible in the further sense of being unlinked with the totality of current physical ideas.

It would seem to be the outcome of the foregoing discussion that quantitative science reveals, and also presupposes, the reign of law, and the hierarchy of laws, provided by what Dr Broad has called macroscopic mechanism; but that science neither reveals nor presupposes a rigid mechanism of microscopic entities.[1] The only science that can be rigidly mechanical is a pure science, not

---

[1] The revolutions in physics, consequent on recent development of theory as to the subatomic, seem increasingly to involve abandonment of the hope that the macroscopic may prove mechanically explicable in terms of the microscopic. During the present phase of reorganisation of theory as to the electron and the quantum, several startling views have been propounded, of which some account will be found in Prof. Eddington's work, *The Nature of the Physical World*. One eminent investigator in this department of physical theory seeks for the governing laws of exact science in symbolic expressions constituting a *non-arithmetical* calculus. Another has been led to emulate a principle, regarded by Prof. Eddington as ranking in importance with that of Einstein, which reduces the old notion of the particle, supposed to have both position and velocity in some exact sense, as an attempt to describe something which cannot exist in Nature. This principle also implies that physics must henceforth be hostile to the idea of a scheme of deterministic law, in that the laws governing microscopic entities such as individual electrons and quanta do not enable science to predict what such an individual will do next. Prediction, it appears, is but statistical; and all that is predetermined is the odds in favour of one course being followed rather than another. Causality, in the sense in which it is invoked by determinism, is thus discarded by the kind of science which professes to deal with the physically ultimate.

Whether or not these revolutionary ideas become established, it may safely be concluded that imagery in terms of the familiar, which hitherto has directed theory in the subatomic field, is now being abandoned as misleading analogy. The view that physical science deals with a world of symbolic entities, or treats of the Actual world in terms of conceptual symbolism, which until lately was held only by philosophers, save for an individual physicist here and there, has now become characteristic of the general scientific attitude of mind. The non-exhaustiveness of science's symbolism is confessed; and the recognition of a background or a Beyond, and of mystery which increases *pari passu* with knowledge, or penetrativeness of thought, has become more explicit and articulate.

physics or science of Nature. The *mikra* that are indicated by empirical facts and are serviceable for investigation are but the macroscopic in essence, retaining somewhat of the qualitative which homogeneous mechanism would fain dissipate. In straining out the qualitative or sensible, theoretical science strains out Actuality also. It does not reach the ontal, but only the conceptual. Inert identicals are but fictions or abstractions. And an abstraction is not an ultimate Reality; metaphysically it is nothing. Science can throw no light on the question what the ontal counterparts to physical bodies and phenomena are. It does not know what matter ultimately is, and has no means of knowing. So far as science can tell, matter may be phenomenon of spirit. The one kind of thing of which it cannot be phenomenal is the non-Actual abstraction. Mechanism is not a phenomenal aspect; it is abstractive description: and, as such, it is neither universally applicable noi in any single instance exhaustive. And as science cannot fathom the phenomenal so as to reach to the underlying ontal, it can attain to no knowledge about the metaphysics of causation; nor, therefore, to any knowledge as to the *modus operandi* of ontal agents, of which observable laws of Nature are the outcome. The mechanical interpretation of law and of change having proved intrinsically impossible, because found to substitute kinematics for physics, the rigidly mechanical theory of the world becomes baseless. Newton's first hope having revealed itself to be vain, it remains to consider whether his alternative suggestion, as to the possibility of some more perfect method of philosophy, promises to be more realisable.

CHAPTER III

Explanation in Science and in Theology: the 'Rationality' of the World

It has been submitted that the rigidly mechanical theory is unworkable within its own sphere of the (phenomenally) material world. As it develops, this theory involves itself in complexity and artificiality, thereby revealing its true nature. Its inert and homogeneous entities, and the ultimate elements which in the theoretical physics of the present hour approximate to the homogeneous, are neither ontal nor phenomenal: they constitute a fictional descriptive scheme, or rather an incongruous set of schemes, partially applicable, into all or any of which even inorganic Nature refuses wholly to fit. Schemes involving thorough-going continuity and schemes presupposing radical discreteness are as serviceable as they are incompatible. Physics brings to light the mathematical relations subsisting between phenomena; but science does not know—perhaps is ceasing to care—what 'matter' ultimately is. The ontal world-elements may be not only heterogeneous but also living. They may be related to one another in ways other than that which mechanism prescribes, without prejudice to the less rigid mechanicalness or regularity of Nature on the molar scale. So far is physical science from threatening the banishment of spirit and spontaneity that it does not necessitate even the dualism of disparate spirit and matter. Spiritualism is equally compatible with science; and while spirit is underivable from matter, matter may well be appearance of spirit. Perhaps, in affording a more satisfactory solution of the problem of the relation of mind to body, the spiritualistic interpretation of matter yields a preferable ontology. But whether there be in our world any ontally material—*i.e.* inert—beings as well as spiritual beings, with instances of which we are acquainted, is perhaps one of the questions which philosophy will never answer, since no empirical touchstone for the decision of it seems imaginable. All we can say is that spiritualism, singularistic as to substance-kind, and pluralistic as to instances of it, is empirically possible: science can neither disprove nor verify it. And theology,

such as is derived from the study of the world and man, is indifferent to the issue. Spiritualism does not imply theism; and it
will be submitted later that neither the argument for theism nor
theistic reinterpretation of the world depends on the establishment
of spiritualism and the refutation of dualism, save in the ancient
and absolute form of the doctrine of the self-subsistence of matter.
More germane to these questions is the conclusion reached in the
preceding chapter: that such reign of law as science has found in
the physical world does not receive its sole explanation, nor a
sufficient explanation, in terms of inertia and negation of *vis
insita*. This means that Newton's second hope may be yet realisable,
whereas his first is hopeless. Only the less rigid kind of mechanism, which asserts no more than a hierarchy of independent
laws, some of which admit of quantitative formulation, is applicable;
and it is applicable only to *Natura* as already *naturata*. If rigid
mechanism be untenable, Nature may also be *naturans*. And, to
put these scholastic phrases to the newer use that is becoming
common, *Natura naturata* is the product of *Natura naturans*.
Law and order are neither self-subsistent priorities nor consequences of inertia and of *vis* that is necessarily *a tergo*, but of
action, whether in all cases due to spiritual *conatus* or not. On the
other hand, the regularity that Nature evinces does not strictly
imply directivity by one Mind: if it did, theism would scarcely
need proving. But inasmuch as minds are known to produce
order of various kinds, and are the only known causes of order
when its ontal causation is assignable, it is not unreasonable,
though logical rationality or coercive proof is out of the question,
to seek an explanation of the world's order by postulating a Mind,
creative and directive of Nature. Such an attempt is at least no
more absurd than the alternative of referring the world's adaptedness, and its suggested meaning for rational beings, to unfounded
coincidence. That the play of *Hamlet* originated in an accidental
scattering of some founts of type would not commend itself to a
reasonable man; and that the world, when all its aspects are taken
into account, seems more or less comparable to such a product of
mind is not *prima facie* a fond and foolish fancy. Moreover, facts
such as that *Hamlet* contains so many letters, and that the number
of its lines is a certain fraction of the number of lines in the whole
of *Shakespeare*, may be established without exhausting the truth

as to either *Hamlet* itself or its relations to the rest of Shakespeare's poetry. A poem is not adequately, if it is truly, described as so many, thus and thus classifiable, black marks on white paper.

As Ward once said, "science might have finished its work and yet be a fool". In other words, there are aspects of the world, to be taken into account in a comprehensive philosophy of it, which science ignores; and, from another point of view than that of sciences, the mechanical and structural interpretation of Nature may be, as Ward observed, the shallowest rather than the most profound. Such representations as these, however, and their import for a theistic argument, can be more justly weighed after examination of the kinds of explanation which science and theology respectively pursue. This inquiry will also serve to make clear what may precisely be meant by such ambiguous assertions as that the world is rational, that its rationality is the precondition of science, or that its rationality is the proof of theism.

It should be observed that the words 'explain' and 'explicate', in their current yet derived senses, have an epistemic ingredient or a psychological reference. To explain is not only to do something to a proposition or an event, comparable to smoothing out a crumpled leaf, but also to do something for minds. Mental habit and economical linguistic device abstract from this subjective reference; but in the case of explanation they do not so completely suppress it, or conceal it from the tail of our mental eye, as in some instances that have before been noticed, in which non-significant indefinables are generated. Few, perhaps, would be prepared to deny that explanation is always interpretation. A bud is explicated when it has unfolded itself into a flower; it is explained when its parts are traceable by us as modified leaves. To explain, in short, is to make intelligible; and intelligibility depends on minds. 'Intelligible', however, bears several meanings; and discrimination between them is essential to philosophy and to clear thinking.

(i) The sense of 'intelligible' which it is suitable here to consider first is that of *assimilable by some apperceptive system*: whether such a one as may form part of the mentality of a barbaric magician or such as a Fellow of the Royal Society may have formed. A phenomenon only calls for explanation when it seems merely contingent, like a bolt from the blue, or as neither continuous nor identical with events already familiar. It is explained when it can be described in terms of conceptions acquired and facts with which there has been acquaintance. What can be understood depends on what is already understood: and so on, in regress to the first acquisition of primary meaning. Indeed the primordial type of the human dealing, interpretation or explanation of things, is what is called reduction to the familiar. From its lowest stage, therefore, explanation involves some classification, detection of similarity amidst diversity, and more or less of elimination of *prima facie* uniqueness. The kind of conceptions which subserve explanation, and produce the satisfaction attending removal of obscurity, perplexity, etc., is primarily determined by the fact that they lie ready to hand. But what conceptions lie ready is an accident of history, a matter of what happened to be learned first. On these lines Mach has suggested that the mechanical trend of modern physics is due to the motion of bodies having been the first subject of scientific study: motion chanced to become scientifically 'familiar' before other things, and so the other things came to be explained in terms of it. That is probably part of the truth, though hardly the whole of it.

Nearest to the original type of explanation, in terms of the familiar in the sense of matter of acquaintance or perception, is that in which perceptibility gives place to imaginability. Familiarity is still the dominant director, but the *explicans* is now but imaginal and no longer Actual, as is the *explicandum*. This second kind of explanation is neither obsolete nor useless in science. British physicists have often preferred to 'understand' phenomena by means of models, or visual and tactual images of perceptual and familiar things, rather than by algebraic formulae alone: as when they have pictured an ether as fluid, as elastic or as rigid, and as having this or that particular structure. Action at a distance is not thus imaginable; it lacks the mediating link supplied, in the case of impact-action, by our causing motion through pushing or pulling: hence to Newton it seemed an absurd notion. But a further venture of imagination is involved in the undulatory theory of light than is needed, *e.g.* in the wave-theory of the propagation of sound. Though air-waves are invisible, the evidence that waves exist in air is little short of being direct; and the air itself is perceptible, whereas ether is not. We connect the phenomena of light with our previous knowledge and our apperception-systems by means of a constructed image, like and yet unlike something perceived: an image to which perhaps nothing Actual wholly corresponds. Then reduction of the [scientifically] unknown (light) to the [perceptually] known (waves) involves reduction of the [perceptually] known (light) to the [perceptually] unknown (ether-waves). The necessary interpolation of the words here enclosed in square brackets indicates that the common saying, 'explanation consists in reduction of the unknown to the known', can be false or paradoxical unless kinds of knowledge are discriminated, and if 'reduction to' be always taken to mean more than 'analogy with'.

(ii) Next in affinity, from the point of view of psychology, with the primordial kinds of explanation thus far described, is causal explanation of the cruder sort. This consists not in reducing to the familiar but rather in deriving out of the familiar, or out of the known past. Familiarity here fades into analogy, and reduction to other external things is largely exchanged for assimilation with self. The instrument used is not perception or imagination, but a 'real' category of the 'understanding', constitutive of thought-knowledge. Scientific explanation has, as a matter of history, consisted mainly in discovering the causes of things. To the working physicist, to whom a cause means a particular bit of Nature of which the *explicandum* is the outcome, an event is unexplained until he has found out how and whence it is produced. It is causal explanation, in this sense, that gives to evolutionary sciences and genetic methods their import and philosophical value. So long as the causes, or conditions *sine quibus non*, are *verae causae* or Actualities, causal explanation is, in a broader than the usual sense of the phrase, natural history. The *propter hoc* exhibits the antecedents out of which, and the stages through which, the posterior thing came to be, and to be what it is. Inasmuch as all such causes are proximate causes, absolute beginnings being beyond science's ken, causal explanation is always relative and bounded by mystery. But it carries us much further than explanation in terms of acquaintance-familiarity, by establishing premises and connexions on which we can rely, and it affords scientific 'knowledge'. It illustrates the dictum, 'like is known by like'; but the knowledge in question involves interpretation rather than reading of the self-evident, and is 'proved' not by logical certification but by pragmatic verification. The relatively crude notion of efficient causation temporarily satisfied modern explanatory science. Doubtless it did so because it seemed to reduce the behaviour and determination of things, as distinguished from the nature and determinateness of things themselves, to the familiar: likening it to that of active and psychical subjects.

If assimilation with a pre-existing apperception-system of any sort, or reduction to the familiar, be the primordial intent of explanation, it is not the essence of explanation in its intellectually higher stages, when another sense is borne by 'making intelligible'. The familiar affords a foothold to the explanation-seeking mind at the beginning of its climb, but no comfortable resting-place to the mind in quest of rational penetration and clarity rather than of reasonable interpretation by successful analogy. From the point of view of the understanding, as contrasted with sense and imagination, the familiar may itself be occult. What is simply given in acquaintance or perception is insoluble in thought. Thought cannot derive, or deduce, or penetrate it: the most it can do is to discover relations within the realm of brute or impressional fact. 'Understanding', in its technical sense, connotes apprehension of relations, and the relational is the intelligible. But this occultness of familiar facts and processes excites the human mind to further adventures, commonly comprised under the one name of 'explanation'. Thus, motion is no more familiar than heat; yet we would explain heat as a mode of motion. A new standard or criterion of fitness to be an *explicans* is here implied: and motion has been adopted as the ultimate *explicans* in science not only for Mach's reason, alluded to above, but also because we are wont to think that motion and the concepts involved in it "lie nearest to the understanding"—the phrase is Kirchhoff's. How much of truth there is in this belief will presently be inquired; but it will already be seen that the more refined and intellectually satisfying kind of explanation, pursued in theoretical science, aims at reducing the familiar, no less than the unfamiliar, to the clear. It regards intelligibility as penetrability by the understanding. And understanding is restricted to the use of those categories alone which, to distinguish them from dynamic or 'real' categories, are called formal. It follows that the kind of causal explanation that has already been described is also then transcended. Although the Cartesian pursuit of the clear and distinct was a recoil from medieval occultism, Descartes was so imperfectly emancipated from traditional thought as to take the familiar but obscure notion of cause, destined presently to give philosophers so much trouble, for a clear idea. Later physicists, however, discarded it as "metaphysical", merely analogical and useless. If it made processes intelligible in the sense of assimilable with the self and its mental dispositions, it did not make them intelligible in the sense of reducible to clear conception and amenable to description in terms of the logical and mathematical categories. Whether such reduction is possible, without disappearance of the unique and indispensable functions for which the causal notion was fashioned, was discussed in vol. 1; here we are only concerned with the influence of criticism of the idea of cause on received meanings of 'explanation'.

(iii) When intelligibility, consisting in absorptiveness into an apperceptive system that may itself be intellectually turbid, gives place to intelligibility in the sense of transparency to the formal understanding, causal explanation becomes the tracing of identity behind phenomenal variety, as in homogeneous mechanism. Change, which is the general provocative of explanation in us, becomes intelligible in the latter sense in so far as likeness is detected beneath diversity, and continuity is traceable behind apparent alteration or substitution. Processes become as explicable as they ever can be if they can be shewn to be cases of the one kind of change, motion, which we suppose to be the easiest to follow, in things that otherwise are immutable and are homogeneous. This is why atomism is indispensable to explanatory science. It provides entities which in two senses are identities: they are self-identical or permanent, and they are qualitatively alike. Conservation of matter, as distinct from conservation of mass, means to the chemist that the carbon in carbonic acid is the selfsame atoms that constituted the unoxidised carbon; and the more rigorous and comprehensive theory of the physicist asserts the atoms of carbon and oxygen to be not qualitatively heterogeneous, but only different constellations of identical atoms of higher order, or differently configured. Atomism was first conjectured for no such empirical purposes as it now serves but, seemingly, to effect a compromise, or a *via media*, between Parmenidean being and

Heraclitean becoming. It embodied the view that there is change, but that the only Real change is change of position in space. Thus it resolved the mystery attending the production of an effect, or the emergence of novelty, since motion purported to be non-mysterious or rationally clear; and the productivity of causation, which in the abstract may conceivably originate anything what-soever, was restricted to effecting displacement alone. Only in this refined sense is causality retained by atomism and rigid mechanism. On the other hand, they abide by the equally "meta-physical"—*i.e.* non-formal, interpretative, and anthropically derived—category of substance or permanence, which is as "imperceptible" as causation, unimpaired. This is requisite in order that motion be cleared of the very occultness that the con-ception of motion, as the only kind of change, should eliminate from physical processes: for, without permanent substances to move, apparent change of position would need to be accounted destruction of a body at one place and creation *ex nihilo* of a similar body at another place. Motion, as an Actuality to be contrasted with an empty concept, is thus not conceivable without a 'real' category, in addition to the formal categories of the under-standing. And if motion is something that comes nearest to being formally intelligible because only the one 'real' category of per-manent substance lies between it and perfect or formal intelligi-bility, both it and its production fall short of being items of pure thought-knowledge. Motion is 'near' to being 'understood', in the sense that is here intended, in that it is a simple change or is change of only one kind, and—substance once being invoked—is the sort of change that it is easiest to follow in imagination. But, as a simply given fact about matter, motion or movability is as brute and alogical as any other qualitative characteristic that we would reduce to a case of it; and its production by impact, however familiar, has no more of logical derivation, of thought-necessitation, or of self-evidence prior to sensory experience, than has, *e.g.* the production of redness in iron by heating it. Perhaps one motivation to the regarding of motion as more ultimate than another property of matter is that we know what it feels like to move a body, but not what it feels like to be red. But in the last resort impact-action is as alogical as action at a distance; and indeed contact-action presents difficult problems to the natural philosopher. Science can never eliminate the occult, or dispense with reliance on the familiar. The most she can do, and what she strives to do, is to retain for her own use no more than the minimal amount of it. The choice of any one of the indefinable and unanalysable ultimates thrust upon us in *Erlebnis* and sensation, all as mysterious as they are familiar, to be sole *explicans* amongst *explicanda*, is interest-guided. Matter, to be distinguishable from space, must have some character, simple or complex; and why it should be credited with only one causal property, in terms of which all its phenomenal manifestations are to be explained, is no more a case of *a priori*, or of logical, necessity than it is of *prima facie* plausibility. The conceit is needful for the 'reduction' of all changes to change of configuration of the changeless; and that reduction is but a human *desideratum*. As Verdet said, "the true problem of the physicist is always to reduce all phenomena to that which seems to us the simplest and clearest, *i.e.* to movement". And we may drop his word "seems" and say 'that which *is* to us the simplest and clearest', or 'that which lies nearest to the understanding'; yet simplicity, and even clarity, will still be determined by *our* understanding. They certainly set the standard of explicability that has urged thought on from 'there is a cause for every effect' to *causa aequat effectum*, and thence to 'the cause *is* the effect'—in a new configuration. But this standard is not purely rational, if that word mean either free from the alogical and occult or devoid of epistemic and anthropic reference. Between science and the world stands human nature.

The actual working of the canon of explicability with which we are at present concerned was examined when homogeneous mechanism received discussion; and that kind of scientific explanation may be said to amount to a revival of Wolff's attempt to extract the principle of sufficient reason out of the principle of contradiction. The present inquiry is epistemological rather than scientific, and it may still be pursued a little further. Clearness has taken, in this type of explanation, the place that familiarity held in types of the less rigorous kind; or rather, it has replaced it so far as was possible without self-stultification. And 'clearness', it may now be observed, bears different shades of meaning when it is predicated of ideas of things or terms, and of relations subsisting between terms, respectively. In the former connexion it should be distinguished from two cognate concepts. It does not mean simplicity, which is the outcome of analysis or partition within some one complex; nor definiteness or distinctness, which is the outcome of isolation or demarcation from neighbouring or overlapping ideas. It rather connotes non-obscurity to the under-standing—to understanding as restricted to the functions indicated by the formal categories alone—which is the outcome of abstraction. The opaque experience-stuff that is strained out in order to yield the clear is sense, which refuses wholly to distil into idea or thought. So the clear idea is such a one as is wont to be described as form without matter. This can only mean the mini-mum amount of matter that is necessary to constitute form, as something distinguishable from nothingness. The image or idea of a three-sided, hilly, fragrant, hay-field is less clear than that of a Euclidean triangle, which is simply shape abstracted from size, colour, etc., apart from one or more of which, triangularity is a non-Actuality. And the clearest ideas, such as those of mathe-matics, are also the emptiest and the furthest removed from concrete things. On this account they are the more useful as fine instruments of thought, of a special kind; but on the same account they are least capable of figuring as things and agents, phenomenal or ontal. The mass-point, because a clear idea, is a nonentity, though it is useful enough as a descriptive symbol.

'Clearness', as applied to relations, seems chiefly to mean capacity to be read-off with the maximum of immediacy, rather than capacity to be reached by the maximum of abstractiveness. Instances of the clearest relations are those of qualitative likeness or difference, temporal succession, and numerical otherness. This clarity is closely bound up with certainty, and with 'rationality' in the sense of logical certification. Hence the importance of clearness to science, and the persistence of the philosophical endeavour to substitute some formal category for the obscure and analogical idea of efficient causation. If the Real is the rational, and the rational is the clear, *i.e.* abstract ideas connected only by logical and mathematical relations, then our world is not Real or rational. As has been argued in previous contexts, science, and therefore philosophy, of the Actual world, cannot subsist on so meagre a provision as that of penetrability by the cold and dry light of the formal understanding. Indeed, apart from further requisites such as alogical sense-data and 'real' categories, both of which belong to the unclear, the kind of explanation that we are at present concerned with needs to rely on another criterion of intelligibility, viz. what is often called simplicity, but may less ambiguously be described as paucity of ultimate concepts and laws.

Unlikeness is at least as immediately discerned as likeness; and plurality, as singleness. When, therefore, rigorously intellectual explanation, such as rigid mechanism, seeks for homogeneity of world-elements and unification of world-laws, it makes selection even within the restricted sphere of clear ideas and relations, in order to render the world intelligible. Plainly another motivation besides that of clarity is then involved. Simplicity will more aptly be discussed in connexion with the type of explanation which consists essentially in reduction to law; but a few words may find place here as to the psychological motivation of the most narrowly intellectualistic type of explanation.

We may ask why it is that we are apt to think that motion or change requires a cause, while rest or immutability does not. Persistence *in statu quo* may involve as much causal activity, in the way of self-maintenance and resistance to change, as does restless movement. We assume that it does not, and that, so far from calling for explanation, it is naturally and obviously the *explicans* of change. Philosophers have often striven to prove that change, and time which is involved therein, are illusions: that the Real is the immutable. Is this but a human prejudice, however venerable? Conceivably, rest may be but the zero-case of motion, and continuance in one stay a case of equilibrium of forces. Previously to investigation, that all things flow is as likely, or as unlikely, to be the truth as that there is no change save in our minds, or save in the one case of transference in space. Yet men study Nature in the *hope* that change can be explained, intellectually reduced, or explained away. If we desired nothing but the truth we should divest ourselves of such hope, and study disinterestedly; or rather, the hope would never emerge. Prejudice, then, seems to be the word that is called for. The predilection for changelessness, evident in the ancient conception of God as well as in natural philosophy, may perhaps have its source in the physiological fact, with its psychological consequences, that our limbs and brains become weary through exercise. It does not seem to have an aesthetic origin, like the craving for unity or monistic explanation; for monotony is dull, if sometimes restful. Nirvana, supposing the popular notion of it to be correct, may owe its conception to oriental indolence; and the assumption that permanent identity and changelessness neither have explicability nor call for explanation may be due to nothing more supernal than the fact that thought is tiresome, or that it is natural to us to think we are in the best position to understand when we have no need or provocation to think further. In this connexion it may be observed that whereas both of the 'real' categories, unchanging substance and causal activity, emanate from the ego, intellectualistic explanation eschews the latter and retains—as when motion is taken for the scientific *explicans*—the former of them. Activity is as much a characteristic of the soul as is permanence and self identity; but philosophical and scientific explanation cleave only to the characteristic that appears compatible with inertia, and interpret or assimilate the world accordingly. The exaltation of immutability into the pre-eminent explanation-principle, and, by ancient theology, into the highest attribute of Deity, thus involves preference of the quasi-materialistic to the unequivocally spiritual.

If it has been made evident that reduction of Nature to homogeneous or identical constituents, of change to the particular kind which lies nearest to the understanding, of epigenesis to unfolding of the preformed, and of science to a network of purely logical and mathematical relations, is impossible, it can now perhaps also be seen that the hope and endeavour to explain the world on these narrowly and rigorously 'rational' or intellectualistic lines arise not from the disinterested desire to transcribe Nature as she Really is, but from desire to satisfy a particular, and a specifically human, need. We wish so to be able to regard the world, or so to make it intelligible, that we shall not feel 'intellectually' lost, but at home, in it. If, further, we persist in substituting the instruments (clear ideas and formal relations), used in this endeavour, for the Realities or the Actualities we would think about, we are merely supposing everything to be something other than it is. The philosophy to which we betake ourselves is not an explanation of the world, but a satisfaction of our wishes and predilections.

(iv) When reduction to the intelligible—by which, in the

preceding section, has been meant the clear and the formal—or any other type of explanation professes to bring us face to face with the ontal behind the phenomenal, explanation claims to be substitution of ultimate or metaphysical truth for phenomenal symbolism. However many so-called explanation-systems, descriptive and analogical, there may be, reducing the less known to the familiar, etc., science such as is sometimes called realistic will then recognise only one kind of explanation as genuine. Moreover the epistemic or anthropic factor in explanation will have been eliminated, if scientific explanation have the metaphysical status thus claimed for it. To explain will no longer mean to explain *to*, or to accommodate to our apperception-systems, but to state *what is*. A fresh meaning of 'explanation' thus emerges. And that is all that here needs to be said, because the grounds for the assertion that science is capable of yielding explanation of this alleged kind have already been examined and dismissed.

(v) The belief that theoretical science, such as rigid mechanism, conducts to ontology is now obsolescent. The prevalent opinion is that such explanation as science affords is not metaphysical truth; and to avoid any possibility of their view being misunderstood, many writers on the scope and functions of natural science have deliberately rejected the term 'explanation', and substituted for it the word 'description', into which a special or technical sense is then imported. 'Description' is as much explanation, in the broad sense in which explanation was here first defined, as any of the kinds that have previously been dealt with; but its new name is bestowed on it in order to emphasise that it is neither ontal, nor causal, nor teleological, explanation, but rather explication in terms of conceptual symbols, and assimilation with an elaborate apperception-system of a special kind.

The ordinary and plain meaning of the word 'describe' is, as Dr Johnson says, to delineate by perceptible qualities; and a description is a direct report or a historical narrative of things or events as they appear or have appeared. There is some deviation from this meaning when description seizes only on some salient point or relevant aspect; and also when it uses imaginative analogy in the place of perceptual delineation. Thus there can be several kinds of description, as there are several kinds of explanation. "Like an asp the wind slips whispering from bough to bough" deviates from plain description in one way; a barometric curve, describing changes in the atmospheric pressure, deviates in another way. Neither re-presents facts, but each represents them. Science, no less than poetry, needs must transcend plain narrative or description, and betake itself to symbolism. And once the original meaning of 'description' is deserted, and the word includes generalisation or reducing phenomena to their simplest terms, there would seem to be no stopping-place left between description and explanation. Science explains or describes in terms of images and concepts; and these, together with hypotheses, postulates, and laws, constitute its apperception-system as well as its instruments for assimilation. When such work is technically called description, in antithesis to explanation, it is implied that scientific symbols are but more or less provisional scaffolding, and that they are on no account to be confounded either with the phenomena which they describe or with the *onta* behind those phenomena. It is also tacitly confessed that the Nature which is described is already largely an artifact. Thus metaphysics (explanation) is disclaimed. Similarly, the causal idea is renounced or dispensed with in 'descriptive' exposition, and law is assigned the pre-eminence that was formerly enjoyed by cause. On these matters, it is true, representatives of the descriptionist school do not speak with one voice. Thus Prof. Hobson maintains that scientific description is independent of metaphysics, while M. Meyerson insists that metaphysic is presupposed. But it would seem that both are in the right, the one speaking of logical, the other of psychological, dependence: or the one adopting the (ps) and the other the (ψ) point of view. Science, as we have seen before, can proceed without professing metaphysical dogma or explicitly invoking causal determination in its exposition of laws; but prediction, verification, and scientific discovery presuppose— however unheedful of it the investigator may be—the determination of natural processes, *i.e.* causality and, ultimately, ontology, and could not be forthcoming unless uniformity of determination subsisted.[1] We may say that descriptionism is all the better, as

[1] The same diversity of standpoint produces controversy in theology, as to whether belief generates doctrine or doctrine belief: and as to the dependence of theology on metaphysics. Many a Christian's belief (believing) has been entirely undetermined by metaphysical arguments or grounds, and in that sense may be called non-metaphysical.

science, for its modest self-limitations and its renunciations; but, as philosophy—which it does not itself profess to be—it is correspondingly superficial. It respects facts, yet slights their determinedness. But, just because it declines to pose as philosophy, we are not justified in condemning it as half-hearted. Laws, indeed, must do more than 'describe', if they are to describe at all; but the descriptionist, as a man of science, is within his rights when he refuses to inquire or to care how much more is involved in law than is relevant to his proper business. He only exceeds his rights when, asserting that it does not matter what the symbols, used by science, are, so long as they subserve the one end of economy in thought. This issues in mere opportunism, or disregard of general principles, compatibilities, and consequences; it overlooks the truth-seeking for which the name of science stands. The truth of science certainly does not consist in the Reality of its symbols, or in their exact copying of Reality: symbolic constructions can apply, and be fruitful in prediction, without that. But there must be some correspondence between symbol-relations and Reality-relations, or science's achievements would be less impressive than they are. Mere economicalness, however, contains no vouch for such validity and verifiableness. And though mutually inconsistent symbols and working-hypotheses may for a time be entertained in different departments of science while it is in one of its tentative stages, science is not lastingly satisfied with such a state of things. In seeking economy or simplicity science also strives after unity, after one principle or as few as possible independent theories; and the descriptionist school might perhaps be more explicit as to whether it is content with opportunism or whether it seeks simplicity, of which unity is the limiting value. Its typical representative, Mach, is unable always to abide by the exaggerated statement that economy constitutes the sole aim and function of science; and he recognises that economical thought presupposes constancy in facts.

Thus, 'descriptive' explication, as distinguished from ontological, causal, and teleological explanation, avoids the error of realism such as is unable to understand how symbols can have

But the *credenda* of an orthodox Christian are metaphysical dogmas; even the distinctiveness of Christian ethics is determined wholly by doctrines, which generally are religious in so far as they are metaphysical.

application without being Realities, as if "fiction which makes fact" must necessarily be "fact too". It accepts the philosophy of *als ob*. But it tacitly relies, in its experimental procedure, on the validity of the 'real' categories, of which, in its exposition, it declines to make explicit use. It uses the concept of law, but is indifferent to the causal implications of law, as no concern of its own. Description is commonly distinguished from explanation by the observation that explanation gives an answer to 'why?', whereas 'description' only professes to give answer to 'how?'. But 'how', in science, does not merely mean 'like what', which would involve reversion to the cruder form of image-interpretation, but rather 'by what stages', 'according to what nomic connexions', and so forth. Indeed the words 'how' and 'why' are both ambiguous, and in colloquial discourse are often equivalent. When all the merits of the descriptive view of science have been recognised, it still remains certain that all scientific explication, whether it be called explanation or description, logically implies, though psychologically it may be independent of, the 'real' categories, and is consequently interpretative or assimilative.

The conception of law, which descriptionism retains, has already been sufficiently discussed. It remains to touch upon the canon of simplicity, *i.e.* of paucity of fundamental concepts and laws, or of approximation to unity and all-embracingness, which is a *desideratum* of descriptive science, and is as regulative of pure mechanism as identity is of homogeneous mechanism.

Subsumption under law is an ingredient in scientific explanation, in the vague and unanalysed sense of the phrase; it is a particular kind of explanation, when the vague complex is differentiated. It is so important an ingredient or kind that explanation in science is commonly regarded as essentially consisting in assigning a particular phenomenon to its place in a scheme of concatenated laws, and rendering it deducible. And it is explanation, if called description, in that it bespeaks assimilation to some apperceptive system, and is a means of eliminating contingency, or replacing it by nomic necessity. Laws need not be simple, nor need science's systematisation of them approach the ideal limit of unification. But simplicity, in the sense of economy of concepts and fewness of independent principles, is a goal towards which science has always felt itself impelled. It is now to be observed that this impulsion comes not so much from Nature as from human nature.

Nature's share in causing hope as to her simplicity to well up in the scientific mind is small. It consists in the fact that the first general laws to be established, Galileo's law of falling bodies and Newton's law of celestial gravitation, were mathematically simple. The laws first established in a science are of course simple, because only simple laws can be discovered while experimental technique and mathematical methods are relatively crude. Were the velocity of a falling body, which, at a particular instant, Galileo could not directly measure, other than a simple function of the time, he would have discovered no law. And previously to the invention of the principles of dynamics and the method of the calculus, the law of attraction could not have been verified, nor have allowed of the deduction from it of Kepler's observations, unless the force of the sun on the planets were a simple function of the distance. But, this conditioning of the discovery of simple laws being overlooked, their simplicity was taken to be a fair sample of Nature's behaviour; and belief in simplicity, as a fundamental characteristic of Nature, waxed strong. Galileo remarked that "Nature uses the simplest means to attain her ends", and Newton that "Nature is pleased with simplicity". Theological convictions led some physicists to regard Nature's simplicity as a representation of the mind of God: indeed the belief in the simplicity of laws, like that in verbal inspiration of Scripture, was a presupposition arising from, and fostered by, religious reverence. And those who, apart from religious grounds, retain belief in Nature's simplicity or regard the simplicity of laws as a criterion of their truth, must be prepossessed by an implicit metaphysic of the world as much as were the physicists of an older generation who saw in Nature's alleged simplicity a manifestation of the Divine Mind. *Simplex veri judicium* is neither an *a priori* nor an *a posteriori* truth. Indeed refinements in experimental accuracy, etc., have dispelled the belief, in so far as it was empirically grounded, that natural laws are always mathematically simple. We now realise that it is better to seek out the ways of Nature than to prescribe them. Science is a struggle of man's discursive understanding with Nature's complexity; and simplicity must underlie induction, probability, the method of interpolation, and so forth. But the simplest form of a law is not necessarily the truest, if it be the most convenient. As an index of the ultimateness, or of the satisfyingness, of our explanation of Nature, simplicity is an anthropic or Subjective test. To God's mind, doubtless, all is simple. Simplicity, for us, can only be defined in relation to our limited faculties. It is a test brought to Nature by our minds, not something read off from Nature. And its motivation is partly economy and convenience, partly of aesthetic kind. A methodological principle, such as Ockham's razor, is not to be confounded with a law of Nature. When it is so regarded, it becomes a superstition, a case of "setting up conceits in Nature's stead".

(vi) So long as 'explanation' means rendering intelligible in the senses of simple, clear, and penetrable by the formal categories of the pure sciences, it is obvious that the world is not explicable, describable, or intelligible, through and through, or without remainder. Scientific explanation such as culminates in rigid mechanism is dictated by the methodological assumptions that the world is a closed system and that Nature is wholly *naturata*. As Nature is undoubtedly also *naturans*, such kinds of explanation, in striving after universality, seek the living among the dead. The part of Nature with which the sciences of biology and psychology are concerned is also intelligible and explicable in some degree and in some sense; but now these terms bear new meanings, irreducible to those just considered. The apperception involved is not purely intellectual; it is partly constituted by conation and reference to practical ends. Categories that may be apt enough for the universal and the formally rational are inapt for the historical and the unique. The interactions that are the *explicanda* are not quantitative, like the action and reaction contemplated in mechanics, but qualitative; and they can only be made 'intelligible' by means of analogical assimilation with the more familiar. Thus the biological realm is only reducible to law when categories such as that of self-conservation or life, as well as that of efficient and internal causation (*vis insita*) are used. Mechanism is unable to predict the emergence in Nature of organic wholes, or organisms manifesting a 'formative principle' of some kind, which differ essentially not only from inanimate natural bodies but also from non-living artifacts such as man-made machines. Life is fact, not theory, and shews no sign of being reducible to motion of inert matter and impressed forces. Entelechies and vital force may be but suppositions, explanations *per obscurius*, restatements rather than *explicantia*; and science may be ignorant as to what 'formative principle' exactly means: but it is certain that the behaviour of organisms is not wholly describable, nor predictable, in terms of the more rigid kinds of mechanical theory, and that reproduction and evolutionary progressiveness cannot be accounted for without resorting to kinds of change such as mechanism does not contemplate. In the higher organisms the existence-for-self, which is a distinguishing feature of the organic, largely admits of explanation in terms of mind, *i.e.* of some degree of sensory awareness, of feeling and striving. But in plants phenomenal science can discover no instincts, reflexes, etc., though adaptiveness is sometimes as impressive in them as in the animal kingdom; and plasticity, determination of part by whole, etc., are evident, where there is no sign of correlating mind traceable by science such as uses some form or other of the causal notion without penetrating beneath the phenomenal to an ontal conception of causality. Ontologically, mind may be co-extensive with life, in that spiritualistic metaphysics is not disprovable by science. And in this connexion we may recall the suggestion of biologists, that plants and animals are descended alike from what was less specialised 'organism': plants becoming earth-parasites while animals developed movability, with all its potentialities in respect of mental evolution.

The mysteries of botany, however, do not further concern our inquiry at this stage; nor is it necessary to speculate as to where, if anywhere, in the organic realm, mentality makes an abrupt entrance. There are organisms lower in the scale than man which evince mentality of some kind as plainly as does the human behaviour that has evoked in each of us the knowledge of other selves. Of such organisms biology gets 'understanding' by attributing to them initiative *conatus*. Individually they are not artifacts of any mind external to them, nor of designing minds transcending those of human engineers, yet lodged in the organisms themselves. But their structure may be determined by function, which in turn is dependent on feeling, striving, and subjective selection. Ontogeny, we are told by some biologists as well as psychologists, is actually and literally a habit. What habit is for individual life, that is heredity for racial life; and the mystery of heredity is explicable in terms of the facts of memory, *i.e.* of 'organic memory'[1]. Thus we have not to choose between the teleology of Paley and the vitalistic doctrine of entelechies; the theory that animal developement is controlled by mind is a sufficient, and apparently a necessary, explanation of the self-adaptation evinced by organisms, of their adaptation to environment and of environment to self. This adaptiveness is sometimes, unfortunately, called inner purposiveness or internal teleology. But it is *Zweckmässigkeit ohne Zweck*, and therefore not teleological at all, if teleology and final causation involve a preconceived idea of the τέλος to be accomplished, and volitional adaptation of means to end. Blind impulse, and what have been called *élan vital*, the hormic, etc., are very different from purposive action; and 'unconscious purposiveness' is a phrase which either ministers to the confounding of things that are distinct or else is a contradiction in terms. Such organic behaviour as has as yet been considered is no more teleological, in the strict and proper sense, than it is rigidly mechanical. Moreover internal teleology, so called, if conducive to the view that Nature is an aggregate of realms of 'ends', so called, carries us no nearer than does mechanism to the view that Nature is realising an end or preconceived goal, fulfilling a purpose, expressing a meaning comparable to that of a drama. To the teleological construing of the world, of which theism is the outcome, it contributes nothing directly: a teleologically ordered cosmos is no necessary result of even a spiritualistic universe in which every organism, or every species, pursues its own self-conservation and self-betterment without foresight and conspiration with others. If in the sphere of the biological we are compelled by facts to substitute contingency for mechanism, and we receive the suggestion that possibly there may be contingency even where, on the surface, there is apparently the mechanical, we still encounter mystery all along the line of evolutionary progress. Variations which made further advances possible, such as the laying of the foundation of a nervous system, which led to coordination of stimuli and psychic control of the whole organism; or the modification of the larynx of some anthropoid ancestor of man, rendering language possible, and developed intercourse and rationality acquirable; or the variations which provided for the

[1] J. Ward, *Essays in Philosophy*, pp. 253 ff.

emergence of aesthetic and ethical sentiments possessing no survival-value: none of these were foreseen and striven for by creatures; and their emergence is left, by what is inaptly called 'internal', or 'non-purposive, teleology', as much a matter of 'chance' as it is by the theory that minds are epiphenomena.

Thus the existence of organic wholes in Nature does not of itself directly imply that Nature is an organic whole, and has no relevance to world-teleology or design unless some further bond of connexion is found. Also the probability that the blade of grass must ever wait for its Newton, and the fact that nests are not built by inanimate things or mechanical forces but only by beings possessed of life and mentality, does not warrant any interpretation of organisms by reading their behaviour in terms of the teleological category. A nest looks as if it were constructed with a view to the rearing of offspring, and a bird looks as if it had been put together by a designer of intricate machinery, be the designer internal or external to the organism: we know, however, that nests are not the outcome of ornithic designing, and that birds or bird-species are not 'special creations'. In colloquial discourse on such matters we harmlessly indulge in the psychologist's fallacy; and in science we likewise need to speak of nests, etc., as 'to the purpose', though we make allowance for the fact that the 'purpose' exists but from our point of view, as explainers, not from that of the bird. But those who, from Bacon to Kant, would banish final causes (proper) even from biological science, because such causes do not reveal Nature's *modus operandi*, and those who would apply the teleological category only to the activities of man and to explanation of the world as a whole, certainly have psychological justification. The adaptiveness evinced by organisms bespeaks internal causes as well as mechanical causes, and that evinced by some organisms involves feeling and striving; but such internal and proximate causes are not final, or guided by preconceived ends, and explanation in terms of them, involved in biology, is therefore not teleological, though it is different in kind from the types of explanation which we have previously studied.

(vii) The kind of explanation to which, for avoidance of confusion, the name 'teleological' is here restricted, differs from other kinds of ejective interpretation in that it regards effects as conditioned by foresight and intention, *i.e.* purpose. It is applicable, consequently, only to what is, or conceivably may be, brought about by beings possessed of ideation, intelligence, and volition. Teleological explanation answers the question why, or for what purpose, a deed was done or a process was initiated. The effect to be produced, the idea thereof previous to realisation, the ultimate satisfaction for the sake of which something is done, the desiring or the designing which leads to the doing, and perhaps other things, have severally received the name of end or final cause; and final causes, as thus described, have sometimes been regarded as also efficient causes. Fortunately it is not necessary, for the understanding of teleology, as here defined, to straighten out the tangle which, as usual, results from this usage of one name where several are needed; it is enough to remark that if final causes are to be more than convenient abstractions for figurative description, like motives, and are to be endowed with efficiency, the only final *causes* will be agents or souls ideating and willing, and the only *final* causes will be such agents when achieving an end which is not merely a temporally last stage of a series but an end that was preconceived, and whose actualisation was intended.

It is only in the sphere of human conduct and history that teleology, or the idea of purposiveness over and above that of non-purposive adaptiveness, is empirically known to have application. Within that sphere it is fact, not theory, that final causes operate; and there teleological explanation is as indispensable as the kinds of explanation pursued by physical science are inapplicable. The realm of history and conduct is the one which, scientifically and 'rationally', we understand (*begreifen*) least; for human life does not admit of much description in terms of formal categories, or of reduction to quantitative laws such as make prediction of particular events possible. But this realm is the one which, in another sense (*verstehen*), we understand best. And this wholly different type of 'understanding' is the predominant factor in reason, when reason includes that which makes the man of affairs as well as the dry light of formal ratiocinativeness which a man might abundantly possess, and yet be a fool. Ends are constituted ends solely by their value to agents; and works of art have a meaning or significance for valuing subjects other than that which propositions present to the grammarian and the logician. Apart from this meaning and purpose, appealing to human capacities and faculties other than those of analytical and formal understanding, such works would not be explicable, and indeed would not be forthcoming. When we meet with a product of any kind which resembles a human artifact, we suppose it to be due to human contrivance until the contrary is proved. The world, as a whole including man, suggests, like a picture or a poem, purpose and design; and whether or not it admits of a self-consistent explanation in terms of teleology, it may be said to be certain that no other explanation is forthcoming of the harmonious relation of causes, whatever they be, in virtue of which Nature and man form a cosmos and a realm of values. Science, such as is concerned exclusively with Nature's structure, does not preclude teleological interpretation of the totality by supplying a sufficient and a non-teleological explanation of its order, in respect of adaptiveness, over and above the uniformity of its sequences. Theism, regarded as a reasonable belief and as a philosophical world-theory, is based on the empirical facts which seem to ask for a sufficient reason in the postulation of One integrating and directive Mind; and teleological explanation is necessarily the type of explanation that is pursued in natural theology.

Leaving teleological interpretation and construction of empirically grounded theology for the next chapter, one may conclude this discussion of the various kinds of explanation by shewing its bearing on the possible meanings of the ambiguous phrase, 'the rationality of the world', which figures in both scientific and theological literature.

Perhaps the most rigid interpretation that this phrase could conceivably bear would be that it asserts the ultimate constituents of the world to be ideas, such as universals, discernible by a faculty of pure or non-sensory intuition, and between which relations subsist that are similarly apprehended, or are read off without any ejective or suppositional instrumentality. If this insinuation lurks in the statement that 'the Real is the rational', it would seem that the statement cannot be true. All beings must be determinate beings, and the determinateness of any thing *per se*, derived or self-subsistent, is not rationally or logically deducible or conditioned: it simply is. And the constituents of an Actual world cannot be ideas. Ideas are derived from the non-ideal; and even if they could be supposed to be prior, *in ordine essendi*, they cannot be supposed to be agents, in *rapport* with which we—who, by the way, at least are not ideas or universals—come by our sensa and phenomena. Our world, as phenomenal, contains the irreducible and uneliminable element of the posited, the alogical or non-rational; and the world, as noümenal or ontal, must likewise contain something alogical, to render it determinate and to enable it to evoke particular and various sensa in us. In this first possible sense, then, the world is not rational but non-rational; and the world-ground is "the last irrationality", to borrow Dr Whitehead's phrase.

Next, 'the world is rational' might be taken to mean that the world is a nexus of relations only, readable by reason; reason being restricted to the formal 'understanding'. In this sense, again, rationality is not predicable of the universe: for relations without terms, relations separable and not merely distinguishable from terms, are neither forthcoming nor thinkable.

Alogical 'terms' having been allowed their necessary place in an Actual or an Ontal system, the world's rationality may next be alleged to consist in these terms being related *only* by such relations as are called formal, viz. the logical and mathematical, which "lie nearest to the understanding". In this sense our world is indeed partly rational. There are like things; genera, universals, common qualities, and repeatableness, are forthcoming. Although there is no *a priori* reason why this should be so, or why any world should also be an intelligible cosmos, it is a matter of fact that in this world things are not so disparate from all other things as to be incomparable or unclassifiable, and that something entirely unimaginable does not always supervene on something else. Somewhat of scientific knowledge happens to be possible. Such rationality as we are now considering, viz. penetrability by thought working with formal categories alone, characterises the ideal worlds of the mathematician, where implication is the only needed kind of necessary connexion, and causality is a superfluity; but it characterises the Actual world only partially. A purely deductive science of this world is not attainable; the apparently contingent is not universally and knowably reducible to the nomically necessary; changeless identities, motion and number, do not suffice for the discovery and the exposition of laws of Nature. The world is by no means rational, in this sense, through and through: to call it so would be to use irony similar to that of the zoologist who devised the name *homo sapiens* for the human race. Moreover, if the world were wholly rational, in this rationalistic sense, and if it were rational in this sense alone, it would supply little basis for natural or rational theology, and no promise of the realisation of human valuations and aspirations. It would be a meaningless, purposeless, valueless cosmos.

We pass to quite a different meaning of 'rational' when, in speaking of the rationality of the world, we refer to its causal explicability. For cause is not logical ground; causal *rapport* is not a formal relation; and the causal category is not logomorphic but anthropic in origin. The rationality now under consideration is not logical, or such as is associated with necessary implication, but alogical rationality, which may be described as amenability to sympathetic *rapport* or assimilability to our egohood, as substantial and active. Causal explanation is thus intermediate between that in terms of formal categories and that in terms of final causes; and it may fairly be said to be more akin to the latter than to the former kind. Reason does not begin to be heuristic, regulative, and interpretative, when it resorts to the teleological idea, but when it employs Kant's 'dynamic' categories, substance and cause. Hence the rationality of the world, which is said to be the precondition as well as the disclosure of physical science with its causal laws, consists largely in interpretableness to human agents. If the 'constitutive' understanding can only be concerned with the manipulation of identities or the substitution of similars, it is a question whether in our world there are any similars such as exact science requires. As we do not begin by knowing that there are, even 'understanding', as directed to Actuality, becomes regulative: seeking not what necessarily *is*, but what must be *thought*, if the world is to be wholly rational in the more formal sense. The guiding principle of science is that the world is rational in the sense of assimilable and interpretable. For causal explanation depends on pragmatic verification, not on logical certification, and so far is in the same case with teleological explanation. In both these kinds of explanation the ultimate justification is "all's well that ends well".

It now appears that there are as many meanings of 'rationality' as there are distinguishable kinds of explanation or of intelligibility. In discussion of the bearing of the rationality of the world on scientific and theological issues respectively, and on the relation of theology to science, it is essential that these different meanings receive the differentiation for which they call. For instance, the rationality of the world evinced in physical laws is almost irrelevant to the question whether the world is rational in the teleological sense of guaranteeing the realisation of our moral and religious aspirations; and the rationality that is the prerequisite of natural science, such as we have, is that which finds expression in macroscopic mechanism, not that which constitutes the goal of rigid mechanism. Again, that the world is rational, in the manner and degree sufficient for macroscopic mechanism, does not imply that the world is completely intelligible or that it will ever be exhaustively reduced to scientific law. Science neither presupposes nor discloses that the world is "infinitely intelligible" or wholly intelligible, either logico-mathematically or causally. Such statements as that "existence must correspond with our ideas", and that "the possibilities of thought cannot exceed the actuality of being", are baseless; for there is no source of information to such effect available to the philosophers who have hazarded them. They are also false; for departments of mathematics are forthcoming to refute them. And in this connexion the statement that the "real" is the intelligible, or that the intelligible is the "real", suggests itself. Sometimes those who repeat this dictum seem to be asserting an analytical proposition, as if announcing that 'real' is intended by them to be a synonym for 'intelligible'. They generally refrain from defining the connotation of 'real' before asserting identity of denotation between that term and the word 'intelligible', or some presumably equivalent phrase such as 'coherent with experience as a systematised whole'. In that case all that is effected is the importation of a superfluous technical term, 'real'. If, on the other hand, their assertion is intended to be a synthetic proposition, like 'dodos are extinct', 'reality' should first be conventionally or preferentially defined—e.g. as the ontal, or the Actual, or the valuable—before its co-extensiveness with the intelligible is affirmed. And then, whatever 'intelligible' and 'real' be taken to mean, a dogma is propounded which, it would seem, cannot be based on anything that may aptly be called knowledge. Until we have had acquaintance with the whole of 'reality', or science has examined every phenomenon in which 'reality' manifests itself, it is premature to assert that 'reality' is wholly intelligible, in any of the senses that 'intelligible' bears. We may deem Kant's usage of 'noümenon' for the thing *per se* a terminological impropriety, a reversal in some respects of the ancient meaning of the word. But if perchance a noümenal realm, in Kant's sense, is referred to by the word 'reality', then the assertion that that realm is noümenal in the earlier sense, or is intelligible in the way in which relations or universals are intelligible, is without warrant from experience as systematised either by the sciences or by fact-controlled philosophy.

CHAPTER IV

The Empirical Approach to Theism: Cosmic Teleology

The classical proofs of the being of God sought to demonstrate that there is a Real counterpart to a preconceived idea of God, such as was moulded in the course of the developement of religion, or constructed by speculative philosophy aloof from religious experience and from avowedly anthropic interpretation, or obtained by both these methods combined. The empirically-minded theologian adopts a different procedure. He asks how the world, inclusive of man, is to be explained. He would let the Actual world tell its own story and offer its own suggestions: not silence it while abstractive speculation, setting out with presuppositions possibly irrelevant to Actuality, weaves a system of thought which may prove to conflict with facts. The *explicanda* which he investigates, and the results of his investigation, alone will determine the content or essence of the explicative idea of God to which he is led, as well as the grounds for belief that such an essence exists. He will thus entertain, at the outset, no such presuppositions as that the Supreme Being, to which the world may point as its principle of explanation, is infinite, perfect, immutable, suprapersonal, unqualifiedly omnipotent or omniscient. The attributes to be ascribed to God will be such as empirical facts and their sufficient explanation indicate or require. And if the empiricist deems the alleged religious 'instinct' and the *lumen naturale* proved to be non-existent, and, previously to the inferential establishment of theism, he must consider the mystic's claims to be untrustworthy, all that he can expect to emerge from his inquiry is grounds for reasonable belief rather than rational and coercive demonstration. Should this seem a mean ambition for the theologian, we need but recall that other selves, as to whose existence each of us has an unshakable conviction, and whose works we can understand or explain only by using teleological categories, are neither directly apprehended nor provable otherwise than by cumulative pragmatic verification.

It has already been submitted that revealed religion, such as the Christian Faith, logically presupposes natural religion, in so far as a distinction between the two is to be drawn, and that religion presupposes some theological notion, crude or refined according to stage of developement, suggested by observation of man and the world. And now it may further be remarked that natural theology is not to be identified with rational theology, though one name has often covered both of them. Rational and *a priori* theology stands or falls with the ontological argument; and if that argument—or some substitute for it, alleged to express its intent —still seems self-evidently cogent to a philosopher here and there, its fallaciousness is self-evident to all the rest. Natural theology, on the other hand, sets out from facts and inductions; its premisses are as firmly established and as universally acknowledged as any of the stable generalisations of science. Here there is at least common ground, as distinct from private certitude, from which argumentation may proceed. Coercive demonstration being confessedly unattainable, it is to be inquired what kind of justification for reasonable belief natural theology can afford. And the first step is to set forth the facts and generalisations which collectively constitute our data or premisses.

The forcibleness of Nature's suggestion that she is the outcome of intelligent design lies not in particular cases of adaptedness in the world, nor even in the multiplicity of them. It is conceivable that every such instance may individually admit of explanation in terms of proximate causes or, in the first instance, of explanation other than in terms of cosmic or 'external' teleology. And if it also admits of teleological interpretation, that fact will not of itself constitute a rigorous certification of external design. The forcibleness of the world's appeal consists rather in the conspiration of innumerable causes to produce, by their united and reciprocal action, and to maintain, a general order of Nature. Narrower kinds of teleological argument, based on surveys of restricted spheres of fact, are much more precarious than that for which the name of 'the wider teleology' may be appropriated in that the comprehensive design-argument is the outcome of synopsis or conspection of the knowable world.

The knowable world, however, is not identical with the universe as to which, as a whole, we have no knowledge. It may be objected, therefore, that to use the phrase 'the world' to denote both of these things seems to beg a vital question. Of course, if trustworthy evidence of design in the limited portion of the universe that we know were forthcoming, a world-designer would be 'proved', and our ignorance as to other parts would be irrelevant. But it is a graver objection—perhaps the gravest that the teleologist has to encounter—that rich suggestions of design in the known world yield no proof of design in the universe, since our ordered fragment may be but a temporary and casual episode in the history of the universe, an oasis in a desert of 'chaos', a chance product of mindless agency in a universe which has had opportunity to produce all sorts of local and ephemeral worlds within A World. To this objection it may be replied that teleology does not profess to base itself on the principle of 'the inconceivability of the opposite', while interpretations of the known cannot be refuted, even if they can be made to appear more precarious, by considerations as to possibilities within the unknowable. Certainly a mechanical theory of the universe must not be tacitly assumed to which our known world gives the lie. More specifically it may be said that the ordered oasis is not an isolable fragment. It and the supposed desert or 'chaos' are interdependent. It is because the desert is what it is that the oasis is what it is; and the one has orderedness only by permission, so to say, of the other. The force of the objection, indeed, seems to be derived from the assumption that our ordered world is due to some evolutionary process within the whole universe analogous to that secured within organic Nature by natural selection out of random variations. This is but conjecture or appeal to the unknown, and, confronted with the second law of thermodynamics, is overwhelmingly improbable. And if it includes the supposition that even unlimited re-shufflings of matter by mechanical forces can produce minds and personalities in a corner of the universe, it conflicts with knowledge. Further, if the nerve of the teleological argument be that design issues in the realisation of ethical values, the spatio-temporal immensities of the universe become less significant than the petty oasis. Teleology, after all, is a value-concept; and magnitude and worth are incommensurable.

Nevertheless the inquiry that is here first to be undertaken, whether the knowable world, or Nature, has been devised by intelligence, is to be distinguished, though it cannot be separated, from the further inquiry, what the ultimate purpose or goal of the world-process is. The latter question may admit of no complete answer by man: reasonable belief as to the former involves but the application of mother-wit to forthcoming facts. A machine can evince intelligent contrivance or design to a man ignorant of engineering and unable to tell precisely what the machine is for. Once more, by way of making relevant distinctions, a teleological interpretation of Nature does not require that every detail in Nature was purposed or fore-ordained. Processes may inevitably produce by-products which, as such, were not purposed, but are the necessary outcome of processes by which a purpose is fulfilled.

The main fields of fact in which adaptation is conspicuous, and which have severally afforded data for particular arguments of the teleological kind and of restricted scope, are those of the knowability or intelligibility of the world (or the adaptation of thought to things), the internal adaptedness of organic beings, the fitness of the inorganic to minister to life, the aesthetic value of Nature, the world's instrumentality in the realisation of moral ends, and the progressiveness in the evolutionary process culminating in the emergence of man with his rational and moral status. A brief examination of these fields in turn will not only enable us to estimate the respective strengths of the more or less independent arguments derived from them severally, but also to appreciate the interconnexions within the world, and the comprehensive teleology which such interconnectedness suggests.

(i) We may begin with the mutual adaptation of thought and things, Nature and Knowledge. The correspondence between human thought and the external world, rendering science possible, has evoked what may be called epistemological arguments for the being of God. Descartes accounted for the marvel, as it seemed to him, of this correspondence by invoking, as its necessary cause, the veracious Deity, whose existence he sought to prove—almost superfluously, on his own presuppositions—by other lines of reasoning. If a subject's 'ideas' were as disparate from percepts and from external Objects as Descartes supposed, each class forming a closed system independent of the other, there might be something to be said for the invocation of divine agency to explain the elaborate correspondence between the two systems. But if our primary ideas of objects are but images of such objects defecated to pure transparency, or are but elements of the objective

of perceptual experience isolated for thought by selective
estricted attention, then that they apply to the objects from
ich they have but been abstracted is no wonder to be super-
aaturally accounted for. And if, as in science, general ideas and
the constituents of developed thought are determined and controlled by things external to thought, and so enjoy validity, there
is no cause for amazement even at the predictiveness of theoretical
physics. The mysterious element in knowledge does not lie where
Descartes would place it: it lies deeper. Similarly, Shelley's
apostrophe,

> O thou immortal Deity
> Whose throne is in the depths of human thought,

supposing it to have any relevance to the present context, errs as
to the location of the "throne". It is in the world, as allowing
itself to be thought about, rather than in our thinking, if anywhere,
that considerations as to the penetrability of things by thought
may lead teleology to enthrone its Deity. Reason might solilo-
quize: world or no world, I must think thus and thus, in order to
think at all. Pure reason may have power to decree *how* thoughts
must be linked in order to yield Thought, and certainly can without
limit form ideas—as in the pure sciences—to which there is no
knowable counterpart in Actuality; but it is powerless to prescribe
to things *what* they shall be, and that they shall satisfy the demands
of any pure science. The world might answer: you must think
me thus and thus, as to my 'what', and not otherwise, if you
would know me. Nature will open to the right pass-word; but
she has chosen it, not we. To revert to plain speech: the primary
epistemological contribution to teleological reasoning consists in
the fact that the world is more or less intelligible, in that it happens
to be more or less a cosmos, when conceivably it might have been
a self-subsistent and determinate 'chaos' in which similar events
never occurred, none recurred, universals had no place, relations
no fixity, things no nexus of determination, and 'real' categories
no foothold. But whether such logico-mathematical order as has
been found to obtain in our world bespeaks 'chance'[1] in self-

---

[1] By 'chance' is here meant absence of a sufficient ground. The word, as commonly
used, carries several meanings; and which of them is to the fore in any context where
the term subsequently appears will perhaps not need to be stated. Among its senses
the following may be mentioned. It may signify an event not as yet included by known

subsistent entities, or purposiveness in a designer or a creator, there is of course no logical method of deciding: the probability-calculus can gain no purchase. We know that similar ordering is sometimes due to human design; that it always is due to design we have no means of knowing. Again, the amenability of things to the more interpretative kind of knowledge, constituted by the 'real' or the anthropic categories, shews that things, or their ontal counterparts, have so much of affinity with us as to be assimilable and to be understood, or alogically interpreted, as well as to be ordered by number, etc.: it does not of itself testify that the adaptedness is teleological.

It is in that Nature evokes thought of richer kind than is involved in scientific knowledge, and responds to thinking such as is neither logically necessary nor biologically needful, thus suggesting a Beyond, that considerations as to the relation between thought and things assume their chief significance for the teleologist. These considerations, however, belong to another context; and those, the logical coerciveness of which has been denied, will later be discussed again when criticism of demonstrative proofs will give place to construction of a cumulative argument for a reasonable, if indemonstrable, teleological interpretation.

(ii) The adaptiveness that is so abundantly evinced in the organic world has already been discussed from the point of view of science and proximate causation. We have seen that if the behaviour of matter be regarded as completely describable in terms of least action, shortest path, dissipation of kinetic energy, and so forth, matter must be regarded also as unable, of itself, to fall into such systems as organisms. There is indeed some tendency to-day in scientific circles to seek an organic conception of the physical atom, etc., rather than a mechanical conception of the organism. But as for the organic at the molar and phenomenal level of description, its formative principle, irreducible to rigid mechanism, is provided by mentality wherever we have reason to infer psychic behaviour; there we can account for the facts of function and structure, heredity and progressive adaptation.

law, or one which, in that it is unique, is absolutely non-subsumable under a general law; or one that is determined by causes as to which we have but imperfect, or perhaps no relevant, knowledge. It may simply exclude final causation, and then denote the non-purposed. It may even suggest the supposed indeterminateness, which can never actually subsist, *e.g.* of a configuration.

Where, as in plants, there is no macroscopic evidence of psychic behaviour, the formative principle, as yet mysterious to science, is further to seek. It may be that only in metaphysics such as spiritualistic monadism, or hylozoism of the microscopic order, is a natural explanation to be found. But in proportion as psychological or other explanation is forthcoming in the organic realm as a whole, resort to external or cosmic teleology, in order to account for adaptations within the organism, becomes superfluous for the special sciences. So long as organisms were believed to have originated, in their present forms and with all their specialised organs 'ready made', the argument that adaptation of part to whole, of whole to environment, and of organ to function, implied design, was forcible. But its premiss became untenable when Darwin shewed that every organic structure had come to be what it now is through a long series of successive and gradual modifications. Gradualness of construction is in itself no proof of the absence of external design: it is not at this point that Darwinism delivered its alleged death-blow to teleology. The sting of Darwinism rather lay in the suggestion that proximate and 'mechanical' causes were sufficient to produce the adaptations from which the teleology of the eighteenth century had argued to God. Assignable proximate causes, whether mechanical or not, are sufficient to dispose of the particular kind of teleological proof supplied by Paley. But the fact of organic evolution, even when the maximum of instrumentality is accredited to what is figuratively called natural selection, is not incompatible with teleology on a grander scale: as exponents of Darwinism were perhaps the first to recognise and to proclaim. Subversive of Paley's argument, it does not invalidate his theistic conclusion, nor even his view that every organism and organ is an end as well as a means. Indeed the science of evolution was the primary source of the wider teleology current for the last half century, as well as the main incentive to the recovery of the closely connected doctrine of divine immanence. This kind of teleology does not set out from the particular adaptations in individual organisms or species so much as from considerations as to the progressiveness of the evolutionary process and as to the organic realm as a whole; but its connexion with the former class of facts belongs to the subject-matter of the present section.

The survival of the fittest presupposes the arrival of the fit, and throws no light thereupon. Darwin did not account for the origin of variations; their forthcomingness was simply a datum for him. It is of no great significance for the wider teleology that variations are not in all cases so indefinite or random, nor so infinitesimal and gradual, as was generally assumed in *The Origin of Species*. But it may be observed that, in the absence either of a mechanical or of an 'internal' explanation of variation, room is left for the possibility that variation is externally predetermined or guided, so that not only the general trend of the organic process, but also its every detail, may be pre-ordained or divinely controlled. Even this observation is pointless save for those who regard a nexus of traceable proximate causes and a theistic interpretation as incompatibilities. Theism such as has over-emphasised the idea of God's immanence denies proximate causes as distinct from acts of God; and advocates of anti-theistic mechanism sometimes appear to think that the traceability of proximate causes bespeaks the superfluity, to philosophy as well as to science, of the idea of God. Thus, in connexion with the topic now before us, Weismann wrote: "It is certainly the absence of a theoretical definition of variability which leaves open the door for smuggling in a teleological power. A mechanical explanation of variability must form the basis of this side of natural selection". But theism, such as is sufficiently leavened with deism to distinguish itself from pantheism, and the world from a deified mechanism, is indifferent to the banishment of the Paleyan type of teleology which relied on particular organic adaptations, any one of which was deemed sufficient to prove a divine artificer; and at the same time it has no need of going to the extreme of asserting that God is "either everywhere or nowhere", or that He is nothing if not all. The discovery of organic evolution has caused the teleologist to shift his ground from special design in the products to directivity in the process, and plan in the primary collocations. It has also served to suggest that the organic realm supplies no better basis for teleological argument of the narrower type than does inorganic Nature. Indeed it suggests that, since the adaptiveness of an organism is non-teleological, the adaptiveness of the whole world may perhaps similarly be *Zweckmässigkeit ohne Zweck*. But this suggestion calls for examination later.

(iii) Although teleologists in the past have generally set out from adaptations in organisms, it has occurrèd now and again to a theistic apologist, *e.g.* to Aquinas, that adaptation in inorganic Nature, where there cannot be a formative principle such as non-intelligent organisms evince, should more unequivocally bespeak external design. The teleologist of to-day, however, would rather call attention to the continuity of apparent purposiveness between the two realms, or to the dependence of adaptation in the one on adaptiveness in the other. Since Darwin, we have realised that organisms can only be understood in connexion with their environment. And more recently it has been argued, as by Mr Henderson, that the inorganic environment is as plainly adapted to life as living creatures are to their environment. The vast complexity of the physico-chemical conditions of life on the earth suggests to common sense that the inorganic world may retrospectively receive a biocentric explanation, which, if 'unconscious purpose' do but restate the facts rather than account for them, and ungrounded coincidence be as humanly incredible as it is logically unassailable, becomes a teleological explanation. Waiving, as here irrelevant, the metaphysical possibility that what we call inorganic matter is an appearance of relatively unorganised spirit, we may say that if science is to be trusted when it regards the organic realm as later in time than the inorganic world, and when it asserts that the processes, which made the emergence and persistence of life possible, would have been precisely the same had life not emerged at all, then there would seem to be a developement of this fitness for life, involving convergence of innumerable events towards a result, as if that result were an end to which the inorganic processes were means. The fitness of our world to be the home of living beings depends upon certain primary conditions, astronomical, thermal, chemical, etc., and on the coincidence of qualities apparently not causally connected with one another, the number of which would doubtless surprise anyone wholly unlearned in the sciences; and these primary conditions, in their turn, involve many of secondary order. Unique assemblages of unique properties on so vast a scale being thus essential to the maintenance of life, their forthcomingness makes the inorganic world seem in some respects comparable with an organism. It is suggestive of a formative principle. But, if there be such a prin-

COSMIC TELEOLOGY 87

ciple, it is not conceivable after analogy with the life and mind of organisms, and cannot be said to be intrinsic or internal; because the inorganic—at the molar and phenomenal level of explanation —is devoid of life, and—at any level of explanation—is devoid of intelligence and foresight. Unless cosmic teleology is invoked, the intricate adaptations that have been mentioned must be referred by the dualist to a mechanically controlled concourse of atoms, and by the pluralistic spiritualist to conative monads that are no more capable of conspiration than are inert particles.

Such is the teleological appeal of this field of facts to common-sense reasonableness, or mother-wit, which regards the 'probability', that the apparent preparedness of the world to be a theatre of life is due to 'chance', as infinitesimally small. It remains to ask whether either science or logic is able to abate the forcibleness of this appeal.

Science does not seem to lessen the convincingness of the argument now before us when it suggests that (as if organic chemistry were irrelevant), had the conditions upon which life, as we know it, depends been wholly or partly different, other forms of organism might equally well have emerged, adapted to the altered environment: silicon perhaps replacing carbon in another kind of protoplasm, and iron replacing calcium phosphate in skeletons. For the point is that, for the existence of any forms of life that we may conceive, the necessary environment, whatever its nature, must be complex and dependent on a multiplicity of coincident conditions, such as are not reasonably attributable to blind forces or to pure mechanism. Nor, again, can science explain the adaptation of the inorganic environment to life after the manner in which Darwinism, its sufficiency being assumed, explains progressive adaptations in organisms without resort to design. Of a struggle for existence between rival worlds, out of which ours has survived as the fittest, we have no knowledge upon on which to draw. Natural selection cannot here be invoked; and if the term 'evolution' be applicable at all to the whole world-process, it must have a different meaning from that which it bears in Darwinian biology. Presumably the world is comparable with a single throw of dice. And common sense is not foolish in suspecting the dice to have been loaded.

But here the logician intervenes. He will first point out that the remarkableness, or surprisingness, of manifold coincidences, evoking our teleological explanation of them, is but a fact pertaining to human psychology, unless 'remarkable' means what he calls antecedently improbable. He will then remind us that a remarkable world might result from 'one throw' in spite of there being indefinitely large chances against it, just as double sixes may be cast in one's first toss of two unloaded dice, although the adverse odds are 35 to 1. But his most harmful observation will be that, if the world be the sole instance of its kind, or be analogous to a single throw, there can be no talk of chances or of antecedent probability in connexion with our question. Sound as this caution is, it does not affect the teleologist; for, when he calls coincidence on the vast scale improbable, he has in mind not mathematical probability, or a logical relation, but the alogical probability which is the guide of life and which has been found to be the ultimate basis of all scientific induction. If teleology here strays from the path of logical rectitude into one marked by logicians with a warning-post, it does so in the light-hearted company of common sense and inductive science. Science has been so continuously successful in its venturesomeness that the wise-head, logic, now lets it pass without remonstrance; but theology, though arm in arm with science, receives a reprimand. The teleologist is told that there is no antecedent probability, as to the existence of the intelligent Being invoked to explain adaptation suggestive of intelligent activity, after observation of the facts in question, unless there was an appreciable probability, before observation of them, that such a Being exists. Robinson Crusoe can be said to have inferred Friday from footprints legitimately, because he already knew that men existed and that they could reach his island; but the teleologist does not know beforehand that any superhuman being exists, and therefore cannot legitimately reason from what apparently are Mind-prints to their divine causation. But some favouritism would seem to be shewn to science in this illustration; for when we inquire how Crusoe originally got his knowledge as to the existence of fellow-men who can not only make footprints but also supply service and friendship, we find that it seems to have been mediated in much the same way as is the teleologist's belief in God. It is true that in the former case there is a psychologically stronger compulsion, a nearer analogy, and a more immediate and constantly reiterated verification-process than in the latter; but the origination of our belief in fellow-subjects, like remarkableness of coincidences, is ultimately an affair of human psychology and life, of teleology and not of logic or of direct apprehension of soul-substance. Moreover, though we have no 'knowledge' of a spirit above man in the hierarchy of spirits that we 'know', neither have we knowledge that there is no such being. Knowledge leaves room for the faith which teleology involves; and the faith-venture is similar *in kind* to that on which all scientific knowledge relies. Previously to verification of his faith the teleologist need ask of science no further recognition than this. He would but insist that, in so far as relations with logic are concerned, it is not true that science rests on reason while, in a corresponding sense, teleology rests on unreason.

(iv) Besides possessing a structure that happens to render it habitable by living creatures and intelligible to some of them, the world is a bearer of values, thus evincing affinity with beings such as can appreciate as well as understand. The beauty and sublimity of Nature have been made the basis of a special teleological argument; and if, as standing by itself, this argument falls short of cogency, the facts from which it sets out may be said to form a link in the chain of evidence which comprehensive teleology presents. The few considerations that lend themselves to either of these uses do not call for lengthy or subtle disputation; and fortunately it is not necessary to enter the scientifically trackless domain of aesthetics in order to ascertain their bearing on theism. Whether the adaptation to our faculties, involved in aesthetic estimation, be, as Kant thought, formal and the same for all, though subjective; whether it be subjectively constituted and not the same for all; whether beauty be wholly Objective and literally intrinsic to Nature: these controversial questions are here immaterial. For the doctrine that aesthetic value is constituted by feeling does not imply that the feeling is not objectively evoked, as if we could see beauty when and where we chose. It has a parallel in the phenomenalist theory of knowledge: that is to say, beauty is not created by minds out of nothing, but is subjectively made out of *rapport* with the ontal. Thus diverse theories as to the constitution of beauty may be said to have in common the implication that the ontal world is ultimately responsible for the evocation of aesthetic thrills and sentiments, though the value-judgements evoked by the same 'perceptual' Objects are different in different percipients. Theories differ but as to what exactly is intrinsic, whether that is intrinsic to Nature as ontal or as phenomenal, and how much is subjectively contributed. And whatever be our proportioning of the shares of the human mind and external Reality in constituting aesthetic value, the dependence or non-dependence of beauty on design will not be affected by it. There is a point in Toby Veck's remark as to the chimes: "If I hear 'em, what does it matter whether they speak it or not?" Yet "We receive but what we give",[1] in this connexion, is a partial truth because it suppresses the fact that our giving is solicited by a prior and different gift to us. If we minimise phenomenal Nature's gift by denying that her beauty is intrinsic, as is form or colour, we must allow to ontal Nature an intrinsic constitution such that minds can make beauty as well as nomic order out of it. And the more we magnify man's part in this making, phenomenalising, and appreciating, the more motivation have we to believe that Nature comes to herself in man, has a significance for man that exists not for herself, and without man is a broken circle. Theologically expressed, this is the belief that Nature is meaningless and valueless without God behind it and man in front; and that is what teleology in its comprehensiveness, and the aesthetic argument in its particularity, endeavour to establish.

The latter argument, at least in its more popular forms, treats the beauty of Nature as Paley treated organic adaptations. That it discusses the beauty of the world, as we now contemplate it, as if it were a 'special creation' with no past history or development, may not signify. The weak spot in what purports to be a special proof of theism lies rather in the assumption that, since in human art a beautiful or sublime production is the outcome of human design, similar effects must everywhere be due to design. This generalisation is all too precarious; it can hardly be maintained that arrangements of matter, accounted beautiful, humanly caused but not contrived or selectively constructed with a view to

[1] "...We receive but what we give,
And in our life alone does Nature live:
Ours is her wedding-garment, ours her shroud!"
                    S. T. Coleridge, *Dejection: An Ode.*

exciting aesthetic admiration, *never* occur. Prescience or purpose is involved in art; but art is not necessarily the sole source of beauty. We may deem some of Kant's criticisms of the teleological explanation of the beautiful and the sublime to be captious, and such explanation to be natural and reasonable; but it is hardly necessitated by the considerations on which this would-be coercive argument relies.

The aesthetic argument for theism becomes more persuasive when it renounces all claim to proof and appeals to alogical probability. And it becomes stronger when it takes as the most significant fact not the forthcomingness of beautiful phenomena but what may be called, with almost negligible need of qualification, the saturation of Nature with beauty. On the telescopic and on the microscopic scale, from the starry heaven to the siliceous skeleton of the diatom, in her inward parts (if scientific imagination be veridical) as well as on the surface, in flowers that "blush unseen" and gems that the "unfathomed caves of ocean bear", Nature is sublime or beautiful, and the exceptions do but prove the rule. However various be the taste for beauty, and however diverse the levels of its education or the degrees of its refinement, Nature elicits aesthetic sentiment from men severally and collectively; and the more fastidious becomes this taste, the more poignantly and the more lavishly does she gratify it. Indeed, from contemplation of Nature, whose "every prospect pleases", the atheist might be led to conclude that processes only need *not* to be fraught with aesthetic design in order to excite, almost without fail, aesthetic admiration. But his generalisation would become untenable as soon as he bethought himself of similar causal *nexa* into which human agency, seeking any end save beauty, enters. In general, man's productions (other than professed works of art), and almost only they, are aesthetically vile. An automobile, with its noises, stench, etc., can disgust all our senses simultaneously, and is not wholly untypical; while human output of larger scale is often not only unsightly and otherwise offensive in itself, but mars the fair face of Nature. Here, then, are two kinds of agency, *ex hypothesi* proceeding with indifference to the realisation of aesthetic values: we might almost say the one never achieves, while the other never misses, the beautiful. And the same contrast subsists between their processes as between their products.

Compare, *e.g.*, "the rattling looms and the hammering noise of human workshops" with Nature's silent or musical constructiveness; or the devastating stinks of chemical works with Nature's fragrant distillations. "In the very act of labouring as a machine [Nature] also sleeps as a picture."[1]

If "God made the country" whereas man made the town—and the black country—we have a possible explanation of these things; but if the theism contained in this saying be rejected, explanation does not seem to be forthcoming. The universality of Nature's beauty,—to speak as if beauty were the same for all and were intrinsic—is a generalisation roughly comparable with the uniformity of natural law. That natural Objects evoke aesthetic sentiment is as much a fact about them as that they obey the laws of motion or that they have such and such chemical composition. And this potency is not coextensive with 'mechanicalness', or absence of aesthetic design, as man's utilitarian productions shew. Nor can Nature's mechanism be regarded as a sufficient cause of the adaptiveness to our subjectivity in which beauty consists; for we may still ask why *Nature's* mechanism affects us in such wise that we deem her sublime and beautiful, since mere mechanism, as such, is under no universal necessity to do so, and what we may call human mechanisms usually fail to do so. Yet this potency, describable as the Objective factor in beauty, belongs to Nature's very texture. And our scientific knowledge that the world-elements are ordered by number brings us no nearer to understanding why Nature is comparable with elaborately polyphonic music, or a harmony of many combined melodies.

It may further be observed that, in so far as the mechanical stability and the analytic intelligibility of the inorganic world are concerned, beauty is a superfluity. Also that in the organic world aesthetic pleasingness of colour, etc., seems to possess survival-value on but a limited scale, and then is not to be identified with the complex and intellectualised aesthetic sentiments of humanity, which apparently have no survival-value. From the point of view of science, beauty proper is, in both its subjective and its objective factors, but a by-product, an epiphenomenon, a biologically superfluous accompaniment of the cosmic process. Once more then lucky accidents and coincidences bewilderingly accumulate

---

[1] J. B. Mozley, *University Sermons*, 6th ed., p. 123.

until the idea of purposiveness, already lying to hand as indispensable within the sphere of human conduct, is applied to effect the substitution of reasonable, if alogical, probability for groundless contingency. If we do apply this category of design to the whole time-process, the beauty of Nature may not only be assigned a cause but also a meaning, or a revelational function. It may then be regarded as no mere by-product, like physical evil, in a teleologically ordered world whose *raison d'être* is the realisation of other values—the moral and the religious. Indeed Nature's potency to evoke aesthetic sentiment, however otiose in the cosmic process studied by science, is efficient in the world's *rapport* with man. From its very origination religious experience seems to have been conditioned by the impressiveness or the awesomeness of natural phenomena, suggestive of an invisible and mysterious presence. Aesthetic values are closely associated, and often are inextricably interwoven, with ethico-religious values. God reveals Himself, to such as have differentiated these valuations, in many ways; and some men enter His Temple by the Gate Beautiful. Values alone can provide guidance as to the world's meaning, structure being unable to suggest more than intelligent power. And beauty may well be *a* meaning. That is the element of sense contained in the romanticist's paradox, beauty is truth, or truth is beauty.

It may be remarked by the way that if sensuous beauty be accounted a world-meaning, so far will the anthropocentric factor in interpretation of the world become accentuated. For as to the ontal counterpart to sensory beauty, or what Nature's beauty is for the Creator Himself, we cannot speculate. If Nature's beauty embody a purpose *of* God, it would seem to be a purpose *for* man, and to bespeak that God is "mindful of him". Theistically regarded, Nature's beauty is of a piece with the world's intelligibility and with its being a theatre for moral life; and thus far the case for theism is strengthened by aesthetic considerations.

(v) Man's moral status, his moral experience and its alleged *a priori* conditions, have provided foundations for a variety of moral arguments for theism, generally purporting to be sufficient in themselves and independent of teleological considerations. In other words, the being of God has been inferred directly from human morality, and from morality alone. One form of moral argument is *a posteriori* and causal. A. R. Wallace, Lord Balfour, and others, have submitted that, inasmuch as natural selection cannot account for the origin of our higher moral sentiments, resort to a supernatural cause is necessary. Natural selection can only explain the emergence and persistence of such moral conduct and principles as possess survival-value for individuals or societies, between which the struggle for existence obtains; and survival-value does not pertain to the higher morality. But it would seem that naturalism can itself supply an explanation, rendering appeal to a divine cause unnecessary. Just as a bodily organ, developed in response to environment so as to fulfil a certain function, often proves, when acquired, to be capable of performing other functions also, and becomes a starting-point for developements in new directions, so may a mental functioning, once sufficiently developed to possess utility in the struggle for existence, be able of itself, or without further evocation from the environment, to develope to higher levels which, from Nature's point of view, are superfluous. The human mind, once having attained in the course of evolution to ideation, social intercourse, and language, is in a position to develope spontaneously, no longer controlled by mechanical selection (which is but rejection) but by its own interests and intrinsic potencies. From intelligence and emotional sensibility that are biologically useful it may proceed to disinterested science, to pure mathematics having no relation to the needs of life, to art, morality, and religion, no one of which products, rather than another, requires the intervention of a *Deus ex machina* to cause its emergence.

The next type of purely moral argument, as we proceed from the more empirical to those of *a priori* kind, is that from our moral aspirations to their fulfilment. It takes several forms, some of which have been considered in earlier chapters: *e.g.*, that which owes its plausibility and its professed independence of teleology to a double usage of the ambiguous word 'rational'. We can only argue from needs and aspirations to their fulfilment when we have established, as a major premiss, that the world is reasonable, or 'rational' in the sense of teleologically ordered. That, however, is identical with what it is wished to prove, and is not datum, or ascertained fact. What is initial fact or premiss is that the world is more or less rational in the sense of analytically intelligible. But such rationality does not imply that the world is so perfectly harmonious a whole that no serious error in human judgements, or no frustration of the nobler and more permanent human hopes, is incompatible with it. Neither certainty nor probability that the universe will respect our aspirations can be given by moral judgements alone, though individuals may hold that belief tenaciously. Philosophical theology is not concerned with (ψ) certitude or religious biography, but with (ps) certainty, or rather—in the absence of that—with Objective or common reasonableness. That certainty is to be obtained, and to be obtained from the sphere of morals alone, is believed, however, by some defenders of theism. And before considering the types of argument on which they rely, it may be observed that in them certainty and certitude are generally treated as interchangeable equivalents. The philosopher cannot plead that if such a view as that our aspirations are to be nullified were conceivable it would remain incredible because outraging the deepest convictions on which our life is built. The 'thinking reed' may face the world as a judge rather than as a suppliant; but so far as moral ideals alone can inform us, the world may expunge both him and them, however intolerable the thought may be. It is of no avail, again, to observe that our moral claims on the world are not private wishes but common rights. Ideals are none the more certain to be realised for being common, and human rights no more compel cosmic forces than do wishes.

The moral value-judgement, which simply predicates value and nothing else, cannot carry us a step beyond itself towards knowledge as to the existence of anything which, if Actual, would possess value. But, self-evident as this negative statement would seem, attempts have repeatedly been made to extract existential truth from ethical principles. It would seem *a priori* inevitable that the plausibility of such arguments, great enough to have captivated great minds, is due to furtive introduction of existential knowledge into a premiss purporting to be purely moral; and it is antecedently probable that the way in which this introduction of a non-moral ingredient, such as must figure in the conclusion, is in each case effected will be determined by the particular philosophical system to which the particular philosopher is pledged. But, whether or not it is plain beforehand that fallacy must be involved, it is not difficult to shew that in each type of forthcoming argument fallacy is involved.

Moral arguments for theism were put forward before Kant asserted the primacy of the practical reason; but they generally held a subsidiary place. From Kant's day to our own they have occupied a dominant position in theistic systems. It is fitting, therefore, to begin an examination of them by recalling the more enduring part of the line of reasoning which led Kant to conclude that the deliverances of our moral faculty afford satisfactory ground for belief in a Divine Being. More than this Kant did not claim to have shewn: he did not intend to provide a theistic proof. He merely argues that God, a regulative idea for the theoretical reason, is a postulate for the practical reason: *if* the moral order of the world (as Kant conceived it) is to stand, and what ought to be is to be, God must exist. It is only more daring venturers than Kant who have sought to extract the permanent standing of the moral order out of the deliverances of the moral consciousness. With the fact that in Kant's own argument the existence of God is postulated in order to secure the final proportionment of happiness to virtue we need not concern ourselves, beyond observing that it indicates that the realm of the moral, in isolation, no more than the realm of Nature, in isolation, evokes from him the theistic postulate. Kant only needs the idea of God in order to secure the adjustment of these realms, as Descartes needed it to secure the adjustment of thought to being. More important, because an element common to other ethical arguments, is Kant's presupposition that moral values, the categorical imperative, etc., are absolute in the sense of being universal, or independent of the cognition and conation of all as well as of any one, and unconditional. Reasons were submitted in chap. vii of vol. 1 for believing that when principles, etc., are abstracted entirely from the Actual conditions which give them their significance and define the scope and range of their relevance, they become non-significant as well as unconditional, thought instead of knowledge, 'empty' because despoiled of all that is 'blind' or alogical, and form as pure a science as a non-applicable geometry concerned only with indefinables, definitions, conventions, and their logical and eternal relations. If those reasons be sound, the plausibility accruing to moral arguments from the presumed absoluteness of axiological propositions is destroyed. They will also suggest criticism of Kant's usage of the word 'ought'. That 'I ought' implies 'I can' is a foundation on which he builds much. So long as oughtness is derived from, and has relevance to, the sphere within which human agents can perform obligations, this implication holds, and indeed the possibility of a performance conditions its oughtness; but when oughtness is made unconditional, by abstraction from its setting, it may no longer involve the 'I can'. There is another sense of 'ought', as Sidgwick observed, in which we say we ought to do only what, in the former sense, we ought to strive to be able to do but cannot do. 'I ought' then does not imply 'I can', or that I ever shall be able to perform what duty prescribes. And Kant does not escape this snare of ambiguity. Moreover, if oughtness-to-be implies possibility of realisation, the highest good must finally be realised; and since Kant held that God is indispensable for its realisation, his argument to a postulate should then be rather a coercive proof of God's existence. Lastly, if the *summum bonum* has its possibility of realisation guaranteed by the concept itself, Kant in principle employs the ontological argument in ethics after demolishing it in theology.

An argument from the moral consciousness to God which differs in important respects from Kant's, but resembles it in presupposing the absoluteness of moral value-judgements, was put forward by Dr Rashdall. The possibility and the forthcoming-ness of absolute morality were thought by this writer to involve the postulation of God for the following reasons. There is an absolute moral ideal: it 'exists'. And 'to exist', for Dr Rashdall, meant to be 'in' some mind. The ideal is not fully apprehended as to its content by any individual; nor is it realised in any human life. There must therefore be a Divine Mind in which its 'existence' is to be located. Our moral experience implies the 'existence' of an absolute and perfect moral standard, and its 'existence' in turn implies the existence of God. In this argument the connecting-link between value and Actuality is supplied by the particular metaphysical system which Dr Rashdall embraced, viz. an idealism of Berkeleian type, indicated by *esse est intelligi*. The fallacy involved consists in a confusion of two different senses of 'exist'. The 'existence' of ideas in a mind has not necessarily any connexion with the existence of Actual or ontal beings, or with the

Actual subsistence of relations between such beings. Presumably the law of the inverse cube 'exists', equally with the law of the inverse square, in the Divine Mind as well as in ours; but the presumable fact does not explain why the one law exists, or Actually subsists, in Nature, whereas the other does not. Ideals and ideas may thus 'exist' without even being valid; and it is a further step from validity to Reality. From an idea, unless it has first been derived from a percept, to an Actual counterpart, there is no direct passage. Moreover, apart from the disputable Berkeleian ontology imported into this moral argument, the initial assumption that *a* moral ideal with content, or a monistic ethics free from internal inconsistency, 'exists', may, as has already been observed, admit of questioning. Our moral experience, evaluation, progress, etc., presuppose norms and ideals; but it is no more obvious that they presuppose an absolute, infinite, or perfect norm than that our growth in stature presupposes the existence, or even the idea, of an infinitely tall giant.

Other words besides 'existence' are sufficiently rich in different meanings to serve to make the directly impassable gulf between ideal value and Actual existence appear, in moral arguments, to have been bridged. The word 'real', when used without definition, often seems to be a name for a hybrid conception involving both value and existence; and, applied now with the one and now with the other reference, it can make a mixture of ethics and metaphysics look as if it were pure ethics implicative of ontology. It is to be feared that this is the case in the argument presented in *The Ethical Approach to Theism*, by Dr Barbour. If 'real' is to have an existential meaning, the assertion that goodness is supremely real and is the final truth of things, so that what ought to be is the ground of what is, is rather the theist's *demonstrandum* than his datum; it can only be taken as known fact, from which to argue, if 'supremely real' mean nothing but supremely valuable. It might also be contended, as against this writer's ethical proof, that the imperative of duty can be categorical without being literally absolute and without directly bringing us into close relation with the central truth, of the existential kind, about the universe. However, Dr Barbour's argument is only adduced here as an example of the usage of 'real' in what seems to be a question-begging way. In so far as its assumption of the absoluteness and universality, in the strictest senses, of moral ideals and judgements, its adoption of Plato's doctrine of universals, its identification of validity with Reality, are concerned, the reasoning on which it relies has virtually been criticised in previous connexions. And if such metaphysical presuppositions be untenable, a moral argument of this type will not enable us to rise beyond the 'finite' God yielded by induction to the Infinite Being, and so play the rôle that used to be assigned to the ontological proof.[1] It is assumed here, as established in the former volume of this work, that our ethical principles are general rules for the guidance of human wills to human ends, owing their significance to the developing society in which they emanated, and presupposing specific values involving human interests, rather than *a priori* forms, or unconditionally valid propositions about indefinables: or that ethics is as much an affair of alogical valuations as of abstract principles and laws of pure reason.[2]

A less ambitious type of moral argument than those which have last been discussed is that which endeavours to avoid the ontological fallacy, or the identification of the valid with the Reality *of* which it is valid, and which is contented with the doctrine of the *universale in re* as distinguished from that of the *universale ante rem*. Moral values subsist ultimately only in persons, to whom they are asserted to be, in some sense, intrinsic; and, thus subsisting, they are as constitutive of that part of Actuality that is personal, as physical laws are constitutive of Nature. They are not asserted to be valid of what persons do or have done, as natural laws are valid of the course of physical things; nor does their

---

[1] For further remarks on this 'proof' see Appendix, Note B.

[2] Of the Ritschlian attempt to find a new basis for theology such as purports to be an Objective science and not merely a body of subjective beliefs, in 'independent judgements of worth' it is not necessary here to say more than that it appears ultimately to reduce to a confusion of the nature of assertions about the soul's attitude to the material world and to human life, the dependence of man on the help of God for his victory over the world, and so forth, with the nature of the value-judgement proper, as instanced in the simple case of an assertion that a given percept is pleasurable. Of course if God be more than an ideal Object, any proposition concerning Him, as well as any about the soul or the world, involves existential knowledge and its methods, though not necessarily those of rationalism. The metaphysics which Ritschl would exclude is presupposed in his data and concealed by a misapplied name. But these criticisms would need to be discounted if he were to be regarded as an expounder of theism assumed to be true, rather than as a demonstrator of its truth.

validity consist in, though it is said to involve, their coherence without contradiction within a comprehensive system. They hold of what persons are free to do and ought to do, of the ideal that it is possible for them to actualise, of human potentialities. It is in this sense that they enter into the constitution of the world. From such premises, which are unquestionable so long as the superfluous claim that morality is wholly unconstituted by conative and cognitive activities is not made, there is no direct argument to the existence of God as the necessary fount or home of ethical ideals; and, as presented by Prof. Sorley in his *Moral Values and the Idea of God*, these considerations are apparently but intended to constitute an essential, and indeed the most significant, part of the data to be taken into account in a synoptic view and interpretation of the world. They supply the coping-stone of a cumulative teleological argument for theism.

And this, it would seem, is the true place of forthcoming facts, concerning man's moral status and experience, in theistic argument. Isolated from other facts, and used only for the sake of their alleged *a priori* preconditions, they can supply no rational proof of the existence of God. Even when asserted to be valid of the ideal or potential, as distinct from the Actual, universal moral judgements form a science more akin to pure mathematics, such as may or may not prove applicable to Actuality, than to applied mathematics; and when, as in special proofs such as have previously been examined, moral laws are abstracted and reified into an eternal *prius*, seeming to call for a supreme lawgiver to give them a footing in 'existence', nothing is proved: the valid and the existent have been confounded.

In an exposition of the significance of the moral order for theistic philosophy, the first step is to point out that man belongs to Nature, and is an essential part of it, in such a sense that the world cannot be described or explained as a whole without taking him and his moral values into account. Prof. Pringle-Pattison, especially, has elaborated the doctrine that, as he expresses it, "man is organic to the world". What precisely this, or the similar phrase "man is the child of Nature", should mean, if either is to be more than a half-truth, needs to be made clear. In so far as man's soul, *i.e.* man as *noümenon*, or (in the language of spiritualistic pluralism) the dominant monad in the empirical self, is concerned, we are not authorised by known facts to regard man as organic to Nature, or as the child of Nature, in the sense that he is an emergent product of cosmic evolution. We are rather forbidden by psychology to entertain any such notion. But, this proviso being observed—it must qualify all that is further said in the present connexion—we can affirm that man's body, with all its conditioning of his mentality, his sociality, knowledge and morality, is 'of a piece' with Nature; and that, in so far as he is a phenomenal being, man is organic to Nature, or a product of the world. And this fact is as significant for our estimation of Nature as for our anthropology. If man is Nature's child, Nature is the wonderful mother of such a child. Any account of her which ignores the fact of her maternity is scientifically partial and philo-sophically insignificant. Her capacity to produce man must be reckoned among her potencies, explain it how we may. And man is no monstrous birth out of due time, no freak or sport. In respect of his body and the bodily conditioning of his mentality, man is like, and has genetic continuity with, Nature's humbler and earlier-born children. In the fulness of time Nature found self-utterance in a son possessed of the intelligent and moral status. Maybe she was pregnant with him from the beginning, and the world-ages are the period of her gestation. As to this anthropo-centric view of the world-process, and its co-extensiveness with teleological interpretation, more will presently be said. But in the light of man's continuity with the rest of the world we can at once dismiss the view that Nature suddenly "stumbled" or "darkly blundered" on man, while "churning the universe with mindless motion". The world-process is a *praeparatio anthropologica*, whether designedly or not, and man is the culmination, up to the present stage of the knowable history of Nature, of a gradual ascent. We cannot explain man in terms of physical Nature; conceivably Nature may be found explicable—in another sense of the word—in terms of man, and can be called 'the threshold of spirit'. Judging the genealogical tree by its roots, naturalism once preached that Darwin had put an end to the assumption that man occupies an exceptional position on our planet; apparently implying that there is no difference of status between man and the primordial slime because stages between the two are traceable. But if we judge the tree by its fruits, Darwin may rather be said to have restored man to the position from which Copernicus seemed to have ousted him, in making it possible to read the humanising of Nature in the naturalising of man, and to regard man as not only the last term and the crown of Nature's long upward effort, but also as its end or goal.[1]

The phrase 'organic to Nature', as applied to man, may serve to sum up other relations between humanity and the world besides that of parentage or blood-affinity. It implies also a denial of the assertion that man is an excrescence upon Nature in the sense of being an alien in a world that is indifferent to his moral aims, or hostile to his ideals. The most forcible presentation of this view, that the cosmic process and human morality are antithetical, is perhaps that contained in Huxley's *Romanes Lecture*. It is therefore here selected for examination. Huxley's first point was that the world, as involving struggle for existence and extermination of the less fit, is no "school of virtue". If that statement merely meant that it is not from Nature that we are to imbibe our ethical maxims, no one would wish to dispute it. But it would then overlook the fact that in other senses Nature may fairly be called a school of virtue. In the first place, Nature is largely a cosmos ruled by uniformity or law; and if Nature's uniformity and impartiality are a main source of the trouble to which man is born, they are also a precondition of all intelligent, and therefore of all moral, life. In this respect Nature is the power that makes it possible for noümenal man to be, as phenomenal man, a moral being. Further, it is partly through his being "the plaything of hazard and the prey of hardship" that man's moral virtues are acquired. The world is thus instrumental to the emergence, maintenance, and progressiveness, of morality. The second charge which Huxley preferred against the cosmos is that the physical world works upon man solely through his lower nature, his ingrained appetites, etc., and against his higher ethical interests. Nature is thus the cause of his 'original sin', and is diabolically provocative of his diverse immoralities. This also is true; but again it presents but one aspect of the facts. For, apart from man's bodily appetites and impulses it is inconceivable that ethical principles should gain purchase on him. Hunger and sex are the bed-rock of human morality; and the self-determination which

---

[1] A. Seth Pringle-Pattison, *The Idea of God*, 1917, pp. 82 f.

human morality presupposes is hardly possible without the conflict
between moral reason and non-moral impulse. Morality cannot
be made without raw material; and in providing this raw material
Nature is once more instrumental to man's acquisition of the
moral status. Morality thus has its roots in Nature, however
indispensable be the innate and non-inherited potentialities of the
pure ego or soul. The non-moral cosmos, personified into a morally
evil world by pessimistic poets for the purpose of giving it, as
Mr Chesterton has said of one of them, a piece of their mind, has
nevertheless subserved the moralisation of human souls, even
when soliciting to carnality. And it is an exaggeration to say that
Nature fosters only tendencies that issue in vice. We have seen
before that there is such a thing as 'natural virtue', or 'original
rectitude', as 'instinctive' as is self-seeking; and Nature plainly
appraises health and vigour, thus inciting to temperance and self-
control. Lastly, Huxley maintained that the world is indifferent
to man's moral aspirations, in that they along with him are destined to be extinguished before the break-up of the solar system.
Here he became unwarrantably dogmatical: for, apart from the
fact that science's predictions are not unconditional, speculations
as to the ruin of a fragment of the universe, based on partial
knowledge of a larger fragment of what, for all we know, may be
possessed of a power to make all things new, are too precarious
to be considered exhaustive of the possibilities even as to our
terrestrial home, let alone those as to a future life.

Nature, then, has produced moral beings, is instrumental to
moral life and therefore amenable to 'instrumental' moral valuation, and is relatively modifiable by operative moral ideas—or,
rather, by moral agents pursuing ideals. Nature and moral man are
not at strife, but are organically one. The whole process of Nature
is capable of being regarded as instrumental to the developement
of intelligent and moral creatures. Acquisition of the moral status
is in line with the other stages of the long 'ascent of man', and is
its climax—unless we reserve that name for the morality which,
tinged with sentiment transcending reverence for duty, passes
into religion.

(vi) The more or less separable fields of fact which have now
been surveyed may each be said to admit of teleological explanation even if explanation of the causal or the descriptive type be

forthcoming in every case. None of them calls for resort to final causes merely because other kinds of causality, or linkage according to law, are not assignable. Theism no longer plants its God in the gaps between the explanatory achievements of natural science, which are apt to get scientifically closed up. Causal explanation and teleological explanation are not mutually exclusive alternatives; and neither can perform the function of the other. It is rather when these several fields of fact are no longer considered one by one, but as parts of a whole or terms of a continuous series, and when for their dovetailing and interconnectedness a sufficient ground is sought, such as mechanical and proximate causation no longer seems to supply, that divine design is forcibly suggested. Paley's watch is no analogue of the human eye; but it may none the less be an approximate analogue of Nature as a whole. Thus the wider teleological argument is not comparable with a chain whose strength is precisely that of its weakest link; it is comparable rather with a piece of chain-armour. And this can the better be seen if the relevant facts be presented again so as to display especially their connexions and their gradually increasing suggestiveness.

There is no intrinsic necessity that a world, or an assemblage of existents and happenings, indefinably and unaccountably 'standing out' as against nothingness, be a cosmos, even to the extent of any one existent being comparable with another or behaving in the same way twice. Reality, or the aggregate of those determinate beings, might conceivably be a 'chaos' of disparates and inconsistencies such that if any of its members possessed consciousness or awareness and the potentiality of intelligence, they would find the world presented to them utterly unintelligible. Our world is, however, a cosmos, at least in the humblest sense of the word, and the original determinateness of its terms or *posita* is such as to make it intelligible. This, of course, constitutes a teleological proof of theism no more than does the existence of the world afford a causal or cosmological proof. The mystery of mysteries is that something exists; and if the one underived or uncaused existent be God, the creator of all things else, God is "the last irrationality", and creation is the next to the last inexplicability. To replace absolute pluralism by theism is to reduce an indefinite number of separate inexplicabilities to these two alone; and so far economy, and therefore explicability of a kind, is secured. It is of no important kind, however: for there is no more wonder about a self-subsistent plurality than about a self-subsistent individual. But when the intelligibility of a cosmos, rather than the mere existence of a world of any sort, is the fact to be considered, teleological theism evinces more conspicuously its advantage, in other respects than that of economy, over absolute pluralism. For over and above the forthcomingness, conceived as self-subsistence, of the many existents, is their adaptiveness, inherent in their primary determinateness and their relations, to the requirements of intelligibility. This further particularises their determinateness and so bespeaks more of coincidence in the 'fortuitous'. For cosmos-quality, or intelligibility, in our world, which conceivably might have been but a determinate 'chaos', non-theistic philosophy can assign no reason. If the world 'made itself', so to say, or is the self-subsistent Absolute, its adaptiveness to understanding has simply happened, and is part and parcel of the pluralist's last irrationality. It gives him more to explain or to refuse to explain: for why should the many arrange themselves to form an intelligible and an organic whole? If, on the other hand, this be due to an intelligent Creator designing the world to be a theatre for rational life, mystery is minimised, and a possible and sufficient reason is assigned. More than this cannot be extracted out of the initial fact that the world is intelligible, in the sense that has as yet solely been in question; but if it be merely a hint that Nature's dice may be loaded, it is to be observed that the hint becomes broader as Nature is further examined, and as the knowledge-process is analysed. For instance, the particular species of intelligibility, in which the knowledge of common sense and science consists, is mediated by the 'real' categories; and they depend for their forthcomingness on the contingency that the dominant monad in man is embodied, or associated with monads such as also constitute Nature but which, in virtue of some mysterious affinity, are not merely bits of Nature to the soul but also its windows and telephonic exchange-office mediating to it all its knowledge whatsoever, even its self-knowledge. Thus, as step by step the machinery which produces intelligibility is scientifically explored and made manifest, the richer in specialised determinateness are some of the world's constituents found to be; and therefore the more suggestive is the intricate adaptiveness, involved in knowledge of the world by man, of pre-established harmony or immanent guidance, or both, and the less reasonable or credible becomes the alternative theory of cumulative groundless coincidence. The doctrine that man is organic to Nature can now be broadened out so as to embrace the fact that it is only in so far as he is part and parcel of Nature that he can ejectively make the knowledge-venture, and only in virtue of Nature's affinity with him that his postulatory categories receive pragmatic verification, and his assimilation-drafts are honoured. When the impossible Cartesian rationalism is exchanged for the humanism or anthropism which, implicit in Kant, is explicitly demanded by more modern empirical knowledge of the human mind, the epistemological argument for theism begins to acquire a forcibleness that was lacking to the arbitrary, if not circular, reasoning of Descartes. It is, however, but a fragment of the epistemological argument to establish the anthropocentric theory of knowledge, which is ultimately based on the fact that between the soul and the world, in so far as knowledge of the one by the other is concerned, stands the body; and the epistemological line or mesh-work is but a fragment of the teleological argument as a whole.

Turning now from Nature's knowability to her structure and history, we may revert first to the fact of adaptiveness in the organic realm, which, so far, has only been found not to yield teleological proof of the narrower kind. Here adaptiveness, unhappily described as internal teleology, is not teleological at all in so far as it is internal to the organism. There is no end present to the agent. It is from the (ps) standpoint of the biologist, not from the (ψ) standpoint of the organism, that reference to the future is involved in organic adaptedness. Again, neither the occurrence nor the progressiveness of organic adaptations, taken *singillatim*, calls for other than natural, if non-mechanical, causation. It is true that the course of living Nature is not mere change, but change that admits of valuation, of one kind or another; of valuation not only in terms of fitness for survival but also in terms of differentiation or complexity of structure and function, and of subservience to further developement culminating, in man, in rationality and morality. Despite cases of stagnancy and of degeneration, which equally with progress may ensure biological fitness, the plasticity, formative power, or *élan* in organic Nature secures not only self-conservation but also progress, morphological and ultimately mental, so that within the main line of developement there has been a steady advance from amoeba to man. But each step and special adaptation, each case of emergence of something new and higher, in this long process, can be sufficiently accounted for in terms of natural, non-teleological causation. So far as the fore-going facts are concerned there is no need to resort to external teleology. It is not *necessary* to invoke design in order to find a guarantee for the stability, in face of the ever-present possibility of deletion of the 'higher' by the 'fitter', of the long and gradual ascent, remarkable as that is. It is rather when the essential part played by the environment, physical and organic, in the progressive developement of the organic world, is appreciated, that non-teleological explanation ceases to be plausible in this sphere, and, conspiration being precluded, external design begins to be indicated or strongly suggested. It is the environment that is the selector, though 'selection' is a figurative expression when applied to non-intelligent Nature. Subjective selection, or the Lamarckean factor, may decide what shall arise; but the environment decides what shall stand. And before discussing the alternatives of theistic teleology and naturalistic Pyrrhonism (if the doctrine of fortuitousness or ungrounded coincidence may so be called), it may be submitted that the fact just mentioned restricts our choice to the one or the other of them, in that, when taken into account, it deprives the only other forthcoming alternative, viz. the theory of 'unconscious purpose', of such plausibility as, *prima facie*, it may seem to possess.

The phrases 'unconscious will' and 'unconscious purpose' are, of course, when taken literally, contradictions in terms. That, however, is unimportant. Overlooking the poetic licence evinced in such forms of speech, we may inquire what the writers who favour them mean by them, or what are their equivalents in scientific terminology. This is not always easy to ascertain with precision; but it would seem to amount to the assertion of an *élan vital* present in Nature as a whole, an intrinsic potency to strive blindly towards, and to attain by changes that we valuing subjects call progressive from the lower to the higher, what, from the same intelligent point of view, are relative goals: not ends of a designer, nor merely temporally later stages in a process, but 'ends' in the sense of later stages that happen to be of higher value, of one kind or another, than the earlier stages, *as if* foreseen and striven for. This kind of *Zweckmässigkeit* without *Absichtlichkeit* has a parallel in human endeavours. Men have sometimes "built more wisely than they knew", and human societies may fashion institutions, beliefs, etc., without any of their members having a preconceived definite idea of the 'end' in which their activities are destined to issue. One thing that was willed leads on to other things that were not at first willed or even imagined, and *sometimes* these other things are found desirable, or are goods to be preserved. Sometimes, however, they are of the opposite kind, so that reforms or revolutions find place in human history. And here, if the theory before us be not misunderstood, this analogy breaks down. For the theory ascribes to Nature an intrinsic potency which, if it is to succeed in the absence of that self-correction by which erring human mentality can change its own course and avoid impending catastrophes, must inevitably go, like animal instinct, straight to its mark in all essentials and on all critical occasions. Nature's 'unconscious wisdom', in other words, must vastly exceed the sapience and foresight of humanity, liable as that is to errors which, save for reasoned amendment, might prove fatal. In fact the theory requires us to believe that Nature keeps her head, which *ex hypothesi* is brainless, through all the changes and chances of cosmic history.

Further, 'unconscious purpose', which has turned out to be as fatalistic as mechanism and yet as value-realising as man, does not seem, on examination, to be one and the same thing in the different kingdoms of Nature. In that part of the organic world that is (macroscopically) psychical it is said to be exemplified in animal impulse, or the non-volitional conation of individual organisms. But this subjective selectiveness of the individual, though essential to organic developement, does not of itself suffice to secure it. The organism, in filling its skin, may get itself a better skin to fill, but on the other hand it might burst its skin; and blind or random movement, such as might secure escape from the painful or displeasing, may land 'out of the frying-pan into the fire'. Natural selection can only secure the progress of species in virtue of such individual catastrophes, misfits, etc., in organisms inspired with venturesomeness and *élan*. Individual variations are mostly indefinite or in many directions, not in the straight path of progress alone; and it is the environment, as censor, that plays the larger part in determining a steady and permanent advance, as contrasted with the sporadic and evanescent experiments which make progress a possibility. Thus the environment, the preponderating part of which is inorganic, as well as its organic denizens, needs to be accredited with 'unconscious purpose'; yet it lacks even the animal conatus and the vegetable 'formative power' which, though they are Actualities, are not unconsciously *purposive*, in that, of themselves, they are not fraught with an exclusively progressive trend. A formative power lodged in the physical, as science has hitherto understood it, making as if for a goal, is not an Actuality known to science. Consequently, it here becomes impossible to find any explanatoriness, and indeed any meaning, in 'unconscious purpose'. If it but asserts that in the inorganic world there is a potency of adaptiveness, that is but a new name for the fact that the environment is adapted; it but restates the fact to be explained, the problem to be solved, and proffers no explanation or solution. An explanation, however, is offered by teleology and theism. It is a fact that Nature, as inorganic, is as much adapted to organic life as organic life is adaptive to physical environment; and it is not a matter of indifference whether we say "God has wisely willed it so" or "Nature has wisely arranged this", simply because Nature has no wisdom wherewith to arrange anything. If Nature evinces wisdom, the wisdom is Another's. The issue narrows to whether what we may generically call the order in Nature is to be accounted an outcome of wisdom or of undesigned coincidence. Indeed, in so far as the question is as to explicability, the issue narrows to the vanishing-point; for assertion of coincidence in the self-subsistent, wondrous in respect of its manifoldness and complex interlacingness, is, again, not explanation but statement of what calls for explanation.

The manifoldness of the coincidences on which the order in the world, including man, is conditional, has already been sufficiently illustrated, though it might be more minutely and extensively expounded. These coincidences, let it be repeated, are present in the determinate natures of the cosmic elements, the world's original existents and their primary collocations, in the adjustment of similarity to difference between them which is the ground of all the uniformity and variety, the stability and the progressiveness, of the irreversible process of becoming; in the alogical *posita*, their logico-mathematical relations, their determinate *rapport* which is such as to provide a law-making, and so a law-governed, world; a world instrumental to valuation and evocative of it, and intelligible in the peculiar anthropic sense which saturates the meaning of 'knowledge' whenever that word denotes the Actual processes in which the human mind comes to an understanding with Actuality. What is here being called coincidence is to be seen, again, in the stages of emergence of novelty which issue not, as conceivably they might and as mere mechanicism suggests they perhaps should, in successive labile configurations of a cosmic dust-cloud blown by a changing cosmic wind, but in an evolutionary process in which much goes that comes, while nevertheless the unceasing flux is such that one whole world-state is, as it were, a built storey and a scaffolding for the erection of another. Emergents 'here' seem to 'take note of', or be relevant to, causally unconnected[1] emergents 'there', in both space and time, since an elaborate interlacing of contingencies is requisite to secure inorganic Nature's adaptedness to be a theatre of life. Any miscarriage in promiscuous 'naturation', such as might ruin the whole, as a puff of air may lay low the soaring house of cards, has been avoided in the making of *Natura naturata*; and though such possibilities do not suggest themselves to science contemplating Nature as a system of Lagrangean equations, the historical process conceivably might be seen to have teemed with critical moments and crucial situations by a visualising compeer of Laplace's calculator. Similarly in the organic world, erratic and venturesomely varying conative individuals may have constantly endangered, as much as they have provided for, the future of the world. Orderly progress, however, has been attained; and it has been ensured by the firm hand and the directivity of already stabilised environment. Organisms, and man in especial measure, have the world with them in their aspiringness. It is not so much the progressiveness displayed in the world-process as the intricate

---

[1] Causally unconnected in the sense in which experimental science must use the notion of causal connexion.

and harmonious interconnexion, rendering progress, intelligibility and intelligence, etc., possible, that in its marvellousness suggests intelligent art. On the other hand, it is the progressiveness which suggests that such art is directed toward an end—realisation of 'the good'.

So long as attention is paid exclusively to the universal, the logical and rational, as is necessary in the case of science but is arbitrary in the case of philosophy, the inner significance of this world, with all its particular 'thusness', will be missed. It is in the concrete or the historical, to which the universal is but incidental and of which the logical or rational is but one nexus among others, that meaning can be, and seems to be, conveyed: and as the history, made by the mindless or by practically infinitesimal minds, is on so grand a scale intelligible to universalising intellect, there would seem to be directive intelligence behind it. It is in the characteristics of *this* world, in the particular determinateness of the collocations prescriptive of its Actual course, and—not least—in the anthropism thrust by Nature on the non-anthropic pure egos out of which she has made men, and its affinity with the world in respect of both genetic continuity and epistemic capacity, that purposiveness lets itself be read. If we thus read things, a unique significance attaches to the realm of the moral, amongst other teleologically suggestive domains of fact, in that it enables us to advance from belief that the world is a work of art to belief that it is constructed for a purpose, and worthily specifies what the purpose is, or includes. If we decline to explain things thus, it would seem that the only alternative is to regard the self-subsistent entities, of which the world is constituted, as comparable with letters of type which have shuffled themselves not only into a book or a literature but also into a reader commanding the particular tongue in which the book utters its unintentional meaning. If the inference from cumulative adaptiveness to design be non-logical, as is admitted, it at least is not unreasonable.

Even critical and iconoclastic philosophers have treated with respect forms of teleological argument such as were current in their day. Hume denied that the argument is logically coercive, but he allows Philo, in the *Dialogues*, to admit that the fitness of final causes in the universe and its parts strikes us with such

irresistible force that all objections to them appear cavils and
sophisms. Kant, again, speaks of it as the clearest of the 'proofs',
and as the one most in harmony with the common reason of mankind. Yet the more comprehensive and synoptic design-argument
that is now producible is more imposing than any contemplated
in their day. Hume almost ignored man and his moral status;
while Kant, who saw in man's moral faculty the central fact about
the universe, so over-emphasised its purely rational functioning as
to overlook its historical developement, its alogical content, and
the respects in which it is 'of a piece' with Nature. The greater
strength claimed for the newer argument consists in its exhibition
of the interconnexion and reciprocal adaptation between systems
of fact which used to be treated as if isolated. It can now be
submitted that if the uniformity of Nature rests on mechanical
postulates, and the 'validity' of moral principles involves a moral
postulate, the evolutionary progressiveness of the world points to
a teleological postulate. And if this evolution is to be explained,
or to be assigned a sufficient ground, instead of being merely
accepted as a brute happening, the historical and alogical aspect
of the world-process must not only be regarded as the primary
reality *in ordine cognoscendi* but also as our clue to the *ordo*, and
the *ratio*, *essendi*. Mechanism and the universalisings of pure
rationality are tools as useless for this purpose as a typing-machine
and a book of logarithms are for landscape-painting: for the
problem is reducible to the question, *cui bono*? Teleological
explanation is comparable with discernment of "the signs of the
times" rather than of "the face of the sky"; and although to fail
to discern cosmical signs of the former kind need not be to class
oneself with the "hypocrites", to be indifferent as to whether
there be such signs may be said to involve venturing less than the
"all that doth become a man". Perhaps no thinking being is thus
indifferent, or even uninquisitive. When the teleological or
theistic explanation of the world is not adopted, it is because one's
explanation-craving is satiated before the limit to which the theist
presses is reached in the regress, or because a seemingly better
explanation has been found, or because one has become convinced
that none has been found that tallies with all the facts. Whether
theism satisfies this last condition will be discussed in another
chapter, and more remains to be said as to certain alternatives to

theism; but it has perhaps already been shewn that no *explanation* is contained in the assertion that the world is an organic whole and consequently involves adaptiveness. That is only a restatement of the occult and wondrous fact that cries for explanation. The world's 'thusness' is explained, however, if it be attributable to the design and creativeness of a Being whose purpose is, or includes, the realisation of moral values. Further back than a creative Spirit it is neither needful nor possible to go. But further back than the world we can and must go, because the notion of a non-intelligent world that produces intelligent beings and makes itself intelligible, that can have no purpose and yet abundantly seems to bespeak one, and so forth, is not the clearest and most reason-satisfying conception that our minds can build wherein to rest. Moreover, as J. Ward has observed, the alternative that the world's evolution is ultimate, or its own sufficient reason, ignores the fact that we rational beings are part of the evolution, so that our demand for a sufficient reason is "a demand that the world itself has raised".

At more than one place in this chapter stress has been laid on the intelligibility of the world to the specifically anthropic intelligence possessed by us, and on the connexion between the conditioning of that intelligibility, on the one hand, and the constitution and process of Nature, on the other hand. Thus a close relationship is indicated between teleological explanation and an anthropocentric world-view; and this relationship may now be more explicitly described.

Anthropocentrism, in some sense, is involved in cosmic teleology. It is useless for ethical theism to argue that the world evidences design unless the only rational and moral denizen of the world, in so far as it is known to us, be assumed to afford an indication as to what the designed end of the world-process is. And, as thus stated, anthropocentrism involves no human arrogance or self-exaltation. It does not assert that man, as a zoological species or genus whose geographical distribution is presumably confined to this planet, is the highest being under God, or the final stage of progressive cosmic evolution, or the end and the whole end of the divine design. It is compatible with belief in "thrones, dominions, principalities, powers", or angels and archangels, and in the possibility that in other worlds there are rational beings akin to us in being embodied and having their

E

specific intelligence moulded thereby.[1] It is content to allow that the divine end, in its completeness, is unfathomable. Nor does it imply that lower creatures evolved in the world-process are necessarily of but instrumental value as stages or means to ends, and, when not figuring in man's genealogical tree, are mere by-products in the making of humanity. Anthropocentrism rather means that, whereas in the realm of Nature beneath man no final purpose can be discerned, such purpose may be discerned in beings possessed of rationality, appreciation, self-determination, and morality. Man may exhibit these powers and attributes in but a limited or humble degree. But, in its essence, intelligence may be common to a hierarchy of beings; and it is in virtue of his membership in that hierarchy, if such there be, rather than in his distinctive or specific and contingent characteristics, the anthropic or human, that man shares the privilege of being a bearer of the highest values, and of being in some relative, rather than in an absolute and exhaustive, sense bound up with the otherwise ineffable divine purpose. Teleology is interpretation of beginnings by *terminus ad quem*, lower stages by higher, process by product, and temporal becoming in terms of realisation of values; and the *terminus ad quem* of the world, so far as the world-process has as yet gone, and in so far as the world is known, is man. It is not that he is the last evolute in time; indeed his parasites should be later: but that he is the highest product in respect of value, and in the light of whose emergence all Nature, to which he is akin, seems to have its *raison d'être*. Hence the necessity of his figuring pre-eminently in theistic philosophy, if that is to be based on facts

---

[1] It is, of course, a matter of indifference to teleology and anthropocentric interpretation whether the material heavens contain a plurality of inhabited worlds. But it is interesting to find recent astronomy, as represented by Prof. Eddington, inclined to the views that the physical universe probably does not greatly extend beyond the range of human observation, and that the number of the heavenly bodies suitable for the maintenance of life (as it is conditioned on this earth) is extremely small. It is commonly deemed absurd to suppose that, out of the immense number of worlds known to astronomy, only one is peopled with living beings; yet it is not a question of numbers but of chemical and physiological conditions. Science pronounces the globes which satisfy these conditions to be, in all probability, very few; while organic life involving only inorganic chemistry, organisms adapted to the temperature of the burning fiery furnace, and so forth, are notions that hardly lie within the sphere of scientific imagination. If anyone likes to maintain that the Creator of the starry heaven is "mindful" *only* of man, neither will science accuse him of grotesque exaggeration nor will theism need to hope that he is absolutely accurate.

rather than on preconceived ideas, and is not to transcend fact save in the inevitable way of fact-controlled and reasonable extrapolation and idealisation. That the investigation, pursued in the preceding volume and in the present chapter, of man's rational and moral status and its conditioning by his physical and social environment, has involved more emphasising of what may be called man's anthropism than of his rationality, etc., in the abstract, is a necessity dictated by facts and by the empirical method. But now that the anthropocentric view of the world has been reached, and the facts which justify it have been set forth, our attention may move on from terrestrial contingencies, creaturely limitations, and specifically human characteristics, to the generic features which, from the point of view of theism, must be common to the mind of man and the Mind of God. The anthropocentric view of the world is a necessary step to the theistic interpretation of the world and man: it need not profess to be more.

The empirical approach to theism being essentially teleological, it is now necessary to raise the question, what an end or purpose, as attributable to the Deity, consists in. The idea of purpose is derived from the sphere of human activity; and such meaning as is imported into it from that context has necessary relevance only so long as that context is not transcended: such is the empirical doctrine as to the scope and validity of ideas or ideational propositions. But when applied to God, whose activities, by definition or *ex hypothesi*, include some that are unique, and whose intelligence is necessarily different in some respects from ours, the idea may become non-significant. Theism that would use the idea, it has sometimes been urged, must be unduly anthropomorphic. That need not be so, however, if such constituents of the complex idea of purpose as involve intrinsic limitations of human mentality and activity can be eliminated from it, while others, essential to the conception of purposiveness but separable from their human manifestation, can be isolated for legitimate transference to the sphere of divine activity. What elements require to be eliminated, modified, or newly related, in such recasting of the idea, has been differently decided by different exponents of theism; and perhaps it is premature to undertake the analysis and re-synthesis until an exposition has been given of one's conception of the nature and attributes of the Deity. In the absence of such preliminary discussion it may suffice to indicate possible divergences of view, as occasion calls.

In the conception of human purpose we may distinguish the following constituent elements: (1) the pre-conceived idea of a situation to be reached, (2) desire for that situation because of its value to the agent, (3) the use—in general—of means for the attainment of it, (4) the actualisation—generally by stages—of what was contemplated in thought and striven for. Into the first of these, and indeed into all of them, the idea of temporal succession enters: idea of the goal is previous to attainment of goal, desire to fruition, and so on. And whether the temporal form, characterising human experience, is to be carried over into the conception of God's activity and experience is a disputed question; that it has been variously answered is the chief source of divergence of view as to what exactly purpose, ascribed to the Deity, is. This question is not to be discussed for the present. It need only be remarked here that *if* it be possible to conceive of purposive activity as not necessarily involving the temporal stages which have been indicated, so that separation of ideated end and accomplished end be non-essential, and if concomitance of plan with actualised volition be as useful a notion as that of succession of the one upon the other, then the purposiveness of the world will consist in its being an organic system, or one in which the natures and interconnexions of the parts are determined by the whole, and in its being an expression of intelligence but not an actualisation of a *pre*-existent plan. According to this attenuated conception of purpose the relation of means to end, generally involved in human purposefulness, also vanishes.

The element of value, of desire and satisfaction, is not eliminable from the idea of purpose. Without it the category of end would lose its distinctiveness and become identical with some other, such as cause or ground, mechanism, or non-contradiction. The tendency to minimise or cancel valuation, in this connexion, and to speak of satisfactoriness as something of logical nature, conceivable in abstraction from satisfaction, is evinced by absolute monists rather than by theists. In whatever sense the world may be said to embody divine purpose, the least that can be meant is that the world contains what is of worth to the Supreme Being.

The third factor in human purposing, adaptation of means to

end, is again one which some theists have been reluctant to admit into the conception of divine purpose: partly because of its temporal implication; partly because it is thought to bespeak limited power and need to overcome difficulties; and sometimes on the ground that the divine end is the world-process, not some perfected outcome of it, and that everything that we would regard as but a stage or a means toward something else is, for God, itself an end. This last issue may be considered immediately; but whether the relation of a determinate God to a determinate world, other than Himself, admits of being conceived without ascription to Him of some kinds of limitation such as do not render the distinction between means or stages and end obviously superfluous in the case of divine activity, is a question that will receive later the discussion for which it calls. The fourth of the factors into which the idea of purpose has been resolved presents no especial problem other than that already indicated when the first was touched upon.

It has been remarked before that Nature and man, empirically studied, may strongly suggest that the world is an outcome of intelligence and purpose, while *the* purpose or divine end which the universe and the world-process subserve may remain unknowable to us. But, as we have also seen, speculation on the latter subject must be allowed to influence views as to the nature of the purposiveness that is involved in the former assertion. The forthcoming alternative views, between which facts scarcely enable us to decide, may be briefly mentioned. The divine purposing may be conceived as pre-ordination, in which every detail is foreseen. An analogy is presented in Mozart's (alleged) method of composition, who is said to have imaged a movement—its themes, developement, embroidery, counterpoint and orchestration—in all its detail and as a simultaneous whole, before he wrote it. If God's composition of the cosmos be regarded as similar to this, all its purposiveness will be expressed in the initial collocations, and evolution will be preformation. On the other hand, God's activity might be conceived as fluent, or even as "increasing", rather than as wholly static, purpose. It might then be compared, in relevant respects, with the work of a dramatist or a novelist such, perhaps, as Thackeray, who seems to have moulded his characters and plot, to some extent, as he wrote. And it would appear that the divine purposiveness must be partly thus conceived if conative creaturely activity may either co-operate or clash with the Creator's, so that providential control and adaptation to the emergent must enter into the realisation of the divine plan.

Again, though the divine end is usually construed eschato-logically, there is an alternative interpretation. It may be that there is no "far off divine event" toward which creation was predestined to move: the process itself may constitute the end. Certainly progress has a unique value, incapable of the absorption or transmutation which some values undergo; and the conception of the divine end as a perfected society of ethical individuals, and a philosophy of history such as is based on that presupposition, are not free from difficulties. At any rate the securing of the consummation will need to be so conceived as not to involve sacrifice of the ethical dignity of the individual person as an end for himself, and no mere instrument to the future perfecting of others. The social good may but be good in that it ministers to the goodness of individuals, each of whom—as the Christian conception of the Fatherhood of God implies—is singly an end for God. Position in the time-series, or the progress-series of social developement towards perfection, may be of no moment as compared with the individual's use of his opportunities, such as they may be: timelessness, in the sense of indifference to axio-logical rank as temporally circumstanced, may characterise the valuation he receives from God, who seeth not as man seeth, and may read the heart rather than 'Objectively' estimate the actual output of the will. If so, asymptotic attainment of ethical per-fection, and the ideal consummation, may be contingent or con-ditional aspects of the divine end, while progressive becoming, throughout all reaches and domains of the universe, may be its ultimate essence. These alternative conceivabilities are here merely mentioned; their relative tenability is not to be investigated. But it may further be observed that if evolution is itself an end and not a means to an end, the hard dualism of means and end must vanish. Childhood, for instance, will not be merely a stage in the making of a man; nor will groping past generations have worked merely to provide their posterity with better opportunities for making further advance. As a rose-bud has a beauty or perfection different from but equal to that of the full-blown rose, so may each stage in the life of the individual or the race have, along with its appropriate work, an intrinsic value, or be an end in itself as well as a means to something beyond. The only conclusion now to be elicited from the foregoing remarks is that teleology and theism may admit of statement in terms of other than the static concepts, and the abstractions such as perfection that is of no *kind*, which dominated thought until a century or so ago, and which, within the spheres of philosophy and theology, still impose themselves on some evolutionists.

The teleological approach to theism, with which this chapter has been concerned, has been made from the fact that conformity to law is intrinsic to the world, and from the conclusion that such order belongs to the world as ontal. It has already been found not to be blocked by science or by mechanistic philosophy of Nature and its law-abidingness. Besides being a cosmos explicable, in one general sense, in terms of its structure and scientific intelligibility, the world is a bearer and a producer of values in that in our *rapport* with it we are affected by it. The world is not completely described if this aspect of it is left out: less than all the data would but then be taken account of. The Actual or historical world-process, from which mechanism is an abstraction, is characterised by irreversibility, epigenesis, progressiveness of developement, and by manifold adaptations which adaptedly interlace. It evokes explanation, consequently, of a different type from that pursued by physical science; and it accords pragmatic verification to use of the category of design for this new kind of explanation, as well as to use of the causal category for scientific explanation. If reason stand to formal rationality in a relation similar to that in which philosophy stands to mechanical science, philosophical reasonableness cannot be a mere extension of scientific, or of logico-mathematical, rationality; and if existential 'knowledge' is allowed its postulates, it seems but partial to disallow to 'knowledge' concerning the value-aspect of Actuality the postulate that is similarly needful to it. *Homo* who provides the *mensura* for all and every kind of intelligibility needs not to blind himself to the fact that he is more than a logical thinker, or to the fact that he stands in other relations with the universe than that of knowing about its structure. He cannot but have other problems besides that of the relation of being to thought. Philosophy, in other words, is an affair of living as well as a mode of thinking. All causal knowledge is, in the last resort, but reasonable and postulatory: teleology is therefore a developement from science along its own lines, or a continuation, by extrapolation, of the plotted curve which comprehensively describes its knowledge. And this is the *apologia* of theism such as professes to be reasonable belief for the guidance of life, when arraigned by science and logic—or by more pretentious theology.

CHAPTER V

The Idea of God: Creation, Eternity, Infinitude, and Perfection

(i) It has been argued that the multitude of interwoven adaptations by which the world is constituted a theatre of life, intelligence, and morality, cannot reasonably be regarded as an outcome of mechanism, or of blind formative power, or of aught but purposive intelligence. The facts do not point to an inscrutable world-ground, as to which no more can be said than that it exists. When Hume asked why should we make mind the one phase in terms of which all others are to be explained, suggesting that the world-ground is something whose nature is an insoluble enigma, and as to which our only reasonable resource is a total suspense of judgement, he had set before himself, as data for contemplation, but a fraction of those that are now forthcoming from the sciences of Nature and man, of knowledge and valuation. The only idea of a world-ground that yields an explanation of these facts in their totality would seem to be that of an efficient, intelligent, ethical Being.[1]

When, at the present stage, we call this Being 'God', we are borrowing a name, but not any idea, from religion. The content of our idea of the world-ground may become richer when we take account of religious experience; but we must not confound the way out from knowledge about the world and man with the way back from knowledge about God to reinterpretation of man and the world, or confuse proof of a *demonstrandum* with exposition of a *demonstratum*. We must gather our sheaves before we can come back rejoicing and bearing them with us. Further, in appropriating the name 'God', no premature assumption of monotheism is intended. What is claimed to have as yet been reasonably

[1] To prevent misunderstanding it may be stated that 'ground', in the phrase 'world-ground' as used here and henceforth, does not bear its logical sense, in which it is correlated with 'consequent'. 'World-ground' denotes that upon which the ontal world, regarded by theism as not self-subsistent, depends for its forthcomingness and its determinate nature: not something from which all else follows with predetermined necessity; because theism ascribes initiation to created beings.

established is that cosmic purposing is embodied in the world. But oneness of purpose does not imply numerical oneness of purposer: societies, as well as individuals, may originate and follow one purpose. Teleological arguments, alone, cannot transcend spiritualistic pluralism. Whether the world-ground is singular or is a plurality of beings may be considered later: meanwhile a name that has become invested with singularistic import by religious tradition and aesthetic sentiment shall be used for convenience in the singular number.

It is an old charge against empirically founded arguments for theism that, even if sound, they do not prove so much as theology needs. But 'theology' then denotes but the more pretentious *a priori* theology, such as describes the Deity as a perfect, absolute, or infinite being. It is here to be inquired what natural theology may reasonably affirm concerning God and His relation to the world, while 'rational' theology will receive some criticism: so the charge is not disconcerting. To Hume and Kant it is willingly admitted that from a finite effect we cannot infer a cause greater than is necessary to produce it. And if the empirical method can attain to knowledge of but a finite God, it is to be debated whether, when the meanings of 'finite' and 'infinite' are gauged by reflection rather than by sentiment, any conception of God save as a finite being can be reached with consistency, and can be either of service to theology or of interest to religion when reached. God's attributes must immeasurably transcend man's attributes of similar kind, but it is a further question whether there is sense in calling them infinite.

It is more important to theism that God stands in unique relations to all the parts of the world, and uniquely stands in relation to the world as a whole. But either that or nothing at all is what is 'proved' by the empirical argument presented in the preceding chapter. There has been speculation as to an evolutionary ascent from the world and man to deity; but among the several senses that 'deity' then has borne can hardly be included the capacity to design and actualise an evolutionary universe. God and souls belong to different ontal orders, if to the same ontal class—viz. spirits.

(ii) It may next be observed that the designing of the world, which implies a Designer, further implies that the Designer is also the world's Creator. One of the shortcomings of which the classical design-argument was accused by its critics is that it attempted to prove no more than a world-architect, working on pre-existent material; on the other hand, within my circle of scientific colleagues there seems to be a preference for the notion of world-shaping rather than for that of creation. But it must be submitted that the designer of the cosmos, required by the facts set forth in chap. iv, could not be its architect without being its creator. The general scope and trend of the cosmic process was implicit in its 'primary collocations', even if we allow for both creaturely spontaneity and immanent divine activity throughout the process; for the universe has no environment to evoke from it the epigenetic, or what may be called the emergent. And if we would confine ourselves to existents or Actualities, and abstain from introducing non-Actual abstractions into our sphere of discourse, we cannot entertain the supposition that the linkages, interactions, and relations of pre-existent but 'chaotic'—*i.e.* relatively orderless—things could be stripped from them or from their determinate natures, leaving them unannihilated, and new linkages, such as should make a cosmos, could be superimposed on them, leaving those natures unaltered. If substance and cause are one category, as has been previously maintained, it is the natures of the existents that prescribe or define their possible *rapport*; and neither the existent nor its *rapport* is separable from the other without the annihilation of both. Natureless substances, matter without form, and form without matter, are indistinguishable from nothingness. And if that be admitted, design in the world as a whole is impossible unless it involves creation. In other words, the ordering of the world as a whole cannot be conceived as transcreation, or as relative creation, or as analogous to the work of a human architect: the initial determining of specific inter-relations, and the positing of *relata* with determinate natures, are necessarily one and the same activity. When man converts clay into bricks, and bricks into a house, he is, according to science, merely altering the configurations of particles of some kind; but if a demiurge arranges particles so that of themselves they shall build a cosmos such as we have found our world to be, providing for the necessary epigenetic 'emergences' throughout its ramifying and interlacing tissue, he must be credited with the initial *determination* of the natures of his particles, and not merely with the collocation of them, so that this world and no other should be evolved from them. That determination can only be creation.

The idea, or rather the notion, of creation, then, has so much of empirical justification as is involved in the fact that it is implied in the teleological interpretation of the world, which vast systems of fact make reasonable or alogically probable. The notion is also both essential to theism and a distinctive characteristic of theism; and it is so on account of both its positive content and its implicit negations. These negations, to take them first, amount to repudiation of other theories as to the relation of the world to God. The notion of creation rules out absolute pluralism, or any form of the theory that the world is self-subsistent, and implies that other beings do not coexist along with God but somehow in Him or through Him. It denies the ancient dualism according to which God only shaped into a cosmos the self-subsistent ὕλη, governed by ἀνάγκη and more or less incalcitrant: indeed the doctrine of 'creation out of nothing', which does but mean production subject to no external limitations, arose in Christian theology from its need to oppose gnostic and Manichaean dualism. It repudiates the neo-Platonic fancy that the world emanated, as by a kind of actual or quasi-physical necessitation, from the 'nature' of God. The use of the notion of creation, again, distinguishes theism from pantheism or absolute monism, be its finite 'modes' substantival or adjectives of the One; and indeed from any theory according to which the derivation of the many from the One is non-volitional, analogous to logical sequence, or in which the many are conceived as ideas or validities contemplated by the One, rather than as ontal beings with existence-for-self. In its use of the notion of creation theism differentiates itself from all such systems, most of which are of the *a priori* type. It would assert that by the 'ground' of the world it does not mean an abstract idea, which cannot be the source of anything actual, but a spirit, possessed of what is called intellective intuition. This postulated activity is not merely one wherein things are known by a transcendent experient, as its name may suggest, but one whereby things exist, are 'planted out' as *onta* other than the Creator, His subjective states, etc. This positing of other *onta*, for which 'creation' is but another name, is the positive item in the notion of creation; it only needs to be added that creative activity is volitional, or involves that in the divine experience to which human volition is the nearest analogue.

Theism must frankly confess that the kernel of positive meaning in the notion of creation, viz. positing, is inexplicable. Indeed if it were explicable it would not be creation. The various analogies that have been employed for its elucidation, such as man's 'creative' art, throw no light on the ultimate mystery. Just as the gradations between the infinite One and the finite many, devised by Philo, Plotinus, Spinoza, etc., conduct nearer to the abyss but do not bridge it, so these comparisons break down at the crucial point—origination of something out of no pre-existent material such as is forthcoming and utilised in the case of causation within the course of Nature, and in all 'creative' imagination or ideation within the minds of men of genius. The *modus operandi* of divine creativity is wholly unimaginable and inconceivable. And this inexplicability is inevitable. For explanation, in all its forms, establishes some connexion, similarity, or continuity, with what is experienced or lies within Experience; whereas creation is the activity through which experients and what is experienced by them come to be. The notion of creation, consequently, is not derivable from experience, and analogies valid within experience cannot reach beyond its bounds. But while the theist must confess that a conception which is fundamental in his philosophy is inexplicable, he may do so without shame and without reproach. Some ultimates, unanalysable and unassimilable, there must be. Theism needs but to allow that creation is one of them. And in invoking it theism sets up no new mystery where there was none before, as seems often to be tacitly presumed by those who regard the notion with disfavour. The ultimate mystery of the origination of the world confronts all theories alike, and to think it does not exist for any one kind of non-theistic world-view is but to hush it up. In giving articulate expression and particular form to the mystery theism is not uniquely burdening itself with a superfluous load. And however much a philosopher may be inclined to disparage the notion of creation on the score of its obscurity, there is certainly no more intelligible a notion which he can substitute for it. If the alternatives are self-subsistence, indefinite regress, emanation, and self-manifestation in a finite many, these are equally obscure or mysterious; and for the same reason. But while all these leave the particularity and diversity, the inferiority and dominance, of the various constituents of the ontal world wholly unaccounted for, and thereby decline to reduce superfluous mysteriousness, they supply no sufficient reason for the forthcomingness of this peculiarly ordered world rather than of any 'possible' aggregate whatever. Volitional creation at least minimises the inexplicability of things; and it is no arbitrary hypothesis, because there is an imposing array of considerations based on fact which bespeaks design, which in turn implies creation. These things being so, and there being forthcoming no substitute for the idea of creation which does not involve at least as great difficulties for imagination and thought, theism may claim that this idea is reasonably justified, while admitting that it cannot otherwise be empirically verified.

Another objection is anticipated, which may perhaps be found to be met in part by observations occurring later in this chapter, and which may in part be considered here. Intelligence and volition, as we know them, involve presented objects: to speak of intelligence and volition such as theism ascribes to God is therefore meaningless, some will say. It may be replied that analogy in some respects between minds of different orders is not necessarily incompatible with difference, and even disparity, in other respects. Certainly creativeness introduces into the conception of divine intelligence an element in virtue of which our intelligence is transcended: intellective intuition, positing its own objects, overpasses a limit to which our experience does but point. But the additional power to posit objects need not cancel all analogy between the intelligence, etc., of the Creator and the intelligence of us who cannot posit our objects. Intelligence and volition in us *pre*suppose objects; and it is perhaps the temporal suggestion contained in the prefix 'pre' that chiefly leads the objector to question the propriety of speaking of intelligent and volitional positing. But creating or positing being allowed, and not figuring (on account of its mysteriousness) as the main ground of objection, the demurrer would seem to owe its forcibleness to insistence on invoking temporal relations where supra-temporality is in question. In this connexion something is said below. Just as the idea of self-limitation, applied to God as creator, does not intend to refer to a prior state of non-limitation, so positing and knowing need not be temporally disjoined.

Even theistic writers, however, have evinced a tendency to minimise or eliminate the element of divine volition when describing the dependence of the world upon God. Their motive is generally avoidance of anthropomorphism, a wish which may over-reach itself; and their method is abstractiveness. Volition, indeed, is sometimes treated as if, by its being indescribable in terms of logical categories, it were constituted arbitrariness or caprice; and as if to assign it a part in God's creativeness were to invoke the quasi-magical. If God is an intelligent, purposive, and benevolent agent, what is called His 'nature' must provide for will as well as for intelligence; but the one of these inseparables is wont to be included in the divine nature, and the other to be excluded. Thus an antithesis between two abstractions, nature and will, is set up; and the creation of the world is regarded as a necessary outcome of the former of them alone. When the idea of a ground, in the sense of a logical *ratio*, is substituted for that of a first cause, or for that of a sufficient real ground which is more comprehensive than a cause as ordinarily understood, the limit of extreme intellectualism is reached, according to which philosophy and science, and even aesthetic and moral valuation, should be reducible to apprehension of the non-contradictory. When the disparateness between logical following (of consequent from ground) and historical or Actual process is not over-looked, another type of 'necessary' world-production may appeal to theology such as is reluctant to accept the notion of volitional creation, viz. emanation.

The ancient doctrine of emanation has not wholly ceased to find favour. But its classical formulation involved quasi-physical analogies which contravene the laws of energy: as a philosophy of Nature it was one of several attempts to read a literature before learning its alphabet. And the emanents which it specified are plainly mythical fictions *ad hoc*, for which modern knowledge has no use. Of more moment, however, than criticism of the out-worn are the reflections that the theory of a volitionless derivation of the world leaves unaccountable the very facts, as distinguished from preconceptions, which commend theism as a reasonable world-view, and that, if volition is to be cancelled from divine creativeness, the ethical must at the same time be cancelled from the divine self-manifestation.

'Self-manifestation' is another euphemism for 'creation', with its suggestiveness of volition. Doubtless, in creating, God manifests Himself; but self-manifestation presupposes creation of recipients of the manifestation, unless it be a theophany of God to God, superfluous in a perfect Being. This, by the way, was not overlooked by Berkeley when he would translate the Mosaic account of the creation of the world as meaning that eternal, archetypal, and imperceptible ideas of God were made ectypal and perceptible, so that things entered upon a relative existence, or were created only with regard to us. If, undeterred by the problem of evil, he reduced the created world to divine symbolism, Berkeley allowed the createdness of finite spirits, for whom the world is symbolism.

The human imagination most forcibly represents to itself the dependence of the world on the will of God by supposing God and time to precede creation. But, as early Christian thinkers found, there is no reason to convert this representation into a theistic tenet. One of them regarded creation as an endless regress, world preceding world; another taught that creation was not in time, but the world and time were created together. Neither of these doctrines gets rid of temporality; and that of Augustine suggests that creation was somehow comparable with an event, and that eternity preceded time. A further refinement is made when God is conceived as *essentially* the world-ground or creator; not another cause in the series, or a being who might or might not have created. God *quâ* God is creator, and the creator *quâ* creator is God: or "God without the world is not God". Causation, as commonly understood, relates to change within the already existent; in this sense it is inapplicable to creative activity. Conversely, if creative volition be called causal, it cannot be a case of transeunt causation. Also, if God is *only* God *in that* He is creative, creation cannot be merely immanent, or change in God. As Prof. Ward has observed, in his lucid exposition of what the theistic notion of creation is not, there is no reason why, because we can distinguish the two elements, will and presentation, in the intellective intuition that must be ascribed to God, we should regard them as separate, and either of them as preceding the other. It is superfluous to entertain the idea of a prior will to create, a posterior selection of a best possible plan, and a final creative fiat: that is anthropomorphism that can be spared. Creation can be conceived as idea and deed together, and the divine transcendence as not temporal priority, but as consisting in the difference between God and His utterance—which pantheism identifies.

Thus conceived, the theistic idea of creation is free from the old puzzles concerning temporal relations. If God be a world-ground, there never could have been no world. The 'possibilities', prior to any Actuality, betwixt which the Deity has been thought to have chosen, are but hypostatised abstractions. The view that God might, previously to creation, be potentially its ground is a reversion to the notion that there was a something external to Him to evoke the transition from potentiality to actuality; and that is just what creation, expressed as 'creation out of nothing', and more correctly by the phrase 'no ground but God', excludes. God, as a determinate being, implies a world; but the world, according to theism, is neither God, nor co-ordinate with Him, nor independent of Him. If we are to speak in terms of time, the theistic doctrine may be summed up in the statement that the world is coeval with God and is contingent on His determinate nature, inclusive of will.

(iii) The relation of the 'eternal' God to the time-process, already involved in discussion of creation, is a question affecting several of the theological issues which are presently to be considered; this, then, is a fitting occasion for its further investigation.

As the word 'eternity' has borne several meanings in theological literature, it may conduce to clearness of exposition if these meanings are distinguished; for the relation of the temporal to the eternal becomes a different problem as the connotation of 'eternity' varies. The first sense to be mentioned is that which the word bears in common speech: everlastingness or unending duration. When eternity is thus defined, its relation to time may be said to be but that of whole to part. And by time will be meant conceptual or common Time, not the private or perceptual time of individual experience.[1] In conceptual Time, whether the clock-

---

[1] For the sake of clearness, 'time' shall henceforth be spelt with a small initial letter when reference is made to perceptual time, and with a capital when abstract concepts are in question. Of conceptual Time several kinds are in use, among which

time of common sense or the more abstract time of Newtonian physics, duration involves succession. An hour is sixty successive minutes to the plain man, and a series of successive and durationless instants to the mathematician. And precisely because duration involves succession, this Time can be called infinite. In its mathematical sense, infinity is only predicable of what is measurable, or consists of members or parts. Endless duration of Time cannot be conceived as successionless without contradiction.

But the first departure from the cruder conception of eternity, in which eternity is but Time, consists in the endeavour to conceive of unending duration as not involving succession. Boëthius defined eternity as "the whole and perfect simultaneous possession of interminable life": a definition which was adopted and defended by Aquinas. This definition is worthless if the temporality or duration implied in "interminable life" be taken to be of the conceptual kind, used by common sense and science, because involving the contradiction that has just been mentioned. But it remains to be inquired whether the definition may stand when for conceptual Time we substitute what may correspond, in the experience of God, to the perceptual time of individual human experience. Such time-perception, if the phrase be allowed, consists in making explicit what is implicit in our fundamental experience of change. We can have experience of change without explicit awareness of the passage of Time; but the presentation of change, as distinguished from change of presentation, involves awareness of perceptual time. Into such experience real duration, which is primarily an intensive magnitude, and is distinct from what in abstract Time figures as duration, enters. But its entrance is detected only by the reflective recognition that what was perceived as simultaneous includes the very recent past, or rather the 'retained'.[1] Duration proper, then, implies both (ψ) simultaneity in the perceiving and (ps) non-contemporaneousness in the parts of what is perceived. Without both it becomes an abstraction and is no longer an actuality. Thus, whether we would

may be included the temporal relations which, according to the doctrine of space-time, are but arbitrarily divided from spatial relations. The capital T is far from being intended to bestow the dignity of Reality, save in the sense of commonness to many experients, upon any temporal conception. It merely points the difference between *ad hoc* thought-constructions and the real temporal element in perception of change.

[1] See vol. i, p. 169.

speak in terms of perceptual time or of conceptual Time, duration involves succession. Further, a 'now' that is temporal at all is relative to other conceivable 'nows', not absolute as the definition of Boëthius assumes. The word 'present', in its temporal sense, is meaningless save relatively to past and future; it refers to time and cannot be applicable to the timeless. The expression 'eternal present' is but a metaphor.

This conception of eternity as a *nunc stans* or a *totum simul*, and as the endless 'specious present'—to use an unhappy but technical phrase—of God, was held by St Augustine.[1] With us the duration-block of a minimum whole experience or single moment, as measured in conceptual Time, is short: but Augustine attributes to God a similar present of indefinitely great span, containing all the past and all the future. This ascribes to the Deity the absence of one human limitation, viz. the shortness of the time-span within which the (ps) past and future are blended in one (ψ) *simul*; but it seems to attribute another limitation, viz. absence of discrimination of the items of experience as earlier and later. With the difficulties attending inclusion of the future, in the same sense as the past, within the present, we need not now concern ourselves; but, however long be the span of an enduring present, it can only be *conceived* as containing Time and as in Time.

Thus eternity regarded as endless duration is a philosophically useless notion. Endless duration *with* succession involves the difficulties besetting the old, or 'improper', mathematical infinity: endless duration *without* succession is self-contradictory if conceptual Time is contemplated, and psychologically unwarrantable if perceptual time is in question.

The endeavour to conceive eternity in temporal terms has not been wholly abandoned, but it is now more common to find eternity construed as timelessness. Several possible alternatives as to the "reality" of time and eternity respectively, and as to the relation between them, then present themselves. Firstly, both Time and eternity may be regarded as "real": that is to say, some eternal existents may be ontal or Actual, and temporality may be other than illusion. Time may then be "truly real" or noümenal, or it may be phenomenal of some noümenal and non-temporal order. Secondly, there is the theory, sometimes called temporalism,

---

[1] *The Confessions*, Book XI, c. 13.

that Time alone is "real", and that nothing existent or Actual can be Timeless. And lastly, all "reality" may be eternal or Timeless, Time being "unreal" or illusory. According to the first view, Time is not a part of eternity, nor does eternity annul Time; the eternal may be the supra-temporal, not limited by the temporal form, and the eternal may be functionally related to the temporal. The last of these theories, on the other hand, annuls Time: the eternal becomes the immutable, since without Time change is not conceivable, and without time change, as such, is imperceptible.

These various suppositions may be now discussed in turn. Taking first the view that 'the timeless' has a "real" denotation or applies to what is Actual and not merely ideal or possible, while Time, or at least time, is not illusory, we need to inquire how any relation of Time to eternity is to be conceived. One particular case of this relation, if relation there be, has already been touched upon; viz. the succession of Time on eternity, or the beginning of Time. If Time mean filled Time as contrasted with the abstraction empty Time, the beginning of Time will be the beginning of change. *Non in tempore, sed cum tempore, finxit Deus mundum*, said Augustine: perhaps recalling the *Timaeus* or the *Theaetetus*. But whereas Time and becoming were "unreal" for Plato, Augustine would fain regard them as in some sense "real". He was confronted with at least as great a difficulty in relating the temporal and the eternal as that which Plato shirked. And when the beginning of Time is dealt with, Augustine and, later, the schoolmen rely on revelation rather than philosophy. Moreover their difficulty was with the causal rather than with the strictly or barely temporal aspect of the problem, *i.e.* with the beginning of change, of which Time is the form. A timeless cause of a temporal order, or an immutable ground of a changeful world, was not found easily conceivable.

To pass now from a particular case to the general question: we may begin by remarking that 'eternal', in the present connexion, may bear either of two meanings. The word may stand for 'absolutely Timeless', connoting unrelatedness to temporality as well as not being 'in Time'—in the sense of being before, after, or contemporaneous with, something else. It may also mean supra-temporal, denoting what is itself free from the form of Time but is functionally related to, and Actual in, Time, and related differently to different portions of Time. If eternity be construed in the former sense, it may perhaps be said that it is admittedly impossible to conceive of any relation or *rapport* between things eternal and things temporal. Such absolute timelessness is a mere negative, and no determinateness is bestowed upon it by contrasting it with the temporal, in so far as it is supposed to denote the Real or existential. Truths of reason are the only entities that are timeless in this sense; and they possess validity, not existence. If God were eternal, in the same sense, He would be an idea, not a spirit, nor a world-ground. It would seem that in order that the absolutely timeless may be related to—*i.e.* have *rapport* with and interest in —the changing, its relations should change: which is a contradiction. We must abandon, then, the possibility of a theological usage of 'eternity' in this acceptation: God and spirits are not eternal in the sense in which truths of reason are Timeless.

But if 'eternal' mean supra-temporal, it may be predicable of existents; and the relation of the eternal to the temporal will be no other than that of the noümenal to the phenomenal. The noümenal or ontal is functionally relatable with the Time-process. Subjects or souls cannot be said to be in Time; for it is through the activity of some of them, and perception, etc., on the part of others, that phenomenal change, of which alone we are authorised to say that Time is a form, is constituted: on the other hand, this constitution of change is a functional relation with the temporal. An apt expression of the truth is cited by Prof. Ward: "time is in us, though we are not in time"—*i.e.* Time. It is in that duration is subjective *erleben*, and as experienc*ed* is not merely a temporal succession of empty instants, that time is in us. It is in that ontal agents make or supply the matter, of which alone Time is the form, that they themselves are not in Time.

While empirically grounded metaphysics compels us to regard experients as noümenal and supra-temporal, psychology teaches that perceptual time is as actual as change, and that experience is change. The charge of illusoriness cannot, therefore, be preferred against perceptual time without involving experience itself in illusoriness, and destroying the foundations of any philosophy whatsoever. But Time, rather than time, has necessarily figured in this discussion. That time is real is inexpugnable fact; that Time is Real is another proposition, and cannot be asserted or denied with significance until 'Real' has been defined. Conceptual Time, of which there is more than one variety in use, is a construction and an ideal, based on perceptual time though discarding some of its essence; it is 'Real' if that word means valid (within limits) of Experience, but not necessarily if it means existent, ontal, self-subsistent, or independent of all experients and all Experience. If the second of the views enumerated at the beginning of this inquiry, viz. temporalism, involves an assertion of the Reality of Time in one or more of these latter senses, and not merely that Time is a conventional construction valid of human Experience; and if, further, temporalism implies a denial of any difference between the noümenal and the phenomenal, it may be rejected in the light of what has been set forth here and in the preceding volume.

On the other hand, it is not possible to deny the reality of perceptual time in individual experience. Experience is not only experience of change: it *is* change. To have one and the same undifferentiable experience is tantamount to having no experience. And it is from the objective side of experience, or by the very nature of sensa, with their protensity, that perceptual temporality is thrust upon us. Nothing, however, can be thrust upon us in perceptual or impressional experience that has no ontal counterpart in the noümenal realm: we cannot make phenomenal bricks without noümenal straw. So, although we are forbidden by the Kantian epistemology to apply the forms of intuition and the categories of the understanding, in the precise form in which they are applicable to temporal phenomena, to the ontal, of which temporal things or sensa are phenomena, we seem to be compelled by the phenomenalistic theory of knowledge, as improved since Kant, to credit ontal existents, if not with temporal relations of some sort, at least with ontal relations of which perceptual temporality is the appearance. The situation is similar to that presented by the category of cause. In a previous examination of causality and its metaphysical bearings it was submitted that, although we may accept the Kantian doctrine that our categories, as they stand, are not applicable to things *per se*, nevertheless the Kantian thing *per se* is useless unless we ascribe to it the activity that is involved in its *rapport* with us, and the *determinativeness* (in part) of what our phenomenalising minds make out of it. But if activity and determination do not enter into, or make up the whole of, what we may please to pack into our causal category when adapting it to the science of phenomena, they do form the essence, the *sine quibus non*, of causality: so that the prohibition to attribute causation to things *per se*, which has been somewhat tamely obeyed by post-Kantian philosophy, is impracticable unless it be legislation in the relatively unimportant sphere of verbal convention. It has now become necessary to plead a like case for the temporality, in the most inclusive sense that the word can sustain, which characterises all that we have any right to call experience. That we and God, as noümenal subjects and agents, are not in Time—the Time of common sense, or of Newton, or of Einstein—goes without saying; but that Time, or rather time, is "in us" must be a profound truth if an obscure one. It cannot, however, be taken for the whole truth. Temporality, in the elastic sense which includes protensity, is in sense-data; it therefore must be, or have some ontal analogue, in things *per se*, whose activity determines our 'perception' of duration and succession. If this be all that temporalism would assert, the phenomenalist, as distinct from the realist or the idealist, cannot but grant its claim; but temporalism is perhaps rather to be identified with the type of realism which looks upon scientific abstractions as ultimate Realities.

To return for a moment to the first of the three theories that were mentioned at the outset: this theory may be said to have been found satisfactory, provided that 'eternal' be taken to mean supra-temporal and noümenal, not absolutely timeless. It admits of relations subsisting between noümena, or the things that are not seen and are eternal, and the things that are seen and are temporal. And such relations must be sustained if the idea of eternity, with other than a purely axiological signification, is to find a place in theistic theology. For, supposing that an absolutely timeless God can be regarded as active enough to contemplate, He could but contemplate timeless verities, and His life would be exhausted in νόησις νοήσεως. On the other hand, a God who is out of Time, only in the sense that He is a noümenal subject and agent, may have the world-process as an object of knowledge and a sphere of activity. The temporal can have meaning for Him, and He can have practical and spiritual value for creatures whose deeds are in Time.

The third type of theory concerning eternity and time, however, remains to be considered, according to which all "Reality" is timeless and all temporality is illusion, or in some other sense "unreal". 'Reality', as applied to Time, may mean various things; but perhaps the meaning that is most generally intended is the one as to which, in the foregoing paragraphs, least has been said, viz. validity. Certainly most of the arguments that have been put forth to prove the unreality of Time consist in endeavours to shew that the conception of Time involves contradictions, or what Dr Bradley and others have called contradictions—viz. notions that are not logically clear or reducible. It is not necessary to reproduce here the various contradictions, etc., with which the conception of Time is alleged to be riddled, or the replies from mathematical logicians to the effect that these allegations generally rest on misunderstandings. It is perhaps sufficient to observe that at the bottom of most of the objections to the Time-concept lies the rationalistic prejudice against the sense-given, perceptual experience, and becoming as distinct from being; also the pre-supposition that the Real (*i.e.* presumably, the ontal) is the rational. If dialectic does not accord with the concrete facts of experience, it does not immediately follow that these facts are illusory or nonsensical; it may be that the dialectic is inadequate to them, or that it is erroneous in itself. Inadequate it must be, because abstractive: even the Time-concept itself is so. But that this concept, admittedly inadequate and abstract, is inconsistent in itself is another matter. And it is less obvious, perhaps, than that the accusing dialectic is not erroneous. Thus, to select one of the ablest attacks on the "reality" of Time, Dr McTaggart[1] seems sometimes to have confounded perceptual with conceptual Time, though the distinction between them is explicitly recognised by him; and he evinced a tendency to deal with abstractions as if they were Actualities. This leads to curious paradoxes, such as, *e.g.*, the assertion that future events exist before we experience them, and that change is from future to present and past. However, it is not intended here to undertake a criticism of arguments to the effect that Time is a self-contradictory notion. It may rather be inquired what, on the assumption that temporality is illusion, is the relation of the eternal to the temporal.

[1] *Mind*, N.S., No. 68; also *The Nature of Existence*, vol. II.

That to any illusion or appearance there is *some* Real counter-part will probably be universally admitted. And if the illusion of temporal order arise from our wrongly reading differences between our subjective affections as differences between Objective events, there must, as was said before, be some Real order of which the Time-order is a misreading. Plato called time a moving shadow or image of eternity; but why there is a shadow, and why one that moves, he did not explain. And philosophers from Plato to Ward have been content to distinguish between the ontal and the phenomenal and to say little or nothing as to the ontal equivalents of relations between phenomena. Dr McTaggart, so far as I know, stands out as the only philosopher who has seriously endeavoured to supply what absolutists and eternalists have omitted, viz. a suggestion as to what the eternal and noümenal order is, of which the temporal order is said to be an appearance.[1] He maintained that the Time-order is determined by the degree of adequacy with which our minds represent eternal Reality, and that it reveals a process or serial order from less to greater adequacy. On this hypothesis, the inadequacy of our representations will finally become infinitesimal, and the eternal is the last stage in a series of which the other stages are those which we perceive as the Time-series. Time thus runs up to eternity and ceases in eternity. Not, of course, that eternity is truly future; for Time and time are unreal: nor that eternity begins, strictly speaking. But that eternity is future is as near the truth as any statement in temporal terms can be.

One could wish that a theory attempting to replace the temporal by a Real non-temporal order were able to dispense with temporal terms; the necessity of retaining them is ominously suggestive. Change in adequacy of representation, and process in adequacy of manifestation, are still change; and change is in Time or in perceptual time. But the main objection that is to be urged against this theory as a whole is that, while it appears plausible so long as we contemplate earlier and later conceptions of the universe entertained by mankind, it offers no explanation of the details, not to speak of the vicissitudes, of the Time-process. It harmonises with what the Christian theologian would call the progressiveness

[1] *Mind*, N.S., No. 71; also *The Nature of Existence*, vol. ii, where Time is more fully discussed.

of revelation; but it does not account for the trivialities of temporal succession, such as 'Mc' coming before 'Taggart', or for the progress of truth, as adequate representation, being subject to haltings and relapses. It is at most explicative of but a fraction of what calls for explanation.

We still lack, then, a theory as to the non-temporal serial order which manifests itself in Time, such as accounts for the forth-comingness of facts. It is once again suggested that, however vast be the difference between noümena and their phenomena, there must be more of structural similarity between the two orders than is acknowledged in the merely negative statement, true so far as it goes, that the forms and categories of phenomenal knowledge have no applicability to noümena. Things *per se* are not causes in the Kantian sense; but if they are anything at all they must be 'agents'. They cannot be immutable universals. And if some of them are experients, it is a question whether 'experience', con-noting utter absence of temporality, has any denotation. We know indeed of experience that is timeless in that it is unaccompanied by explicit awareness of duration or succession; but that is not to be identified with Timelessness, or with timelessness regarded from the epistemological or (*ps*) point of view. This confusion of things that differ is sometimes a basis of eternalist theology. For instance, Baron von Hügel (*Eternal Life*, p. 27), after emphasising the fact that "all states of trance, or indeed of rapt attention, notoriously appear to the experiencing soul, in proportion to their concentration, as timeless; *i.e.* as non-successive, simultaneous, hence as *eternal*", observes that this eternity "is the very centre of the experience itself, and is the chief inducement to the soul for holding itself to be divine". Such facts, however, do but establish that the rapt subject is not attending to the temporal aspect of his experience, not that it is non-temporal: whether they bespeak Real or Objective Timelessness can only be decided by reflection on the experience, or from the (*ps*) standpoint.

The general conclusions to which the foregoing examination points may be stated in few words. If 'eternal' means lasting for ever in conceptual Time, eternity is but Time, and the conception is without special significance for theology. If the word means absolutely timeless, it is predicable only of truths or reason, which may or may not be valid of our world, or be actualised in it, and is not predicable of the existent. If, instead of the logical and timeless, it denotes the noümenal, in the Kantian sense, or the supra-temporal, the eternal must be functionally related to the temporal. In this case temporality cannot be purely illusory, though it may be phenomenal of some serial but non-temporal order. What this supra-temporal order may be has seldom been inquired, and no satisfactory formulation of it is forthcoming. If it be not essentially identical with the temporality of perceptual experience, as distinct from conceptually elaborated and conventionally idealised Time-Experience, then the activity, the determinative potency, the experience, and the functional relation to time, of noümenal beings such as the soul and God, are not only not explained but seem to be inexplicable and unthinkable. At any rate the eternal or unending 'specious present', without succession, is an untenable conception. When, lastly, 'eternal' is used, e.g. in the fourth gospel, as a predication of spiritual value, it has no reference either to time or to timelessness, but is indifferent to both. But the most important consideration for theistic philosophy is that, however inadequate conceptual Time be for purposes other than those for which it was fashioned, perceptual time, with its alogical factors which the abstract concept ignores, does not seem to admit of being expunged from experience unless experience itself, or all that we have any right to bestow that name upon, vanishes with it into a contentless abstraction. Whether or not the desire to interpret eternity and the divine experience as timeless emanate from aesthetic preference and anthropic predilection for the logical, it cannot be said to be induced by disinterested study of psychological or other facts, while it can be said to have engendered more hopelessly intractable puzzles than the alogicalities which it would explain away. It may well be that duration and succession are unique modes of ontal as well as of phenomenal being, which cannot be, as well as have not been, translated into terms of another type of serial order: that becoming, not static perfection, is the fundamental nature of all created Reality, and also of the life, as distinct from the 'substance', of the Creator. If the world-ground, the Supreme Being who designed and created the world, be also The Eternal, His supra-temporality must be so conceived as not to leave souls and the world-process matters of indifference to Him, or to preclude *rapport* between Him and beings in whom "time is" and whose deeds are in Time.

(iv) Theism such as renounces the *a priori* method of proof is justly chargeable, we have seen, with inability to infer from its premisses the existence of a Supreme Being who is other than finite. It is therefore incumbent on a theologian who would empirically establish his theism to shew that this charge is not damaging to his theology on either its philosophical or its religious side. This can best be done by inquiring what precisely may be meant when God is called an infinite being, and by shewing that, when 'infinite' is used in this connexion, the word, as Hume said, savours more of panegyric than of philosophy.

The notion of infinitude, as applied to the Deity and the divine attributes, was imported into Christian theology from Greek philosophy, where it appears in more than one form. The earliest equivalent to the infinite is Anaximander's ἄπειρον; but this term soon became a synonym for ἀόριστον, and signified in philosophy the boundless, not so much in the sense of exceeding all limits as in that of devoid of all defining limitations, hence the indefinite or indeterminate.

The second sense of 'infinite' to emerge is that which characterises the mathematical usage of the term from antiquity until the nineteenth century, and according to which the infinite is the limitless in number, time, or space: that which cannot be reached by successive acts of addition or division.

Thirdly, some early Greek philosophers spoke of a boundlessness that is neither quantitative nor identical with indeterminateness, but is rather completeness or perfectness, as illustrated by the circle, which is an endless line but a definite figure. And when the tendency to replace Anaximander's ἄπειρον by a teleological ἀρχή, promoted by Anaxagoras and Pythagoreans, had culminated in Plato's idea of The Good, or of God, notions of perfection took the place, in theology, of those of infinitude. The term ἄπειρος was not applied to God, but to the finite world or its formless matter, with which God was contrasted in virtue of His immutability—the essential characteristic of perfection with Parmenides and Plato. The influence of Plato led philosophically minded Christian theologians to conceive of God in terms of perfection rather than of infinity. But the Aristotelian view, that the highest

is that which possesses the greatest wealth of attributes, was really
more congenial to Christian theology than the view that the highest
is the most abstract, despite the use made of the negative way and
pursuit of the analytically simple. Earlier Fathers who followed
the abstractive method were saved from its dangers by happy
inconsistency; but the late Eastern compilers of doctrine, towards
the close of the patristic age, in virtue of their leaning towards
neo-Platonism, developed a tendency to subtle disputation about
empty or vague words which was transmitted to Aquinas and
other schoolmen.

Thus, when Aquinas (*Summa Theol.*, I, Q. 7) discusses the infinitude of God, he does not define 'infinity', nor seem to be aware
that he is using it, as well as 'perfection', in more senses than one, and
with somewhat of arbitrariness; and he largely follows the Platonic
canon and the abstractive method. Pure being, he says, is the
emptiest and most comprehensive of all forms; yet this empty
form or abstraction is said to be the most perfect of all "things"
(I, Q. 4) because "actuating" all things. And it is because the
being of God is pure, self-subsistent, or not received, that it "is
called infinite". Thus non-limitation by other self-subsistents is
all that 'infinite' then means. If elsewhere it suggests more than
this, 'infinitude' would seem to be merged in 'perfection', a term
the vagueness of which will later be exhibited.

The earlier philosophers of the modern period also regarded
infinity as identical with perfection, or as implied therein. They
shew a tendency to identify determination with negation and
finitude, along with a desire to attribute to the Deity an infinitude
of a positive kind, different from endlessness conceived mathematically. Transition from the highest abstraction or emptiest
form to the concept expressible as *omnitudo realitatis* is observable;
while in Leibniz the perfect is also identified with the good.

This fragmentary historical introduction will perhaps serve to
shew that, in so far as the notion of infinity has lent itself to theology,
its meaning has changed from indeterminateness and from quantitative endlessness to something qualitative, and positive rather
than negative. Infinitude has been preparing for abdication in
favour of perfection. And now it may be remarked more fully that
neither of the ideas of infinity that may be distinguished from any
of the various meanings of 'perfection' is of use to theism. The

world-ground is not an infinite, in the sense of an indeterminate being. "I am that I am" may be an incorrect translation of a non-ontological scriptural phrase; but it is aptly ascribable as an utterance to God, and it implies a nature that is neither nothing in particular nor everything in general. God is not an Absolute in whom all differences are included or lost, nor an *omnitudo* of all qualities however mutually incompatible. To be this and not that, *e.g.* to be wise and not foolish, may be to be finite, if to be infinite means to be indeterminate; for determination is in one sense negation: but such finitude involves no subtraction from the majesty with which theology and religion invest the Deity. Here, then, is one sense of 'infinitude' in which that term cannot be predicated of God or His attributes. And if 'infinitude' be not, as apparently with Aquinas, but a synonym for 'self-subsistence', the only other definite sense that the term has historically borne is likewise out of place in theology of any type. The mathematical idea of infinity applies only where there are magnitudes, or parts correlatable with numbers. It is not relevant to qualitative attributes such as wisdom and love, nor to a Being without body or parts. It might be deemed relevant to the divine knowledge and power if these be regarded as knowledge of, and power over, an infinite or endless number of things; but such usage is fruitless. However, this old conception of the infinite, accused from the time of Zeno of involving difficulties when applied to Actuality, and more lately called the improper infinite, has comparatively recently been replaced by the proper (*eigentlich*) infinite; and occasionally a philosopher or a mathematician has sought to apply the latter conception to theological problems.

Some account of the newer infinity is provided for the non-mathematical reader in the Appendix, Note C, where a critique of recent attempts to put it to theological use will also be found. It may suffice here to observe that while the newer conception of the infinite implies determinateness, and its characteristic is self-representativeness (in a highly technical sense) rather than the more negative endlessness, it is still applicable only to classes and series composed of discrete terms or members, and only to such of them as are purely ideal or non-Actual. It can therefore have no more relevance to the subject-matter of theology than has the older conception.

We may conclude that 'infinity' has not borne any definite connotation that is essential to theism or appropriate to the theistic characterisation of the world-ground. If it be merely used to affirm that God, in abstraction from the world of which He is the ground, is unlimited by anything self-subsistent as Himself, its signification is not so distinctive that theology needs to retain the term; for that is already implied in the notion of creation. And 'infinite' is not an appropriate term by which to express that signification; partly because the word already stands for quite different ideas, and partly because creation itself, apart from which God is but an abstraction, involves self-limitation. The popularity of the word 'infinite' has protected it from scrutiny, and traditional use has invested it with honorific value.[1] Philosophical theology, however, should confine itself to definite ideas and appropriate terminology; and inasmuch as the one definite and distinctive sense that 'infinite' can now bear is mathematical, it should be surrendered to the mathematician.

(v) We have already observed that, in order to be more appropriate within the sphere of theology, infinitude was deprived of its quantitative or mathematical significance and tended to be conceived qualitatively. Thus the conception gave place to one or more of the distinguishable notions for which the name 'perfection' has been used. Inasmuch as empirical premisses can no more establish the existence of a perfect being than the existence of an infinite being, properly so called, two questions arise for the empirical theologian. It must be inquired whether theology has a right to, and a real use for, the *a priori* idea or ideas of perfection; and also, if that prove not to be the case, whether reasonable, *i.e.* fact-derived and fact-controlled, extrapolation or idealisation, such as is requisite to make theism explanatory without otherwise transcending experience, involves retention of the term 'perfect', in any of its historical senses, for the characterisation of God.

To answer the former of these questions involves examination of the various meanings which the word 'perfect' has borne.

---

[1] Perhaps, as popularly used, 'infinity' means no more than that the divine powers and attributes surpass any limits that we can imagine, and the infinitude of God is a 'practical infinity'. Otherwise, it is an honorific epithet, expressing reverence rather than connoting a definite idea; it is then comparable with 'pre-existence' as used by ancient Jewish writers who, we are told, spoke of the Law, Jerusalem, etc., as pre-existent, with no metaphysical intent, but simply by way of laudation.

Firstly, 'perfect being' has meant pure being. Thus the perfect being is described by Dionysius the Areopagite as in Himself ὑπέρσοφος and ὑπέρζως; wisdom and life are unworthy of Him, though unintelligence is ascribed to the fount of all reason not by way of defect (κατ᾽ ἔλλειψιν) but by way of eminence (καθ᾽ ὑπεροχήν). Similar abstractions are the Good which in dignity and power transcends existence, the absolute non-existent of Basilides, Erigena's conception of the God who cannot know Himself, and Nicolas of Cusa's very modern notion of the Super-Absolute. But none of these conceptions of indeterminate being, nor yet the One of Plotinus or of Spinoza, the Absolute of Hamilton, or the Unknowable of Spencer, can be entertained by theism which asserts the ground of the Actual world to be God, and God to be a living Spirit. The negative way, confounding the highest abstraction with ultimate Real existence or with the worthiest divine appellation, arrives at a 'perfect' being that is indistinguishable from non-being.

Theology has perhaps fared no better when, going to the other of two extremes which seem to meet, it has conceived the perfect being after the model of τὸ ὅλον or τὸ τέλειον; as *ens realissimum*, or *omnitudo realitatis*, or *actus purus* in which no potentiality or possibility remains unrealised. A being that is universal yet individual, containing all Reality or all Real predicates as well as the 'material of all possibility', is scarcely more determinate than nominally deified nothingness.

Determination certainly involves negation of what is left out, but also affirmation of what is put in; and too full a content, as well as one that is too meagre, destroys such determinate perfectness as theism can significantly claim for its Deity. Perfection cannot be completed endlessness, for that, when predicated of anything Actual, is a contradiction; nor can it consist in possession of an infinite number—or even an indefinite number—of unlimited attributes, for positive attributes sometimes circumscribe one another. Leibniz pertinently remarked that, before the ontological proof of the existence of the perfect being could be regarded as coercive, it was necessary to shew that the idea of that being is possible or self-consistent. Unless its component ideas are compossible among themselves, it is not realisable, and therefore no considerations could prove its realisation in an existent being. When scrutinised in the light of this comment, the vague notion of perfection shews itself to be non-significant because of its abstractness, as well as inconceivable because housing incompatibilities. In other words, 'perfect' is a non-significant term unless it means perfect in some particular respect, and connotes perfection of this or that kind. Idealised to the limit in all ways and respects at once, perfection becomes a bundle of contradictions or incompatibilities.

'Perfection' has also meant completedness in the sense of excluding all unrealised 'possibility' or potentiality. The word then becomes synonymous with 'immutability'; and unchangingness has ever been an eminent ingredient in the theological notion of God as a perfect being. The Parmenidean doctrine of the immutability of the truly real, grounded apparently on the idealistic confounding of the kind of existence that may be predicated of the ideal with that which belongs only to the Actual,[1] became, through the influence of Plato, a determinant of much theological speculation, as was observed when eternity was being discussed. The unchangeable substantiality of God was unfortunately conceived after the model of inert matter or of the static idea rather than that of active spirit; and scholastic ingenuity was unequal to shewing how an absolutely unchangeable being could be the sole ground of a changing world, the very knowledge of which should be precluded to its Prime Mover. A God Who is a creator and the strength and stay of an evolving universe cannot in an unqualified sense be called immutable; and again, in that sense, He cannot be called perfect.

The notion of perfection, when unqualified as to kind or as abstracted from specific respects in which a being may be said to be perfect, will now have been seen to be no clear and distinct idea or possible concept. It embraces incompatibilities within its comprehensiveness: immutability, e.g. cannot subsist together with ethical excellence, which involves doing or willing. Again, the inclusion of positive attributes alone within the *omnitudo*

---

[1] Parmenides inferred from the proposition 'whatever can be thought of is', that the past still is, and therefore change is impossible in the truly real. But 'is', in 'is thought of', and 'is', which expresses existence or 'position' independent of thought, have not the same meaning. Thus an influential dogma emanated from a linguistic fallacy.

realitatis is arbitrary or nominal, because in some cases it is as much a matter of verbal convention, which of two qualitative opposites we would call positive, as which of our two hands we name the right; and evil, in the concrete, is no less positive than the good, of which it is said to be the negation. When qualification is introduced, so that perfection admits of being spoken of with significance and without inner contradiction, as perfectness in some one or more definite respects, the perfection ascribed to the Deity is, before all else, ethical. Thus when the perfect being, contemplated in Anselm's ontological argument, is described as *quo majus nihil*, we might substitute *melius* for *majus*. And now at last we meet with a meaning for 'perfect' which is compatible with theistic doctrine concerning God, provided that theism discard the notions of divine immutability and impassibility.

'Impassibility', in the patristic age especially, was used by theologians with great laxity. Sometimes the word signified no more than freedom from bodily pain and passion, disturbing anger, and such like human affections. Sometimes it was intended to mean that God cannot suffer save by way of sympathy with human suffering, which nevertheless is suffering, and in human beings is heart-wringing mental distress. Perhaps impassibility was never understood by Christian theists so rigorously as to exclude what would nowadays be called feeling, and is involved in all valuation; but the heavy yoke of Greek theological philosophy, academic and aloof from religious experience and life, sometimes imparted a docetic bend to supple orthodoxy, and evoked reluctance to extrude apathy from its 'alienated' conception of divinity. More recent theology, inclined to substitute ethical categories for the unassimilable and now largely unintelligible formal and ontological ideas in terms of which antiquity expressed its doctrine of God, is not averse to the notion of passible Deity. And certainly theism such as sets out from the empirically suggested idea of God as designer and creator of the world, rather than from a quasi-physical force or quasi-logical ground whence things indifferently flow, must image the divine blessedness as of richer affective content than uninterested contemplation of an 'intelligible' world.

It should be mentioned that the distinction which has been drawn between the ontological and the ethical sense of 'perfection'

would be annulled if there were anything more than verbal play
in the ancient identification of the good with the existent, and any
force in the argument by which Aquinas would confirm the
Platonic teaching of Augustine that "inasmuch as we exist we are
good", or as Aquinas himself expresses it, that goodness and being
are "really the same, and differ only logically".[1] This identification, historically of interest because it appears to be the source of
the once prevalent doctrine that evil is 'non-existent', seems
paradoxical to anyone familiar with the psychology of valuation;
and the modern student may perhaps be curious as to the grounds
on which it commended itself to the scholastic mind. The argument of Aquinas will be found to hinge upon the ancient assumption that existence or being (as distinct from growth of what
already exists) is a matter of degrees or stages; whereas any
'thing' either exists or does not exist. He does not refute the
anticipated objection (No. 3 in the context indicated) that "being
cannot be more or less", but tacitly sets it aside in asserting that
everything is perfect *so far as* it is actual, and that a thing is perfect
so far as it exists. So long as perfection is thus (ontologically)
conceived, bad deeds and villains, being as actual as good deeds
and saints, should be as perfect; and it is far from "clear that a
thing is desirable [or good] only in so far as it is perfect". For
if there were a gradual process from non-existence to existence,
the desirableness or goodness of a thing would not necessarily be
proportionate to its degree of self-actualisation: things are desirable solely in that they affect our subjective states. In this
argument Aquinas does not come within sight of the ethical sense
of goodness and perfection, unless the incidental and illustrative
remark "all desire their own perfection" betrays his confusion of
two disparate senses of one word. The most he would have
achieved, were his curious assumption, implied in the phrase 'so
far as', tenable, is the identity of being with a non-ethical goodness.

Ethical perfection being now taken to have no connexion with
completedness or richness in attributes or in their immensity such
as expressed by the terms 'omnipotence', 'omniscience', etc., we
may inquire what perfection of this distinct kind may be. Perhaps
the theist who puts such a question to himself will find it difficult

[1] *Summa Theologica*, I, Q. 5, E.T. by Fathers of the English Dominican Province,
vol. I, pp. 52 f.

to give an answer that is at all precise. Certainly his conception of The Good God cannot be reached by idealising to the limit the virtues imperfectly manifested in man; for some of these are exclusively anthropic, owing their specific nature to the conditions of human life. On the other hand, elimination of all that is thus conditioned will still leave somewhat of community between God and man in respect of moral experience and activity; and this element may with some appropriateness be called 'perfection', because necessarily free from creaturely imperfection. There may be real meaning in the statement that God is a moral being, though the morality that is predicable of the Creator must in certain important respects be different from that of the developing and sensuously conditioned moral creature. The statement asserts, *e.g.* that the righteousness and holiness of God are not quasi-logical or quasi-mechanical necessary consequences of a will-less 'nature', non-moral or supra-moral, but are to be ascribed to volitional self-determination and consistency. And it embodies the import of the empirically reached conclusion that the world, of which God is the ground, realises an ethical design in that the moral status of rational creatures is a stage in the ordered world-process, if not its climax in respect of value. But the morality thus ascribed to God does not imply the conflict of motives, the temptability, and so forth, which occasion and constitute moral behaviour in embodied selves such as live and learn. In that God is what He is, creator and designer of all rather than a superior member of a commonwealth, His moral activity is free from such conditioning, and His moral nature is largely incomparable with ours. And where it is both gratuitous and incongruous to suggest developement from lower to higher, clash of conative tendency with moral reason, struggle and attainment—in a word, imperfection—it is at least more reasonable to speak of God's ethical perfection than it has been found to be to speak of God's infinitude. In this connexion we may even apply the idea of immutability, in a particularised sense. In God there may be said to be "no variableness, neither shadow of turning" in respect of His world-purpose as a whole: for again there is no ground for supposing the possibility of variableness. But such immutability is to be distinguished from the static perfection that leaves no place for providential control or divine action of any kind upon the world.

If some of God's creatures be in turn (in a relative sense) creators, and especially if human freewill be found to involve limitation of divine fore-knowledge, variation of activity upon or within the world would seem to be involved in realisation of the invariable purpose. The divine immutability, in fact, can only be self-identity and self-consistency through change; and the divine perfection, if it include more than morality, cannot be static completedness, but is rather self-manifestation of the Eternal in the temporal process of ethically significant history. That they have been conceived predominantly in terms of the Parmenidean doctrine of Reality must be said to be an unfortunate accident.

CHAPTER VI

The Idea of God (continued): The Absolute; Divine Personality and Self-Limitation

The theistic argument presented in an earlier chapter may be said to involve little more than an exposition of accepted knowledge concerning the world and man which, when synoptically regarded, forcibly suggests, and receives explanation (of the only kind that is possible) in, the view that the world-ground is an intelligent and purposive spirit. This argument has already needed to be contrasted with others whose premisses, inferential procedure, and criteria of satisfactoriness are different; and reasons have been given for asserting that the world-ground, reasonable belief in which is evoked by empirically conducted inquiry, cannot be described in terms of static concepts such as completedness, perfection, infinitude, immutability or timelessness, in the unqualified forms in which they have been cherished by abstractive speculation, or have been used in dialectic operation on thoughts and unsifted word-meanings. In the further characterisation of the world-ground or God that remains to be undertaken it will still be necessary to reject certain conclusions reached by speculation aloof from facts: partly, as before, with a view to illustrating the gain which accrues to theology in ridding itself of the age-long influence of pre-scientific philosophising, and partly to avoid the appearance of not reckoning with types of theology other than that which is here constructed in accordance with the method of philosophy expounded and applied in the first volume of this treatise.

To set out from the historical and perceptual is to begin with the *terra firma* of primary reality under our feet; and to use the sciences of mind and matter is to keep in touch with, and under the control of, the Reality of which our conceptualised sensible and psychical facts are at least functions, versions, or manifestations. On the other hand, to proceed from thought-created entities, or to set out 'from above', is to begin in essentially the same kind of supposition as that which, in grotesque forms, is exhibited in primitive cosmogonies. In this respect, however great be the difference in other respects, it must be alleged that Platonism, neo-Platonism, and modern forms of absolute idealism are on a par with pre-scientific creations of poetic or mythopœic fancy. Again, the theism to which empirically established knowledge points is, in virtue of the process by which it is reached, an explanation evoked by the world itself. On the other hand, it must be affirmed that, in general, the systems of *a priori* theology yield no explanation of the Actual world with its particular nature, but rather render it the more inexplicable. If, by pure intuition and intellectual searching, the great minds that have devised apparently deductive systems of theology have found something on which to bestow the name of God, the fact that they have taken mathematics or logic to be the paradigm of knowledge and philosophy precludes all possibility of the Deity or the Absolute which they affirm being a sufficient ground of our 'rough and tumble' world. The alogical essence of the world, on which mechanical description and logical concatenation are contingent, by which value is borne, and in which meaning is lodged, has been strained out or spurned.[1] And what is retained can afford no explanation of the rejected content. That these charges are not groundless may, it is hoped, be seen by briefly examining a few of the outstanding instances of the kind of theology in question.

A typical example, and the fount of most other examples, of *a priori* theism, is that of Plato, the founder of philosophical theology though not a framer of a co-ordinated or consistent body of theological doctrine. What is generally understood to be Plato's metaphysics, and is called his idealism, though it is not perhaps what in all his moods and all his works he meant to inculcate, is better described as a logical realism. The ideas, constituting the

---

[1] Perhaps the following extract from *Pride and Prejudice* affords as happy an illustration of my meaning as could be found.

"I should like balls infinitely better", she replied, "if they were carried on in a different manner; but there is something insufferably tedious in the usual process of such a meeting. It would surely be more rational if conversation instead of dancing made the order of the day."

"Much more rational, my dear Caroline, I dare say, but it would not be near so much like a ball."

Hegel ascribed the contingencies and apparent sportiveness of the world, which present trying limitations to rationalistic philosophy, to the "impotence" of Nature. Even so, the inadequacy of panlogism is confessed.

intelligible or non-sensible, and therefore the truly real, world, are validities reified into supposed existents and regarded as prior to experience. God, apparently, does not owe His Actuality, as things owe theirs, to 'participation' in an idea; rather is He a personification of the highest idea, the Good, on which those of reason and power are superimposed. Plato was somewhat indefinite as to the relation of God to the ideas, and as to the ideas being efficiently formative of 'things'. With which of his statements on these and cognate matters he was most in earnest is a question differently answered by different commentators. Our concern, however, is rather with his teaching as to the relation of God to the sensible world.

When dealing with this problem in the *Timaeus*, Plato resorts to absolute dualism. He recognises two causes of the origin of the world, νοῦς and ἀνάγκη, each of which produces its separate effects, rational and irrational respectively. The formless matter was not created by νοῦς, and God does the best He can with it. It has been suggested that, like the account of the origin in time of the primitive chaos, all this was intended by Plato to be myth; that the doctrine is contrary to the whole gist of Platonism, and that dualism is but dallied with in a single passage. Others, on the contrary, urge that this passage is the only one in which Plato *seriously* tackles the problem of the sensible world and its physical evil. Of more importance, however, for our present inquiry, is what becomes of Platonism as a philosophy of the Actual world if this dualistic element be removed as non-essential and perhaps non-Platonic. It would seem that then God is conceived as an absolute subject with none but absolute and intelligible objects; the outcome should be acosmism. The finite or created world has no Reality of any kind. It can be but an appearance to God, and an appearance that should be superfluous in that He is perfect without it. The divine creativeness, ascribed to love, is purely immanent causation. Thus, on the latter interpretation, Platonism does not explain the world, but explains it away; while, if its dualism be retained as essential, Platonism is incompatible with theism. In either case God, without the world, is regarded as yet God; and the taking of such an abstraction as Real is responsible for many of the difficulties in which abstract speculation has entangled itself.

Aristotle, again, needs the theistic idea, especially in the form of the conception of an unmoved Mover. He does not first obtain it, however, by inference from the nature of the world to the nature of its ground, but rather by hypostatising thought. According to this *a priori* theology, God's sole activity is thought. From such a conception of the Deity there is no transition to that of God as prime mover; and there is no deduction of a world from a prime mover, Himself unmoved by will or desire; nor of the world's particular determinations and alogicalities from the ideal laws or validities in the contemplation of which the life of the self-sufficing Deity should consist. The whole finite process lies beyond the sphere of the activity ascribed to God. He is of purer eyes than to behold contingency: contingency needs Him, but He has no need of it. If there be an Actual world, the Deity of Aristotle should have no awareness of it, not to say no relations with it.

Thus if God be conceived as an absolute subject with intuitive consciousness of self, over against Whom are Really no objects save timeless validities holding of no ontal terms, there is no accounting for the concrete Many, nor even for there being the appearance of a Many. The sensible world may be appearance, though scarcely appearance of timeless universals, to the imperfect apprehension of finite selves; but these selves cannot in turn be appearances of timeless verities, especially to the one subject who apprehends perfectly. The Actuality of selves and the world was of course accepted by Plato and Aristotle; but that should have been an impossibility for them, had their *a priori* theology been such as to command their unwavering allegiance.

Plotinus carried the abstractive method further than did his predecessors. His absolute One is neither a unity of absolute subject and object, nor a subject apart from objects, but a being indeterminate enough to transcend the distinction between the subjective and the objective. The One, however, has a sufficiently determinate nature to enable it to overflow, or to manifest itself in emanations, images, or products, other than itself. It is, in an indefinite sense or senses, perfect: a high abstraction and also a being complete even to repletion. Its necessary tendency to overflow into the imperfect, into a lower degree or a lower kind of perfection—phrases which, by the way, imply ideas of perfection different from that of the perfectness of the One itself—is no latent imperfection, as one might naturally suppose, but is part of the essence of the One's perfectness. Plotinus uses the metaphorical notion of emanation, and presents an account of the origination of the Actual world which may be compared with a Fall-story. Successive emanations at the same time produce the best possible of worlds, each kingdom within which is perfect after its kind. The first emanation leading to plurality is that of reason and the intelligible or non-sensible world, which, to repeat once more, owes its supposed existence to man's inveterate habit of linguistically reifying his own abstractions. But so far is the νοῦς of Plotinus from possessing any explanatory value that it may be said to admit of no translation into terms possessing denotation for minds such as can only think at all about Actuality by using the more or less definite and scientific concepts which knowledge about Actuality, forthcoming since the third century, has thrust upon us. By no effort of sympathetic imagination can we recover the mental apperception-systems of Plotinus and at the same time retain our own more modern mental furniture. By his νοῦς the following things, that for us are incongruities calling for distinct names, and fancy-bred entities whose Actuality is not thinkable, would seem to be meant: (1) potential reason, an 'image' of the One which 'turns' toward the One in order to comprehend it, and thereby becomes 'reason'; (2) reason that has thus come out of potential reason, and undergoes differentiation into knowing (νόησις) and the known (νοητόν), so that its objects—the supra-sensible ideas—are immanent in it and not external to it; (3) these differentiated νοητά. Conspicuously absent is the knower (other than the One, which ought not to have νοῦς), apart from whom νόησις is a nonentity. Enough has perhaps been reproduced, without further unfolding Plotinus' thought as to the equally non-existent emanations, the world-soul and formless matter, to illustrate that neo-Platonism is a poetic treatment, largely of spurious concepts and non-significant words, abounding in results so fantastic as that souls or knowers emanate from knowing or reason. It may fairly be called mythology, intellectualised in a fashion which was natural and perhaps inevitable before there was a sufficiency of knowledge, as distinct from thought, on which a great intellect could operate. It is not explicative, for us, in any of the senses which 'explanation' has been found to bear. And these ancient systems of thought, determinative as they have been of theistic speculation throughout many centuries, must, from the point of view of modernity, be now assigned to the province of imaginative art rather than to that of business-like pursuit of knowledge, or reasonable belief, about man, the world, and God.

Aristotle alone among the giants of antiquity clearly recognised that the problem set to the philosopher involves tentative procedure from the confusedly but better and earlier known to the more adequately but later known: from common sense and special sciences to 'first philosophy'. Had he worked more in accordance with this insight, instead of becoming rather a second Plato, the history of philosophy might have been very different, and the waste—save for refinement of logic, and little else—of two thousand of the race's years of discretion might have been spared. For every advance in philosophical knowledge, as distinct from delectable additions to unproved speculation, has been due to practice of the method which the potential Aristotle descried and the actual Aristotle largely forsook. Philosophical theism, however, has generally preferred the *a priori* way, constructing thought and mistaking it for knowledge, and has consequently tended to become pantheistic. And pantheism satisfies aesthetic sentiment and a kind of religious yearning rather than either exhibiting logical concatenation or proffering explanation of alogical facts. Its deficiency in the latter respects stands revealed in its classic model, the system of Spinoza. All 'causality' is lodged by Spinoza in God or the absolute One; but when he would account for the finite modes he needed to invoke another kind of causality in place of deducibility (*more geometrico*) from his concept of God, and a causality which presupposes the existence of the things for whose derivation he would account. Similar defects, it remains to be argued, appertain to the recent doctrine of The Absolute propounded chiefly by the neo-Hegelian school, and borrowed sometimes as a philosophical basis for what is professed to be theism, if of a somewhat indefinite and heterodox type.

Before undertaking the examination of absolutism of any kind a preliminary inquiry is desirable as to the connotations of 'absolute', the denotations corresponding to them, and the compatibility of instances of either with ideas essential to theism. The connotation of 'absolute' has often been defined as 'independent of anything other'. But 'independent' is an ambiguous word. When it means uncaused, ungroundable, or self-subsistent, it expresses what is essential to the theistic conception of God. For God, as *naturans*, is the ground of the world as *naturata*: it is derived from, or owes its existence to, Him. But there is neither need nor justification for conceiving God in separation from the world from which theism would distinguish Him. God as potential creator before creating, or as subject of none but 'intelligible' experience, is an abstraction for which empirically derived theism has no use, and which has already been found to lead *a priori* theology into superfluous difficulties. In another sense of 'dependent' than that of derivedness, God is as dependent on the world as is the world on God: for God without a world is not God.

So if, when God is called absolute, independence in the latter sense is intended, theism must reject the term: if no more is meant than that God alone is self-subsistent, the word is inappropriate, and is not wanted. 'Absoluteness' can also be dispensed with when its meaning is identical with infinity, static perfection, 'necessary' being, etc. But the most usual signification of 'absolute' is constituted by antithesis with the relative or the related. To the common representation that the relative implies the absolute, as west implies east, it is sufficient to reply that the only implicate of the relative is the correlative. If, on the other hand, the term connotes unrelatedness, its denotation is at once determined: for then the whole of Reality or of the existent can alone be called absolute. If God be absolute in this sense, however, the only possible theology is pantheism or acosmism. And this would seem to be the sole clear, distinctive, and univocal sense, in respect of both connotation and denotation, that 'absolute' can bear, when predicated of God. Short of embracing the All, or—as the phenomenal will be ruled out—the whole of Reality or the ontal, the term 'absolute' or 'non-relative' like 'perfect', etc., is meaningless save within some restricted context or sphere of discourse. That restriction removed, and the All being called absolute because there is nothing to which it can stand in relation, the term conveys no information, explanatory or other, about the particularity of the Actual world, save that it is a totality. Nevertheless systems which are designated by the name 'absolutism' have hazarded more special views as to the nature of The Absolute, which, previously to inquiry and determination, conceivably may be One or a Many, personal or impersonal, ethical or non-ethical. Thus some philosophers identify the ontal totality with the formally or logically intelligible; Plato's Absolute is the Good, having also the significance that is bound up with value; often The Absolute is described as a self-consciousness inclusive of no more than thought or cognition, will being deliberately or unintentionally reduced to attention; sometimes it is regarded as an experience into which volition enters; and the absolute experience has been conceived as essentially love, or as a perfection of which goodness and truth are distorted shadows. Sometimes the perfect experience or self-consciousness is spoken of as if it involved no subject, but was a personification, in the poetic sense, of one or more of the over-individual concepts, ends, etc., of art, religion, morality, and philosophy. There are absolute idealists who maintain that The Absolute cannot be a personal God because such a being implies relations with other existents, whereas The Absolute is the unrelated. On the other hand, there are theologians who would combine absolute idealism, of one kind or another, with theism, and identify The Absolute with God. So diverse are the conceptions of what The Absolute is, both with theistic and non-theistic absolutists, and so far from easily intelligible (to one whose apperception-systems are constituted by the ordinary concepts of psychology, the sciences, and historical philosophy) are the metaphorical terms in which absolute idealisms are usually expounded, that it is hazardous to make generalised statements about the common tenets of this school. But perhaps it may be affirmed that, as a rule, two distinct and not easily reconcilable ideas of The Absolute are used as if they were interchangeable: the one being the ontal universe, the All or the Whole, and the other an individual Experient whose Experience (*i.e.* experiencing and what therein is experienced) constitutes Reality. In this Experience our experience, deemed full of "contradiction" because containing alogical incompatibilities and oppositions, is said to be "somehow" transformed and freed from "contradiction".

The transformation in question has been described by analogy with that which characterises the progress of human thought from crude facts and opinions to theoretical science and philosophy; but inasmuch as this is a temporal process, whereas the absolutist's transformation is not a case of becoming but of what eternally is, the analogy entirely lacks elucidatory value and is irrelevant. It would seem that if any explanation of the alleged transformation is to be found, it must be sought in the contrast between ontal and phenomenal knowing. This should imply that whereas we can only know in part and see as in a mirror, The Absolute sees the ontal face to face and without what (by a confusion of contradiction between propositions with incompatibility between things—kinds of opposition which are disparate) is called 'contradiction'. Such a doctrine, apart from its abuse of the idea of contradiction, is compatible with theism. But absolutism is not contented with it. The dualism between the absolute One and the phenomenalising Many is done away by philosophers who would resolve finite selves or subjects into appearances of The Absolute, and would apply the 'transformation' or 'fusion' to them as well as to their sensory and other objects. This dissolution has been effected by confounding the relation of part to whole with that of adjective to substantive, and by absorbing subjects of experience into "organisations of content" within The Absolute, or 'finite centres" of experience, which should be as disparate from subjects as are centres of disturbance in the 'fields' which the physicist describes.[1] It is especially in this connexion that the type of absolutism now under consideration is to be accused of being mythological and at the same time non-explanatory. Poetic metaphor as to the fluidity, not only of personality but also of the active, individual, substantival souls which synthesise personality, is allowed to usurp the place of fact and its natural interpretation; and free composition replaces the translation of set copy, in which metaphysics should consist if it is to have any relation to forthcoming knowledge. Further, behaviouristic psychology of the most paradoxical kind would seem to be involved in explaining away the *continens* of a finite mental life as mere content; and it seems to be overlooked, as by the extreme behaviourist, that in seeming to themselves to be subjects while accused of not being

[1] On these representations, and their incompatibility with logic and psychology, see vol. I, pp. 95 ff.

Really subjects, the centres of experience are all the time but being subjects. If this last charge be obviated by appealing to the One subject of all experience, in lieu of the many experients which have become organisations of content, the resulting acosmism certainly explains nothing, but vastly increases our philosophical perplexities. What is ultimate is *ipso facto* inexplicable. But when the ultimate or absolute is said to be an experient with an experience involving no *rapport* with an Other, it is an added inexplicability that this experient should call up pseudo-experients, or organise itself into centres which, if only they were truly experients, would be doomed to delusion, and which, if they are not experients at all, and therefore cannot even be deluded, exist only to undergo the fusion and transformation in which the experience of the self-sufficing Absolute would seem, at least in part, to consist. Moreover the supposed 'transformation', besides being both inexplicable and non-explanatory, really involves the subjecthood and otherness of the existents which *ex hypothesi* should be but adjectives of the One subject: for otherwise an untransformed experience, *e.g.* a man's bodily pain, which *as such* is not comprised in the experience of The Absolute, is an experience without an experient. The existence of finite minds has always been the chief obstacle for absolute monism. The shew of surmounting this obstacle is made by a temporary desertion of idealism for behaviourism or presentationism, *i.e.* by regarding a subject's mind not as it is for him but as it presents itself to an external observer. Psychology, however, forbids us to entertain the possibility of regarding what for it is a subject as an adjective of another subject, and to speak of illusion or appearance as if it involved no subject. Some less rigorously monistic absolutists blur the line between monism and pluralism by hinting that there are other kinds of inclusion than that of which common sense and the sciences talk. But where precise definition is vital they are content to be vague. An assertion such as that human spirits are essential elements in the life of God conveys no definite meaning. Interpreted in consistency with theism it is irrelevant; and interpreted relevantly it is pantheistic. Others, such as Prof. Royce, are more explicit in declaring that their experience is part of, and identical with, God's experience, or a unique constituent of God's life. This should imply that The Absolute, or God, is an individual subject

comprising many individual subjects: which, in the present state
of our psychological knowledge, is unassimilable or unthinkable.

It would seem that one objection, of such absolutists as embrace
theism, to the Reality of finite selves is that the existence of Real
egos would derogate from the perfection and infinitude of God,
whom they would fain conceive as literally all in all. A preference
is then evinced for some metaphysical notion of perfection rather
than for perfection of the ethical kind, bespeaking relations of love
between a Person and persons. And an abuse of metaphor seems
to be substituted for clear thought when it is represented that love
does away with mutual exclusiveness; for numerical diversity of
subjects, together with qualitative likeness of objects and affections,
is what love implies. Philosophy and explanation are not advanced
either by courting ambiguity or by indulgence in rhetorical
figurativeness.

Another objection that is often urged against theism, such as
would not identify God with The Absolute, is that it is essential
to conceive of God as able to know, if not to foreknow, all our
thoughts, volitions, etc.; which is taken to imply that God cannot
be completely distinguished as one subject from the many subjects,
or that His experience must in some sense contain ours. It will
presently be inquired whether unlimited foreknowledge can be
ascribed to the Deity, consistently with our knowledge about
knowledge. But if it cannot be ascribed without denying the
otherness of finite subjects, it may prove less disastrous for theology
and religion to recognise a limitation to the divine omniscience
than to identify man's experience with God's, or finite egos with
centres at once set up and transformed within The Absolute for
Its own manifestation or enrichment. In any case philosophical
theology cannot uncritically take over a dogma expressive of a
religious prepossession, however venerable and reverential, as if it
were a self-evident axiom, and thereby determine its concept of
God. Empirically reached theology rules that religion must wait,
in so far as intellectual grounding of its ideals is concerned, upon
the deliverances of philosophy with reference to the compatibility
of these ideals with such knowledge as we have.

If by 'The Absolute' is denoted the whole of ultimate Reality
or the ontal, then, whatever be the connotation of 'absolute',
there is an Absolute: the empirical proposition 'something exists'

vouches for so much. This Absolute, however, may be a One, or a Many, or a One and a Many. The last of these alternatives is identical with the theism which has here been partly expounded, and which has been argued to be the most reasonable metaphysical system in that forthcoming knowledge about the something that exists, when not put to torture, suggests it and testifies to it. Of the other two alternatives, the former alone has as yet been considered; and it has been submitted—one trusts with as much of outward respect as is consistent with candour—that in all its outstanding forms it has secured its plausibility by rhetoric and vagueness rather than by coherent argument embodying clear thought. There remains to be noticed the pluralistic and non-theistic type of absolutism, in so far as it claims to be based on *a priori* or deductive reasoning and eschews empirical knowledge and conditionings as much as is possible. One instance only of this kind of metaphysic needs to be selected; and the less is here called for in connexion with it in that a large part of the first volume of this treatise may be regarded as a sifting of the nature of its premisses and of its method. I share the opinion of Dr Broad[1] that Dr McTaggart's work, *The Nature of Existence*, "is equal in scope and originality to any of the great historical systems of European philosophy", and am almost persuaded that "in clearness of statement it surpasses them all". It is certainly refreshing to exchange the relaxing atmosphere of monistic figurativeness and ambiguity for the bracing, if rarified, mountain-air of this clearly expounded absolutism. But its premisses cannot be allowed. I would submit that there is no intrinsically necessary axiom concerning Actuality that is not purely formal, unless we regard as non-formal the proposition 'an existent cannot at the same time be non-existent': and even that did not appear always to be self-evident to Aquinas, as we have seen, or even to Leibniz. And, if there were such propositions, 'a substance' needs so to be defined as possibly to have no Actual denotation when among these 'axioms' Dr McTaggart includes the dogma that every substance must consist of substantial parts and be divisible *ad indefinitum*. Ontal existents can be conceived, without self-contradiction, as having no parts; and it may be submitted that the idea of a part is sometimes as much abused, if in a different way, by this writer

[1] *The Proceedings of the British Academy*, vol. XIII.

as it is by Dr Bosanquet. No further inquiry, such as a discussion of Dr McTaggart's 'principle of determining correspondence' and of its being the sole possible means of avoiding contradiction between one of his main axioms and deductions from certain others, is now needed in order to justify the assertions that his wonderful edifice "only lacks a good foundation", and that knowledge as to the absolute or the ontal can be obtained no more by his almost completely *a priori* method than by any of the other magnificent attempts to dispense with the phenomenal or the empirical as the sole datum and the sole external control for thought such as may also be knowledge or reasonable belief. But there is one doctrine, common to this and other absolutist systems, that is of the highest importance in connexion with a metaphysical conclusion previously reached in the course of the present work: one on which Dr McTaggart has characteristically written with explicitness and clearness lacking to his monistic fellow-exponents of absolutism. His presentation, therefore, must needs be selected for controverting. The doctrine in question is that our minds, which admittedly misperceive—I would prefer to say, phenomenalise—in external perception, also misperceive in introspection of their own processes, etc.; though each mind, according to Dr McTaggart, is a 'primary part' of the Real universe, and possesses knowledge as to itself of the kind called acquaintance, as contrasted with reflective and mediated cognition. How it is possible for the perfect parts of a perfect totality, or of The Absolute, to misperceive the timeless and immutable as temporal and changeful, Dr McTaggart sought to explain in his critical examination of the conception of Time, which has already been briefly discussed; and there he has also done more than has any other advocate of *a priori* absolutism to enable us to understand how these perfect parts see themselves but as imperfect and misperceiving. Our misreading of Reality is largely bound up, he teaches, with the illusoriness of temporality. But it also involves, in a more general sense, the phenomenality of the acquaintance of a mind with itself, or—according to the view adopted here—of reflective apprehension by the soul of its own nature, acts, and states. Now this, for reasons previously assigned in part, seems to be a dogmatic assumption, unwarranted by any psychological facts. We have every right to speak of sensory cognition, or external perception, as phenomenalising; indeed it is our knowledge concerning perception and its conditioning that compels us to distinguish between the phenomenal and the ontal. But inasmuch as so-called internal sense, or introspection, is not sense at all, we are not authorised by fact-knowledge and its necessary presuppositions to assume that introspection involves any phenomenalising or distortion. The difficulties generated by this assumption have already been found to be grave. On the other hand, difficulties are not raised for the translator of facts, but only for the *a priori* theorist, by the alternative and more natural supposition which entails no indefinite regress. Indeed the groundless and directly untestable assumption, that phenomenality attaches to introspection of the psychical or subjective, is largely responsible for what Dr Broad has called "the ghost which haunts every system of Absolute Idealism": viz. "the seemingly hopeless conflict between the error which must exist if the negative results be accepted and the perfection which must exist if the positive results be accepted". This seemingly hopeless conflict is familiar to readers of *Appearance and Reality*. In the latter part of that book tools are used which, by logical sleight of hand and confusion of the formally unintelligible with the contradictory and the nonsensical, have been blunted and hacked, if not demolished, in the earlier part. Dr McTaggart must be said to have made a more sustained and coherent effort than did Dr Bradley to abate the conflict between the negative and the positive results of absolutist philosophy, and to relate appearance with Reality; but it may be that what one has ventured to call a baseless assumption, having more affinity with aesthetic predilection than with scientific or metaphysical exigency, is the gratuitous cause of superfluous troubles, met more than half-way with heroic fortitude and wondrous ingenuity in *The Nature of Existence*. If we abide by the maxim *entia non multiplicanda praeter necessitatem*, the assumption that introspection is phenomenalising is methodologically *de trop*. Psychology has no need of such a supposition, and gives no hint that activity, change, time (as distinct from Time), etc., are misperceptions of the functionings of the soul. To suppose that the soul utterly misperceives its own functionings has proved to be a courting of trouble and a creation of puzzles which strenuous and clear thinking has been unable to resolve, and which have elicited from more misty and metaphorical thought only fantasy with which forthcoming knowledge is incompatible. That immutability is an essential characteristic of the ontal is a hypothesis for which nothing in the world or in human experience gives the slightest ground; it must therefore be ascribed entirely to subjective motivation which proceeds, by criticism of the 'real' categories, etc., to secure for itself a rationalised expression. And in that the hypothesis remains as yet unsupplemented by a tenable theory as to how the immutable causes the appearance of change for any subject, finite or Absolute, it may be said to leave an open field for metaphysical explanation in terms of no more, and no less, than forthcoming knowledge necessitates.

That phenomenalising, similar to that involved in sensory perception, attaches also to introspection of subjective activities and states, is an assumption which not only underlies systems such as have been described as types of absolutism, but also much of the agnosticism which accounts teleological theism unsatisfactory. A few remarks may therefore be offered here concerning certain agnostic objections to the theistic argument previously set forth. The Actual course of Nature, it will be urged by some, even if we are driven to regard it *as if* it were due to design, is phenomenal: in its ontal counterpart there will be something of which design is an appearance, but which we have no right to call design, since our categories cannot be carried over unchanged from the phenomenal to the noümenal realm. This counterpart, so far from being identical with design, may not even be analogous to it; we cannot imagine, and have no means of knowing, what it is. Thus the agnostic may regard the teleological explanation of the world as the most plausible that is forthcoming, but as involving a venture which his reason cannot make or justify. By way of reply to this demurrer it may be repeated that, unless certain constituents in our 'real' categories are carried over into the ontal realm, the notion of the thing *per se* becomes useless, while on general grounds it is nevertheless indispensable. And in the particular case of the category of design, which presupposes intelligence, valuation, and volition, a further reply is contained in what was said just now about the alleged phenomenality of knowledge concerning such activities and affections of the ontal soul. There is reason to believe that the distinction between Reality and appearance here vanishes; at any rate it is not empirically called for and serves no purpose when postulated. Nothing seems to be gained by entertaining the notion that intelligence and volition, as actually experienced, are appearances of non-intelligence and. non-volition; and no reason seems to be forthcoming for such a supposition, save that a similar one needs to be made in the case of sensory perceptions: which is no reason at all. Thus the agnostic who is prepared to admit that there is overwhelming evidence to shew that the world is *as if* designed, and who also allows that to designing there is some ontal counterpart in the world-ground though we have no right to identify it with the essential core of human designing, is not in a demonstrably more rational position than that of the theist with whom he may regard himself as at variance. *Practically* it comes to the same thing whether we say that the ontal activities of the world-ground and of finite souls are design, etc., or are such as to produce appearances which we call design. And *theoretically* it is but a question of where we choose to stop in a regress that, once started, admits of being pursued *ad indefinitum*: a regress, however, which cannot be carried a single step with any gain in philosophical explanatoriness, or under any compulsion from science of forthcoming facts.

To return now from the consideration of *a priori* guesses at truth to the more congenial task of further characterising the idea of the world-ground which, with minimal reading between the lines of 'knowledge' and with only such reading as is suggested by the actual context, offers the most reasonable interpretation of science without offering it violence or explaining it away. It is scarcely a step, beyond what the foregoing criticism of absolutism has positively suggested, to assert that the world-ground which, as designer, is creator, is also personal. By 'personality' is here to be meant something more than subjecthood and its inalienable individuality. Within the human sphere personality includes the self-consciousness which distinguishes the adult man from the infant and from non-rational animals, together with all else such as the moral status, the pursuit of ends, the synthesis of character, that may be superimposed on subjecthood when individual experience has attained to the common standpoint through social intercourse. And inasmuch as the world-ground, as reached by inquiry into the natures of the world and man, is a satisfactory explanation-principle solely in virtue of its possession of intelligence and ethical purposiveness, it must needs be conceived in terms of the notion of personality. The divine nature may include more than the potentialities of man indefinitely perfected, even capacities as far removed from our ken as human science is beyond the range of a worm's cognition; but, whatever else it may or may not include, it is at least characterised by intelligence, valuation, and volition. Empirically derived theism does not profess exhaustive knowledge of God as He is in Himself; it would affirm no more than so much as it finds Objective reasons for believing. It can allow that human personality is but "a pale copy" of divine personality, or that God is the only perfect Person. But that is not to renounce speaking of the Deity as personal.

Personality can be conceived as divested of conditions and limitations that are specifically human, and the resulting concept may then be relevant to the Deity without being exhaustive of the divine nature. If no more than transcendence such as this is meant by 'supra-personal', theism can appropriate that term. But if it connotes something essentially different from all that we mean by human personality, such as agency that is non-volitional, non-purposive, and non-ethical, the expression becomes a synonym for 'impersonal', and must be rejected. For 'God', as used by theism, is not a name for universal reason, ineffable being, or even for absolute morality or a tendency that makes for righteousness, but rather for a determinate spirit who is an artist and a lover as well as a geometriser, etc. Theism professes to be based on indications, apart from the satisfaction of religious experience, that God stands in 'personal' relations with creatures which may literally be said to bear the divine image or likeness, and less literally be said to be partakers of the divine nature, in the sense that they possess the potency of indefinite advance in fellowship and communion with Him.

Absolute monism, with its predilection for attributes such as infinitude, unconditionedness, and metaphysical perfection, disallows the identification of its One with the God of theism, because personality, even as applied to God, must bespeak somewhat of limitation and relationship with what is other than Himself. But theism, as we have already seen, is indifferent to the outcome of attempts to construe human experience from the imagined standpoint of an absolute experience. The theism which purports to have been here established maintains that the many are as Real, and Real in the same sense, as the One on Whom their being depends. It likewise cannot identify its world-ground or God with the Absolute, or the whole of Reality; and its preference for the highest category that our minds can conceive, viz. personality, wherewith to describe the Supreme Being, is not a groundless predilection but in accordance with the dictates of forthcoming knowledge. Yet even theistic writers have sometimes evinced reluctance to speak of God as a Person. In some cases this is due to a leaning towards absolute monism; in others, to the adoption of a particular interpretation of the doctrine of the Trinity; but most commonly, perhaps, to the belief that to ascribe personality to God involves difficulties suggested by our knowledge concerning the conditions of human acquisition of the labile status of personality. These difficulties call for discussion; and consideration of them will serve both to explicate the idea of divine personality and also to raise the question, hitherto postponed, whether the world-ground is more aptly comparable with a single subject or with a society of persons.

A self or subject does not depend, *quâ* an existent or as to its being, upon any object to which it stands in the relation of presentation and attention; but that relation or *rapport* is essential for any existent's assuming the rôle of, and being, a subject. This conditioning of bare subjecthood must apply universally, to God and man alike. Subjecthood, however, is not self-consciousness; and self-consciousness is requisite for personality. It was shewn in vol. 1 that there can be no self-consciousness in man without objects from which the ego distinguishes itself; and, assuming this conclusion to be established, it may be asked whether a like conditioning must be affirmed in the case of the self-consciousness of God. Lotze maintained that we need not think so: on the ground that God's states of consciousness, as subjective modifications, may provide the objective or presented factor of His experience, and so mediate self-consciousness apart from evocation by any 'other'. But Lotze was anxious to justify the attribution of perfect personality to a God more akin to the absolutist's One than to the Deity of theism: a God of Whom finite souls are parts or modifications. It is not necessary, therefore, to pass criticism here upon the subjective idealism which seems, in this connexion, to dominate his psychology. Moreover, if we accept at the outset the view that God without a world, or a Real other, is not God but an abstraction, the question now before us becomes superfluous.

But if personality involves self-consciousness it also involves more. And, in the case of human beings, personality has been found to be conditioned by embodiment: it is not predicable of the pure ego. Rationality and morality are socially mediated, not innate or intrinsic to the unbegotten soul. Personality grows as knowledge of the world and of other selves increases; and there is no reason to believe that it will otherwise advance to what it may become in "spirits of just men made perfect". The absence of these conditionings of human personality, in the case of the Supreme Being, does not render the ascription of personality to Him inconsistent or meaningless, however. There must be a hierarchy of souls in the cosmos, or degrees of 'dominance' in its monads, else the same Objective environment should elicit rationality, etc., from all experients alike. And if we needs must assert the existence of souls humbler than ours, there is no inconceivability in the notion of higher souls, or even of a supreme spirit possessing, without mediation or evoked developement, faculties and capacities indefinitely transcending those which human souls acquire only by means of embodiment, or symbiosis, and social intercourse. The idea of a developing God who, like us, progresses to self-consciousness and personality, is indeed incompatible with theism. For theism primarily consists in the assertions that, as ground of this world, God must be an intelligent and ethical being, and that, when conceived apart from and prior to His world, God becomes a cosmologically useless idea, in that then we can no more conceive an actual transition from a worldless God to God and a world than we can find a logical way from the absolute One to a finite Many.

It is a further question, however, and one that has sometimes been raised, whether perfect personality and perfect love can be attributed to God, even if He be conceived as eternally confronted with His finite world, so long as He is also conceived as the sole supreme spirit, or the single member of the class designated by the class-concept deity. If God's personality may be supposed not to be mediated by social relations with compeers, it may still be argued that perfect—in the sense of perfected, actualised and not merely potentially perfect—personality and love can only be attributed if the preconditions of their actualisation be forthcoming. And these, it has sometimes been maintained, could only be forthcoming if God be conceived as a society rather than as a supreme individual.

When raised in this way, the question before us involves the precarious assumption that the theistic idea is theologically and philosophically inadequate unless it excludes the notion of any unrealised potentiality in the Deity, or at least of any lack of actualisation within the sphere of ethical life. Reasons have previously been submitted for abstaining from attributing to God perfection in the sense of complete actualisation of all potentiality, as inconsistent with the idea of a living spirit, if not with the idea of a determinate being. And theism such as is chary of asserting more than explanation of facts requires, as distinct from theism such as would assert all that religiously or aesthetically directed metaphysical craving demands, will not attach so much importance to the considerations on which theology of the latter type relies when arguing from the conditions of actualised potentiality in the ethical sphere of the divine life to a pluralistic conception of Deity. These considerations nevertheless deserve to be set forth.

If we are to regard goodness and love as essential attributes of God, and God as an ethically perfect being, then, it is urged, He must ever have been able to realise in the highest degree the capacities for love with which His nature was eternally enriched. And this implies that within or besides Himself there must eternally have been an other to be known and loved with all the fulness of His capacity to know and to love. The created world, with its imperfection, could not exhaustively express or engross such a being. His love for it could only be of the kind that bespeaks condescension: love indeed, but not the only kind, nor 'perfect' love. For perfect love there must be perfect reciprocity and communicability, a perfectly loveable and loving recipient or recipients, an other that is only adequate in that it is equal to God, or is God. Thus the conclusion is reached that plurality within the Godhead is a condition of attributing eternal and perfect love to the Godhead. Aristotle's saying, "He who has no need of society because he is sufficient for himself must be either a brute or a god", is

amended by the assertion that such a being could not be a God
in the theist's sense. Of this nature is one form of the philosophical
argument for the Christian doctrine of the Trinity, a discussion
of which will be found in the Appendix, Note D; but obviously
unless Trinitarianism becomes tritheism it cannot make use of
such speculative support.

There is another line of argument in favour of the pluralistic
conception of Deity, which does not involve the assumption that
divine perfection must consist in the actualisation of 'infinite'
potentialities. This rather relies on what is sometimes miscalled
the 'law' of continuity, which is rather an aesthetically pleasing, and
a more or less reasonably grounded, hope than a logically demonstrable principle. Human beings owe their pre-eminence over
lower denizens of this world to social organisation into an organic
and over-individual unity, though doubtless their capacity for such
organisation is ultimately determined by the higher rank of the
human soul, or the dominant monad in man, in the hierarchy of
ontal subjects. The principle of continuity, as Prof. Ward has
observed, will then suggest that individuals of higher order are
in like manner organised into over-individual unities, or societies,
and so on: possibly *ad indefinitum*. This view would lead up to a
society rather than an individual personal being as the supreme
unity. Here again we are in the sphere of speculation rather than
of inference from knowledge, save for the fact that as yet there
has been nothing in our empirical argument for theism to require
us to advance from unity of world-purpose to singularity of
purposer. Perhaps none of the several fields of fact which have
evoked teleological explanation point to the directivity of a sole
supreme being rather than to the directivity of higher beings and
eventually a supreme society. Whether there are further considerations decisive in favour of the former alternative will be
inquired later; but here it may be submitted that if there were not,
there is nothing philosophically, or even religiously, shocking in
the supposition that the world-ground or the ultimate One is a
divine society rather than a sole individual. Polytheism is regarded
as an obnoxious creed chiefly because of its historical associations,
or because the "gods many" which it has imagined have been
individuals at cross purposes and with undivine characters and
habits. But such diversity of natures and wills is not an essential

accompaniment of a supreme society. We can eliminate these irrelevant historical associations and postulate equality of nature, *homoousia*, and harmony of will. It then becomes no longer true that 'God' is a word which "defies the possibility of a plural". There cannot be a plurality of discordant and conflicting world-grounds, from the point of view of either philosophy or religion; but there would seem to be no *prima facie* reason why the one unity embracing the universe should not, like the universe itself, be a many in one, though self-subsistent. Such a view would only conflict with inherited preconceptions and sentiments associated therewith, and perhaps not seriously with those of a Christian, wont as he is to interpret his monotheism in terms of implicit tritheism when putting it to practical or devotional use. Moreover the objectionableness attaching to the use of 'God' in the plural form is removed if that name, in the singular number, is applied only to the divine society. God would then be personal but not a Person. And though the word 'society' needs must be used in exposition of this conception of the Deity, its objectionableness is somewhat toned down when its human associations are transcended or discarded. The divine society for which 'God', on this supposition, will be the name is rather to be conceived as intermediate between a society and an individual, as these entities are known to us within the sphere of humanity. For the divine *hypostases*, though distinct subjects and agents, may, or rather must, be conceived as much less individual than human persons: more penetrable or less impervious than the selves which we know, or know but in part. A human self presumably cannot directly know another self's experiencings; but a subject free from limitations besetting the human self may be able directly to be aware of another's states, etc. It is not necessary to suppose all subjects to be individuals or *atomoi* in the same degree as that in which we ourselves are individuals. Those forming the highest unity in the hierarchy may possess so much of mutual coinherence, in respect of cognitive and volitional experience, as enables each to be concerned in the activities of the others, and to be transparent to one another. The notion of *perichoresis* or *circumincessio*, which can only be used figuratively by Trinitarian theology such as stops short of regarding the divine *hypostases* as subjects, may be applied literally by theology such as takes the idea of the sociality of God in all seriousness. The 'persons' of the Godhead, as thus conceived, would be "members one of another" in a much higher degree than are the units of a human society; and being, *ex hypothesi* self-subsistent and of the same nature or substance (*unius substantiae* rather than *una res*), they would constitute a unity and one world-ground no less explanatory of all the facts that have previously been presented as suggestive of theism than is the Singularity asserted by rigid monotheism. The unity comprising the supreme plurality would be a unity of concurrent wills, of joint purposes, or moral harmony, and of co-operant agencies.

The foregoing paragraphs are not an advocacy of the view which they have set forth. They are rather intended to indicate that, in so far as facts concerning the world and man guide us, there is little or nothing to compel us to choose between the conceptions of the world-ground as an individual and as a society. The latter interpretation of theism, if the name 'theism' would still be allowed to it, is philosophically neither more nor less requisite than the former. It is only preferable if we adopt the one or the other of two precarious assumptions. It is preferable if we postulate that the perfection to be attributed to the Deity is of the kind that excludes unactualised conceivable potentialities; but that view forms no part of a philosophical theology arrived at by the empirical method. It only becomes objectionable if we incorporate into our theology ideas due to aesthetic predilection for numerical singularity and to the contingencies of anthropo-morphically conditioned developement in the sphere of religious experience and traditional belief. The social interpretation is also preferable if we postulate continuity; but then it is based on nothing more secure than analogy, while it must not be overlooked that the alternative view has the same kind of basis and support. For if the idea of dominance, as something original and not acquired in a process of developement (as is its manifestation), is essential to the pluralistic theory of the world, analogy suggests that the world as a totality is constituted an organic whole by its *one* supreme monad, its creative and indwelling spirit. The issue does not lie within the sphere of fact-controlled thought; and religious experience, if it was correctly analysed in vol. I, can offer no decisive testimony because it has already *assumed* one of the alternatives in constituting itself what it has become. Polytheism, of the kind contemplated just now, has never been a candidate for religious or for philosophical recognition, save in so far as Christian doctors have dallied with it before recoiling from it, and popular Christian theology sometimes implies it.

The theistic idea obtained by seeking an explanation of the world has now been made somewhat more definite through comparison with ideas, of like function, yielded by other methods of reasoning. And thereby have been brought to light several respects or senses in which God must be conceived as limited and as self-limited. If we would refrain from using the phrase 'a finite God' because it suggests limitations other than those which philosophy compels us to specify, it is necessary to assert that God is non-infinite. He is not an indeterminate being but a personal spirit. And He is not The Absolute in the sense of the All, since the created world is not Himself, nor His modes, but His utterance or deed. And it is not only in creation that limitation is involved. Divine attributes, such as power and love, in order to be compossible, cannot be infinite or perfect in the more unqualified senses in which those terms have been wont to be used. In particular, the attributes of omnipotence and omniscience, which have not as yet been discussed, call for some diminution of the plenitude of connotation with which they have been religiously invested before they can consistently be predicated of the Deity. The notion of omnipotence may await investigation until, in the succeeding chapter, the problem of evil, in which considerations as to divine omnipotence become central, will be dealt with. The notion of omniscience may receive some scrutiny here.

There is only one method of reasonable inquiry concerning the knowledge that can be attributed to the Supreme Being. It is to begin with analogy, without which no discussion is possible, and then to eliminate from human knowledge such characteristics as are known to be humanly conditioned, subtraction of which will still leave what can legitimately be called knowledge. Pursuing this method, we can set out from the fact that knowledge implies objects. But whereas the primary objects of our cognition are the data of sense, posited for us and not by us, the objects of God's knowledge are posited by and for Himself; and sense-knowledge is precluded to Him in that embodiment, such as mediates our sensory perception, cannot be attributed to Him. Thus in two fundamental respects the divine knowledge of the Actual world will necessarily differ from ours. With regard to the former of these differences, it may be useful to recall a difficulty in which Berkeley was placed by his idealism, and from which he failed to extricate himself when, in his later works, he leapt from sensationism to Platonism. The *esse* of a thing, he at first taught, is its being perceived by us. But the *percipi* which enters into individual experience described by the formula $S—p—o$ is fleeting; continuous existence of the thing, (o), when not perceived by us, he ensured by transferring its *percipi* to the experience of God. Yet to God he could not attribute sensory perception. If $G—p'—o$ be now the formula required, the p' of divine cognition must be essentially different from the p of human sensory experience. Accordingly, Berkeley later identifies p' with pure reason, or intuitive apprehension of the 'intelligible', so that o also is exalted from a sensory ectype into an archetype, or a Platonic universal. Then, however, all the particularity, the concrete or historical, in virtue of which the Actual world differs from any possible or purely ideal world, vanishes; and divine knowledge of our world, whose *esse* is *a Deo causari*, would seem to be precluded to God, since no means of knowing it is left. Such a means is provided, on the other hand, when this unworkable idealism is replaced by the phenomenalist theory of knowledge, or when for the noümenal of Plato we substitute the noümenal of Kant. The p' of divine cognition then becomes but that seeing 'face to face' which is the ontal counterpart of our p, the phenomenalising of sensory perception, etc. And if, as has previously been argued, there must be as much of structure in the ontal as there is in the phenomenal, knowledge of our world in all its detail is as easily conceivable in the case of the Deity as is phenomenal knowledge of the ontal in the case of human cognition. The first respect, then, in which divine knowledge must be conceived as differing from our knowledge of the Actual world, is that God's objects are things *per se* whereas ours are phenomena.

Another difference that can safely be asserted is constituted by the fact that God stands not only in the relation of knower, but also in that of creator, to His world. His knowledge, if 'knowledge' be used with proper strictness, will not be *identical* with the 'intellective intuition' in which His creative activity consists; but room must be left for the possibility that His knowledge may differ in nature even from such ontal or non-phenomenal knowledge of the world as might be ascribed, *e.g.* to an archangel, in virtue of God having posited the *onta* which are only presented to the archangel. The limits to the scope of the activities, even the activities of creatures that are secondarily 'creators', and to the 'emergence' that succeeds upon primary collocations, may thus be knowable to the Creator as they cannot be knowable to the highest beneath Him in the hierarchy of spirits. But, not to pursue speculation on matters beyond the range of fact-controlled thought, it may be added to what has already been said that the divine knowledge of the world, as existent and in so far as it is *natura naturata,* is to be distinguished from our knowledge, in that the Creator's cognition is not derived through sense, discursive understanding, and ejective interpretation, nor perspectively from some standpoint within the whole. God, conceived as uniquely related to every part of the world and to the world as a whole, must be, so to speak, ubiquitous or omnipresent; and, in virtue of an unrestricted range of attention, He must be said to be omniscient as to all that is and has been, and also as to all that will be, in so far as it is the outcome of uniform causation.

Here, however, a limitation is suggested. For it is only in case the world-process is mechanical, in the rigid sense, that its future can strictly be called knowable. The astronomer has not fore-*knowledge* of an eclipse; what he predicts is but a probability, a possible experience whose actualisation depends on contingent conditions which he does not know, but only assumes. He could only have foreknowledge if the world were known to be no more than a pure mechanism. Unless we are thus in earnest with the latter half of the compound word 'foreknowledge', we but talk of we know not what in attributing foreknowledge of Actuality to the Deity. That which He can be said, with strict and proper usage of terms, to foreknow is but what the world tends to become, and what it *must* become only in so far as it is mechanical, or is evolutionary in the sense of being an unfolding of the preformed and predetermined. But some at least of God's creatures are in turn 'creators'; *i.e.* their utterances are not of His positing. Human beings, *e.g.* are not mechanical automata, actuated by a *vis a tergo* alone, or determined solely by their pasts. Their future, awaiting naturation, is not a part of *natura naturata*. Their life consists not in eduction of the predetermined but evinces epigenesis, or emergence of what is not implicit in the primary collocations. God has created, and may be supposed to sustain and inspire, these free agents, but not to coerce them. Nor can He be said to experience or to *erleben* their states, feelings, conations, etc. Knowledge of these spontaneities, immediate or inferred, is only conceivable once they are 'uttered'. Thus, as Prof. Ward has argued in *The Realm of Ends*, the self-limitation involved in creating free or 'creative' creatures, so that in God's world there is much that He does not create, in turn involves a limitation to divine omniscience in respect of foreknowledge. Foreknowledge implies predestination or predetermination, and is incompatible with the freedom or self-determination of human souls. It is limited to the tendencies, the possibilities, and the limits of the scope of free activities, and cannot apply with necessity or universality to particular future cases of such activity. God is thus beyond surprise, and His purpose beyond frustration; but as that purpose is to allow His creatures some initiative and to associate them with Himself as fellow-workers, it leaves room for contingency and for non-omniscience as to particular forms which free action will take. This limitation involves no derogation from the divine majesty, however: it is part of what may be called the self-abnegation that is implied in the enrichment or perfection which religion calls divine love. And in comparison with that the so-called metaphysical attributes, *e.g.* omnipotence and omniscience, are scarcely evocative of worship.

There remain to be considered two ways in which it has been sought to turn the force of the foregoing considerations. One of them is to admit their cogency so long as fore*knowledge* is in question, but to claim that there may be divine fore-*intuition*, or cognition not belonging to any of the types technically denoted by 'knowledge', pertaining to what is neither divinely created nor divinely predetermined. But while we may shrink from dogmatic denial of a possibility as to which we cannot know, it is open to us to observe that something is then supposed for which no warrant is furnished by experience, analogy, or reasonable extrapolation. Such intuition is unimaginable and inconceivable; we can say nothing about it save that it involves appeal to mystery transcending philosophy, and to alleged truth that is above reason.

The other way is to sacrifice the import of the former half of the word 'foreknowledge', and to construe foreknowledge as eternal knowledge. According to which of the senses of 'eternal' is adopted, omniscience as to what we call the future will then admit of different interpretations. If God's vision *sub specie aeternitatis* means but that His time-span or specious present is of boundless duration, or that a thousand ages in His sight are but a moment, the upholder of divine omniscience must imply that what for us is future must be known to Him *in the same way* as is knowledge of what for us is past. In other words, the future must be presented, as already 'uttered': *futura jam facta sunt*. But that is an obvious contradiction. So long as eternity is thus conceived as unending time compressed for the divine spectator into a moment, the difference between past and future, what is and what is not, is still contained within it unless the undone is really done. We can only take in a symphony as a whole after we have heard its successive notes; and if the world-process is similarly presented as a finished whole to God, it can only be presented to Him as composer, not as hearer or spectator. Then, however, it is implied that there is one sole composer, not many. The world-process is but a performance of a perfected score; epigenesis is replaced by preformation; prescience becomes predetermination, and the fore-seen is the intended, down to the veriest detail. Thus if fore-knowledge be replaced by this kind of eternal *knowledge*, it involves either identity of the done with the not-done, as in the assertion of S. Augustine quoted above, or else the identification of freedom with necessitation.

It is sometimes alleged that in the experience of God, which transcends time, there can be nothing corresponding to the differ-ence which exists for us between memory and foresight. Eternity would then seem to be regarded not as an embracing of all time in one present, but as either absolute timelessness or supra-temporality. In the former of these new senses eternal knowledge is a contradiction in terms, because it involves relation of the unrelated and unrelatable. In the latter of these senses it is know-ledge of the ontal. But, as has been submitted before, there must be something in the ontal corresponding to temporality in the phenomenal, and something corresponding to the difference, in our experience, between memory and anticipation, else that difference could not be forthcoming. In other words, the ontal equivalent to futurity cannot be identical with the ontal equivalent to pastness. So the difficulty from which eternalism would escape is only postponed. It is relegated from explicability to absolute mystery: a realm as to which anything can be asserted and can be, with similar groundlessness, denied. With us, the very power to anticipate or to foresee is derived from experience of the past: memory involves traces of past presentations, or of what *has been*. There is thus no analogy between memory and foresight. The significance of psychological facts is ignored when it is assumed to be a mere accident that memory does not work forward as well as backward, or that memory and anticipation differ no more than x differs from $-x$. This attempt to interpret divine foreknowledge as supra-temporal knowledge, in which memory and foresight are either identical or are both non-existent, involves application of the supra-temporal version of S. Augustine's *futura jam facta sunt* to ontal activity; and if that saying be a glaring untruth when referring to the temporal and phenomenal, there must be some equivalent to its falsehood in the version of it that is appropriate to the ontal world, of which the temporal is an appearance. Thus, whichever of the several senses of 'eternal' be adopted, no light is thrown on the possibility of divine prescience as to the outcome of human freedom. A world which is timeless, in the sense of having no real counterpart to temporality, is incapable of accounting for our temporal experience: an ontal world which has some such counterpart, and whose activities can (in any legitimate sense) be declared *knowable* to the divine mind, must be a 'block-universe' in which there is no freedom, or a static world in which all that phenomenally ever will be is Really done.

The difficulty involved in extending omniscience to include foreknowledge of the output of human freedom could hardly be better stated than in the following passage from Book ix, chap. 5, of Lotze's *Microcosmus*:

To attain by inference to a knowledge of the future which has its causes in the present is a prescience possible for us in a limited degree and belonging to God to an unlimited extent; but what can be the meaning of saying, as people do, that God foreknows that which is to happen through freewill in the future, not as something that *must* come, but as something that *will* come? If the future does *not exist*, how could this non-existent (unless represented in the present by its causes and thus *not* free) stand in any other relation to cognition than that which never will be, and how therefore could it be distinguished from the latter?

Lotze himself endeavours to surmount this difficulty chiefly by the assertion that free actions also find their place in the timeless (supra-temporal) and ontal whole; "not as non-existent and future, but as existent". Although not conditioned by the past, they have reference to the present, and their place in the supra-temporal order is determined, he says, by members which are co-ordinate with them; so that omniscience can observe free action as something real, rather than foresee it as something that will be. But to be determined by co-ordinate members is not to be free; and Lotze offers no more explanation than do other upholders of his view as to the ontal counterpart to the phenomenal difference between pastness and futurity. Foreknowledge of free activity is thus left by him a mystery, or a groundless belief.

CHAPTER VII

The Problem of Evil

Theism has been found to provide a sufficient explanation of the intelligibility, the adaptiveness, and the progressiveness of the course of Nature, and to offer the most reasonable and satisfying interpretation of certain wide ranges of fact and of their interconnexions. It now remains to be inquired whether, like some alternative theories as to the world-ground, it sets up any new difficulties, and whether it is consistent with all the facts as well as with most of them. The outstanding fact, or group of facts, with which a teleologically grounded world-view may seem to be incompatible, is the abundant forthcomingness of the apparently dysteleological in a world-order alleged to embody the moral purpose of a benevolent creator. And before theistic faith, however sanguinely it may be entertained by individual believers, can be redeemed from subjectivity and be pronounced to be reasonable from the point of view of common or Objective 'knowledge', a solution of the problem of evil must be found. It is as incumbent upon empirically reached theism as upon theology of the *a priori* kind to provide a theodicy, or to afford grounds for a belief equivalent to the rationalistically derived assertion that this is the best possible world. It is commonly held, however, that the problem of evil is the *crux* of theism, and that though it does not exist for theism alone amongst theories as to the world-ground, this problem is graver for that than for any other world-view, in that theism regards the rationality of the world as including more than its intelligibility to the analytic understanding, to wit the ethical purposiveness of a creative will which is wholly good. For materialism and mechanistic naturalism, for spiritualistic pluralism, and for singularism which conceives The Absolute as above, or indifferent to, the distinction between good and evil, no such problem exists, be the world as replete with evil as a pessimist could wish; and upholders of one or another of these anti-theistic theories have declared the question, how the evil in the world of a good God is to be accounted for, to be one which has received many replies but no answer. Indeed there have been convinced theists, *e.g.* Lotze, who have professed ignorance as to the lines along which a solution of this problem is to be sought. On the other hand, more recent exponents of theism have argued that the problem of evil, as such, is not thus hopelessly insoluble, but that the existence of both physical and moral evil may reasonably be accounted for if the *raison d'être* of the world be, as theism maintains, the realisation of moral values. Even the remoter question, why the world is evolutionary rather than statically perfect, is not left wholly unanswerable if theism be true. And Prof. Sorley has emboldened theists to go even further than this and to declare what has been called the *crux* of theism to be its glory. So far is theism from being the one philosophy to which the existence of evil presents an insuperable difficulty that it alone assigns evil a meaning—whereas singularism accounts it to be illusion—and a place within that order which non-theistic pluralism, etc., must be content to regard as an accident of luck.

Such are the various views as to the possibility of a theodicy, between which a decision must be reached by consideration of the relevant facts.

The fact that evil exists in the world is a primary datum for the empirical theist, knowable with much more immediacy and certainty than is the being of God. And he cannot approve of either of the chief ways in which pantheists and theists respectively have sought in the past to explain the reality of evil away. He finds no comfort in the supposition that evil is an illusion of finite and temporal experience, an inadequate idea, or an appearance which would dissolve away if only we saw *sub specie aeternitatis*. For, if evil is illusion, the illusion is an evil; and if no evil would confront timeless vision, it is an evil that we see *sub specie temporis*. The problem of evil is raised by the world as we find it, and is not to be solved by diverting attention to other-worldly cognition of a world-order other than the phenomenal and temporal.

Nor, again, can the theist of to-day resort to the view that evil is unreal or "non-existent" in the sense of being mere deficiency or negation, having and needing no efficient cause: he possesses psychological knowledge to the contrary. The privation-theory of evil owed its plausibility to the ease with which abstractions can be verbally manipulated. It abstracts moral evil from moral

agents, and, because the resulting concept no longer includes
subjective activity, asserts that it denotes nothing actual or active,
substantial or causative. Of course if good were similarly regarded
in abstraction from its agents it would likewise be reduced to the
unsubstantial. Evil in the abstract is indeed nothing existent, and
cannot be said to resist the good; but evil wills none the less resist
good wills. S. Augustine, in teaching that the evil will or act has
no efficient cause, stated that it is due to *not* setting the will upon
God; but he overlooked the fact that evil volition also consists in
actually setting the will upon something other than God. Thus
the positive element in moral evil was suppressed by substituting
an abstraction for a concrete fact, and by adopting a negative form
of words where a positive form is equally called for. Even the will
is an abstraction: the only actuality is an agent willing; and he is
the efficient cause which the deficiency-theory failed to find
because, by a mere verbal device, it had left him out. When
S. Augustine[1] and other defenders of the privation-theory have
sought to present it in such a form as to escape the force of these
considerations, they have relied on the special assumptions that
only the immutable really exists, and that goodness and existence
are the same. But, as has been observed in previous contexts, the
former assumption is baseless, and the latter is derived from word-
play. Lastly, when the theory identifies moral evil with so-called
metaphysical evil, which is but morally neutral finiteness, it
obliterates the morality of the evil. For these reasons all forms of
the theory in question must be discarded as useless for the purpose
of theodicy. The error in the theory is nowhere more vicious than
in such reasoning as that evil is non-existent, *therefore* God cannot
be its cause, or in the ingenious argument (said to emanate from
Boëthius): there is nothing that the omnipotent God cannot do;
He cannot do evil; therefore evil is nothing. At best the privation-
theory is a misstatement of such truths as that evil is never an end
in itself, nor a power or 'principle' co-ordinate with goodness
and absolutely antithetic to it, since moral evil is always choice of
a lower good, while physical evil may be instrumental to ethical
goodness, and may be inevitable in a world which is to be a theatre
of moral life. Such facts, it may be observed by the way, preclude
the possibility, logically open so long as Actuality is not consulted,

[1] *The Confessions*, Book VII.

that the good in the world is but a necessary condition of the maximum of evil in a worst possible world.

What is meant by the assertion that this world, in spite of its evil, is the best possible, needs to be explained, else it may seem to state an absurdity. And explanation may begin with clearing away certain gratuitous errors which have been historically associated with the dictum. It is not necessary to analyse the divine creativity into the actualisation of one best world subsequently to the choosing of it, and choice of it subsequently to contemplation of an infinite number of unrealised, purely ideal or possible, systems presented to God's thought or imagination. It is not only unnecessary, but also inconsistent in several ways with the requirements of thought and knowledge, so to represent the origination of God's world. God without a world is a superfluous abstraction, and a God who might have 'chosen' a different seminal world from this, or different 'primary collocations', would be a different God. The supposed possibilities with which the Creator is alleged to have been confronted are not to be conceived as eternally independent of Him; nor are ideas, properly so called, prior to actualities, but are derived from them. Possibility, in the sense that is here relevant, presupposes actuality; and to speak of possible worlds as prior to an actual world is but to indulge in the reification of abstractions that are meaningless apart from relation to *some* actuality. When possibility rules out not only, *e.g.*, the round square, but also non-compossibility with other possibles within one system and with the determinate nature of God, apart from which He is nothing, the supposed infinity oɩ possible worlds vanishes: unrealised possibilities become im possibilities. What is possible for God is not determined by a *prius* of eternal laws, for there can be no such thing, but primarily by His nature and secondarily by that of His one world. As Lotze has shewn, empty images or ideas of other possible actualities can only be said to arise with the actual world and its logical and other kinds of order. God and his world are the ground and cause of the distinction between the possible and the impossible, and between the possible and the actual. Having derived the notion of the possible from the actual, the human mind has been apt to invert the order, and to regard the actual as but one case of illimitable possibilities, 'existentially' and logically prior to it.

Similarly, when it has not regarded the true and the good as arbitrarily determined by the divine will, it has tended to conceive them as a *prius* which the Creator must recognise, as if He had once been an indeterminate being for whom truth and goodness were not as yet valid. But, once more to quote Lotze, as there is no motion without velocity and direction, on which they can be afterwards imposed, so is there no power that has not some mode of procedure, and no empty capacity which somehow hits upon definite modes of activity. Determinateness excludes what are called possibilities, or other subsequently conceivable modes of action; choice between them, as if none were ruled out by the determinate nature of the Deity, is thus a superfluous supposition. The world is what it is because God is what He is.

That God might have 'chosen' another world than this out of the unlimited sphere of the possible, and one in which there was less evil or none at all, has sometimes been urged as an objection to ethical theism. To suggest this as a bare possibility is easy. Imaginatively to construct such a possible world is less easy, as is also a demonstration of the alleged possibility. Such initial attempts as are forthcoming are trivial, and have been described as specifications for a fool's paradise. Thus it has been surmised that the physical world might have been framed with a view to safeguarding man's physical well-being at every turn. It is a question, however, whether this happy state of things is compatible with the world being a cosmos, and a further question whether the world would then be instrumental to the realisation of moral worth. The particular incompatibilities involved in particular suggestions as to how the elimination of physical and moral evil from a world such as ours might have been effected will be exhibited in due course. At this stage it may but be observed that a world characterised by static perfection is incompatible with a world characterised by evolutionary process, and that ours is of the latter type. This brings us to a remoter problem, of which the problem of evil is an outgrowth, and to the alleged ultimate insolubility of which that of the narrower problem is due. Why God created a world at all is a superfluous question if by 'God' we primarily mean the world-ground; but why His world is evolutionary rather than already perfected is a question that is perhaps not quite futile, nor so wholly beyond a reasonable answer, in the light of the fundamental tenets of ethical theism, as some would pronounce it to be. A world, as a sphere of existence objective to God, must be composed of finite beings: God cannot create Gods, because 'God', in the theistic sense of the term, connotes unoriginateness. And if the world is to realise the good, that being its *raison d'être*, it would seem that it then must be characterised by developement or epigenesis. For moral goodness cannot be created as such; it cannot be implanted in any moral agent by an 'almighty' Other. It is the outcome of freedom, and has to be acquired or achieved by creatures. We cannot imagine a living world, in which truly ethical values are to be actualised, save as an evolutionary cosmos in which free agents live and learn, make choices and build characters. If there be theists who think otherwise, they must be content to regard the evolutionary character of the world as but part of the ultimate nature of things, and as inexplicable because ultimate. At any rate philosophy must start from what simply is; and it deserves no blame if it modestly withholds inquiry as to how and why things came to be. Theism would only go so far further as to apply its doctrine that God is love which seeks reciprocation.

Apart from all variable and incidental qualities which may belong to love as possessed by mankind, and from such enrichment of the conception of divine love as is supplied by religion, it may be said that love must everywhere and always involve self-imparting and seeking the highest welfare of the beings on whom it is bestowed. In God it must also involve self-limitation in respect of power. Love, in this sense, has always been assigned by theology as what we can only speak of as the 'motive' of God in His volitional creativity. Taking this cardinal doctrine and also the reality of the world's evil for granted, the theist needs to shew that in and behind this evil there is a soul of good, or at least to afford reasons for disbelieving that the world, in so far as it is due to God's making and not to man's mismaking, contains absolute and superfluous evils. If he can do so, he will not need to seek refuge from an intellectual difficulty by merely assuming a wholly incomprehensible divine love, or by faintly trusting the larger hope: his faith will remain reasonable, supported by what passes for knowledge—knowledge which, however, itself ultimately rests on other faith.

Since theism teaches that the world-ground is an ethical Spirit, or that God is love, it must also teach that, in some sense, the world is the 'best possible' of its kind. And it may now be submitted that this implication is defensible, so long as we are consistent and in earnest in the use of both the words 'best' and 'possible'.

There is no sense in calling a world a best world unless we specify the *kind* of goodness or worth which that world is said to manifest in the fullest measure. Different values may not be actually compossible, especially if each of them is to be present in its superlative degree; so the notion of a world as an *omnitudo* of values may be as 'impossible' as is the notion of God as the *omnitudo* of all positive attributes. What the theist means by 'best', in this connexion, is best in respect of moral worth, or of instrumentality thereto. But those who have allowed themselves to "charge God foolishly" have substituted for this meaning that of happiest, or sensuously pleasantest. Certainly our world is not, in this sense, the best that we can imagine. Equally certainly, the theist maintains, it was not meant to be. If it were, it would not be truly the best; for we cannot go behind our judgement, rational or non-rational, that the highest value in the hierarchy of values is moral worth, or—what is the ultimate essence of all morality—personal love. The hedonistic theory that pleasure is what gives worth to life, the ultimate good to be striven for, is generally acknowledged to be untenable: at any rate it is out of court for the theist. Happiness may be a constituent element in the highest complex good that we can conceive, and may accompany the attainment of a higher good; but the ultimate standard for the valuation of human life it cannot be. The 'best possible' world, then, or the world that is worthiest of God and man, must be a moral order, a theatre of moral life and love. Moral character and moral progress must be its purpose, as the best things which any world can realise. To dispense with them would be, for the Creator, to prefer a worse world. Unalloyed pleasure is condemned by man himself as unworthy to be his "life's crown". No pain or want, no effort; no effort, no progress; no progress, no attainment. *Necessity* is the mother of invention; experience is the "becoming expert *by experiment*": mere happiness would entail stagnation.

Thus we cannot have it both ways: the best world cannot

be the most pleasurable; and it cannot lack its crown in moral agents.

The word 'cannot' leads on to a discussion of our second leading term, 'possible': on this occasion in connexion with the notion of divine omnipotence. It has already been found vain to speak of a *prius* of possibilities independent of actualities. It may now be added that, possibilities and impossibilities being once constituted by an actual order, omnipotence cannot be conceived as power or control over the possible and the impossible alike, as if both were the same to God. That leads to absurdity. Yet when theism has been rejected on the ground that the evil in the world furnishes an argument against the goodness, or even the existence, of God, it would seem to have been generally assumed that such a being must, by arbitrary exercise of will, be the author of possibility as well as of actuality.

That whatever power may be called omnipotence must be limited by the impossible has been maintained in at least two ways. One of these is to assert that the laws of thought, *i.e.* the laws of identity, contradiction, etc., are valid independently of God as well as of the world, and impose themselves upon Him as well as upon ourselves with necessity. If this be so, we at once reach a distinction between the possible and the impossible which must be eternally binding upon the Supreme Being. Such a doctrine will not be unacceptable to common sense, but it does not commend itself to all philosophers. It has several times been insisted in this work that the valid, abstracted from that of which it is valid, is a mental figment, not an 'existent' *prius*. And it may be argued that this is so even in the case of the fundamental laws of thought, as well as in that of the empirical laws of Nature. The sum of eternal truths cannot exist, so to say, *in vacuo*, prior both to the things in which they are embodied and to the thinker in whose mind they are ideas, etc. When we speak of God as recognising truths independent of Him, or as establishing truth or validity by fiat, and when we try to conceive of God as able to obliterate the difference between the logically possible and impossible, or to set up that difference as if it once did not exist, we are endeavouring to think of Him as a being for whom truth is not as yet truth, and therefore as an indeterminate being eventually indistinguishable from nothing.

On the other hand, if the thinker of the eternal truths is deter-minate, self-consistent, and so forth, with a definite nature and mode of activity, other modes of being and conceivable or possible activities are *ipso facto* precluded. Hence the sum of eternal truths becomes the mode of God's being and activity, and is neither their *prius* nor their product. And this is the better answer to the sup-position that the possible is an arbitrary creation of God, and that the possible and the impossible are alike to omnipotence. In that God is love, He is not hate: in that He wills a developing moral order He is not the creator of a paradise of angels. Possibilities are thus determined by what God is; and God is limited by His very determinateness, not an indeterminate Absolute in whom all differences are lost. Theism has no concern with such an Absolute, and the puzzles set up by the adoption of such a notion constitute no difficulties for theism. Nor is determinateness, or the kind of finiteness which it implies, any derogation from such 'almighti-ness' as theology can predicate of the Deity without self-stultification.

But, granted that God is a determinate being, restricted to consistency and compatibility in His action, and granted that His world is to be a developing moral order—the highest ideal of a world that we can conceive—then it must follow that there be a possibility and a risk of moral evil in that world. There cannot be moral goodness in a creature such as man without the possibility of his sinning. Without freedom to choose the evil, or the lower good, a man might be a well-behaved puppet or a sentient auto-maton, but not a moral agent. But the best possible world implies the existence of moral agents; its crown cannot be the puppet or the automaton. Were our conduct determined like the movements of the machinery of a clock, our world might manifest a pre-established harmony and fulfil the purpose of a clock-maker. But it could not fulfil any ideal of its own, and could not have one. Nor could it realise the purpose of a God willing a best possible world. In both these respects a world from which the possibility of moral evil was excluded would be other than a moral order. It is idle, then, wistfully to contemplate the happiness which the world might have known had its creator made us capable only of what is right; to profess, like Huxley, our readiness to close with an offer to remove our capacity to do wrong and cause misery; or to indulge the wish that we had been made good at the expense of freedom. There is no moral goodness in a clock, however perfectly it may keep time. Freedom to do good alone, except after suppression of lower motives by moral conflict, is not freedom. Such regrets as these, to which the ablest of men have occasionally allowed themselves to give expression, do but shew how hard it is to avoid playing fast and loose with plain words when we would apply logic to a question which excites emotion.

The best world, then, must include free agents, creatures that are in turn 'creators' in the sense that their 'utterances' are not God's positings but their own. And freewill introduces contingencies, new causal series, and new possibilities. God stands "a hand-breadth off" to give His creatures room to act and grow: and here another limitation is involved—the self-limitation of love. The Actual world, including human society and human achievements, is due to man as well as to God. We are fellow-workers together with God in the actualisation of a moral order: otherwise the world were not a moral order at all. For the possibility of moral evil entering into this moral order, God, who foreknew it, is responsible: He permits, so to say, the evil in order that there may be the good. But for the actual emergence of man's moral evil we cannot say that He is responsible: our sin, when 'sin' is strictly and correctly defined, is not God's act but the product of our volition, or devolved freedom. Conceivably moral evil *might* not have emerged, though the basic motivations to it, themselves morally neutral or non-moral, are inevitable consequences of the evolutionary process through which phenomenal man came to be. This vindication of the goodness of God is indeed sometimes alleged to be worthless, on the ground that in creating human wills God created all their volitional issues. But this objection involves the crude notion that a will is a concrete thing, like a machine, instead of a name for an activity, or a trend of activity, of a substantial subject which has nothing in common with a machine. Although, according to theism, God assigned to each soul its specific nature or individuality, determinative of its original responses (when it should become embodied) to primary presentations, and prescribed the scope of certain of its capacities and faculties, this was not to foreordain, as a chain of quasi-mechanical effects, all its future actions, and so to be responsible for its misdeeds. Freewill consists in subjective activities of a plastic person, in directivity of assigned capacities, etc., in choice and trans- valuation, in selective distribution of attention such as determines the strengths of motives, and so on: doings which are not quasi- mechanical issues of a preformed 'will', on the one hand, nor creative acts of God, on the other hand. Whatever be the begin- nings of a man's natural history, his moral history begins with himself. And it begins not in the affective response evoked willy- nilly in a subject of determinate nature, but in the governable responses which a more or less rational being makes to more or less rationally synthesised value-complexes.

Such freewill is the human being's burden at the same time that it is a condition of "the glorious liberty of the children of God". And the demand that it should be the one of these things, and not the other, is but the child's cry for the impossible or self-contra- dictory. Morality, in an evolved creature such as man, involves the possibility of moral evil, and entails conflict and warfare. The objection raised against theism on the score of the prevalence of moral evil is that there is too much of contingency in the world. It will presently appear that the objection raised on the score of the prevalence of physical evil is that there is too much of rigid regularity. As they stand, these objections cancel one another; and the theist's reply to them is that neither the contingency in the human realm nor the uniformity in the physical realm is a superfluity, but both are essential conditions of moral life. Con- ceivably Nature's regularity and man's waywardness might be tempered by divine intervention; and it is sometimes urged that such intervention ought to be forthcoming if God be both bene- volent and omnipotent. Moral evil alone being for the present under consideration, it suffices here to repeat that though safe- guards which would make us immune from temptation might secure Objective rightness or correctness in conduct, such right- doing would possess no moral worth. They would not secure the morality which, in the last resort, is love—the only real fulfilling of the law—and would not conduce to moral character. Character is made, not born nor given ready-made. The developement of morality is naturally not continuous or uninterruptedly progressive; but to coerce it to be so would be to destroy its morality. Sup- pression of freedom might reduce human suffering, but it would mean surrender of the ideal which the world embodies; and the omnipotence invoked would be inconsistency or indeterminateness such as the idea of God excludes. A world "in leading-strings" may realise *an* ideal, but can have no ideal that is its own or is moral. To preclude moral evil would be to preclude moral goodness, to do evil, to prefer a worse to a better world.

Thus the difficulties raised by the existence of sin are of an insuperable kind only on one or both of the suppositions, (1) that to God there must be no difference between the possible and the impossible, and (2) that the best possible world must be the happiest world and not a moral order. But theism repudiates omnipotence, in this sense, in its characterisation of the Deity; and it asserts that the instrumentality of the world to the production of a moral order is an expression or revelation of the nature of God, the empirically suggested world-ground. And if the moral ideal be the best or the highest that a world conceivably can fulfil, the process by which alone it is attainable is also good, despite the evil incidental to it. Theism *requires* that the world be an imperfect or mixed world, in that it takes the purpose of the world to consist in the realisation of the highest values by finite and developing creatures, with which an omnipotent establishment of non-moral or static perfection would have nothing in common.

If we suppose the ethical status of man to be less than the whole of the divine purpose, and but a stage to something higher but transcending our power to conceive, the further elements in the world-purpose may condition the evils with which we men are confronted, in respects that are beyond our ken. But, however this may be—and it is practically useless, if theoretically wholesome, to invoke the limitations of our knowledge and the inscrutability of the divine purpose in its fulness—theism is not unable to find a place and a meaning for moral evil in the world of an all-good God, in so far as the world is knowable and its purpose can reasonably be assigned.

Thus far God's purpose has alone been contemplated. And the theodicy which has as yet been constructed in part would not be satisfactory unless man, in struggling through many sins and miseries, could account himself to be striving for his own ideal, as well as fulfilling a divine end. This, however, mankind acknowledges through those who represent it at its best. Indictments of

God based on the facts of human sin and suffering seldom imply a denial of the claim of moral values to be the highest in human judgement. We deem the prize worth the cost, and life without moral strife and attainment to be not worth while. If there is no "peace in ever climbing up the climbing wave", there is zest in warring with evil, and the supreme joys of life are found in love such as is not mere passion. Confronted with the choice between the happy and innocent life of the brute, without thought before and after and pining for what is not, on the one hand, and the life of moral endeavour and spiritual progress, on the other hand, human beings would be practically unanimous in deciding that it is better to have risen above the non-moral level and to have tasted of the tree of knowledge:

> What were life
> Did soul stand still therein, forgo her strife
> Through the ambiguous Present to the goal
> Of some all-reconciling Future?

If the best things we can conceive are bound up with moral character, or rather with personality which includes much more than morality in the barer sense of the word, the best possible world we can conceive is a world which affords opportunity for their attainment. The worser man generally recognises the supremacy of goodness, while the morally advancing man, from the standpoint he has gained, condemns any other sort of life than that of moral growth as incapable of satisfying his soul's needs, and as unworthy of him as he now is. Had mankind never appeared, had Nature stopped short of her crowning in a rational and moral species, the world's falling short of being a moral order would have remained both unregretted and unapproved. The moral race which has emerged, though born to suffer through its freedom, nevertheless rejoices in living, approves its creator's ideal, accepts the chance of the prize of learning love: at least so long as it can believe the cost to be inevitable and the possibility of moral evil to be not superfluous.

To these qualifying conditions, which have been found to be satisfied, another will be added by those who would regard the divine purpose as finding fulfilment, not in the world-process, but in the far off consummation toward which they believe all creation

THE PROBLEM OF EVIL

moves. Reasons have been given for rejecting the notion that evil is absolutely and exclusively evil, ministering to nothing but further evil, never subservient or instrumental to good, and not necessarily or contingently incidental to the actualisation of moral good. But some will also require theodicy to supply reasons for believing that moral evil is not ultimately insuperable, that it will eventually give place to the good, or at least that it is not destined to become supreme over the good so that the world, though a moral order in one sense, would mock our highest moral aspirations. When self-limitation is ascribed to God in place of that omnipotence which is but inconsistency or indeterminateness, such possibilities as these, it is urged, present themselves to be reckoned with. They therefore need to be considered.

Looked at in the abstract, freedom in antithesis to external coercion, and contingency in antithesis to external necessitation, imply the possibility that universal goodness will not be finally realised, and even that moral evil may ever assert and reassert itself until it culminates in moral anarchy. But bare possibilities, like sheer impossibilities, need not be taken too seriously. Probabilities reasonably grounded on experience are another matter; and it is a question whether the theist may not claim that, in so far as the defeat of the divine purpose by man's delegated freedom is concerned, probability favours the view which theism would prefer. Moral advance, in spite of relapses, has undoubtedly marked mankind's history, on the whole, hitherto; and though it cannot be argued from that fact that progress will continue throughout future ages, neither are we at liberty to regard humanity's past progress as a mere accident, or as a state of things which is likely to be permanently reversed. We may reject the view that the contingencies of history are somehow ruled by a dialectic process of which the world-process is a manifestation; we may renounce the Victorian notion of progress as intrinsic and necessarily involved in the world as a whole including man, and regard such optimism as the outcome of a false analogy between spiritual and physical evolution, ignoring human freedom and over-emphasising the influence of environment; we may refuse to appeal to God's supposed power to subdue all things, including freewill, to Himself, so as to conserve the good and exterminate the morally evil; we may deem an inductive inference from the fragment of history up to date to the far future to be absurd; and we may reasonably assume that, in so far as this world is concerned, and while human nature remains essentially what it now is, motivation to evil will never be lacking and sinlessness may never be universal: yet there is good reason to disbelieve in the possibility of evil becoming supreme over good in the world. Man is not merely an organism, and moral evolution is by no means wholly determined by natural heredity and environment. Moreover the environment, in the present case, is partly moral, as is also adaptation to it. What is called social heredity is an important factor in moral evolution. And when we contemplate this latter determinant we find that there is something in goodness which promotes its own conservation, and something in evil that promises disruption—if not self-extinction, at least impotence to become supreme. And this is so, contingency and freewill notwithstanding. The wicked are like the troubled sea which cannot rest: the double-minded man is unstable in all his ways. Accordingly, the encroachments of moral evil upon the established good do not become consolidated. Apparent gains are apt to prove vanity, even loss. And it is plain that no universal conspiracy in evil is possible, such as would produce a hell on earth. If that be what is meant by defeat of God's purpose through human freedom, it seems to be precluded by the intrinsic nature of both human goodness and human badness. Evil desires and evil purposes conflict with one another, so that evil as well as goodness resists and thwarts conspiration in evil. On the other hand, conquests in moral goodness and truth, despite their temporary obscuration, when once made are made for ever. The world always has knowledge that it is the better for them. There is a unity of aim, a co-operation in purpose, a solidarity of interest, a growing consensus, amongst men of goodwill. The moral law, in spite of its continual violation, survives and increases its dominion: the good is self-conservative.

Again, moral evil does not come out of moral goodness, but good does come out of evil and error. Error exposes itself, to the further elucidation and definition of the truth: evil, in its very acquisition, reveals itself to be the lesser good, and learns by bitter experience that it is evil. Nor does each new generation, or each fresh individual, advance *wholly* by first-hand experience, though experimenting for self is a right that never will be renounced, in whatever disasters it may issue. For in human society the social inheritance, or stored experience, counts for much. The higher the moral tone of the many, the more difficult to realise and to entertain become the evil inclinations of the few.

For these reasons, then, it is no flimsy and sentimental optimism, but a reasoned and reasonable expectation, that, as history establishes the fact of moral progress up to date, that progress is not an accident, but will maintain itself. In future ages it may proceed with accelerated speed: for the gains of the good over the evil would seem to be cumulative, although evil may ever take new forms. The tendencies inherent in goodness and badness, as such, preclude the possibility that the purpose of a self-limited God, supposing it to include the final victory of goodness over evil, should be defeated by the freedom of His creatures. There is no more reason to believe that moral evil is destined to become supreme than to believe that its possibility, or even its actuality, is incompatible with a moral order such as the 'best possible' world must be.

It is another question whether moral evil is destined, here or hereafter, to become extinct through the response of freewill to fuller light: conceivably, evil may continue everlastingly while unable to become universal and supreme. But this question is not vital for the theodicy of theism such as confesses to limitations besetting its knowledge or probable belief. If natural theology is able to supply reasons for belief in a future life, it is utterly unable to imagine the conditions of such a life or of knowledge accessible to souls that are disembodied or embodied otherwise than they are in this life. It is impossible to foreknow individually, or non-statistically, the issues of the freewill of moral agents in any imaginable circumstances. And theism, while able to adduce reasonable grounds for believing the cosmic process and human history to reveal the purpose of establishing a moral order, in the sense of a theatre for the life of persons possessed of freedom and the moral status, cannot supply similar reasonable grounds for the conjecture that cosmic and human history are but a means, or a stage, towards a future and final consummation in which nothing evil will remain. This is not a necessary corollary of the doctrine that God is a lover of free persons. It is a belief motivated by religious yearning for the fleeing away of all sorrow and sighing, and by the ancient predilection for the static and perfected, or for the conception of God as, figuratively or literally, all in all. Natural theology, however, cannot make use of either cravings or pre-dilections, and possesses no data for the construction of an eschatology. Theism is not pledged to the doctrine of universal hope, or of the perfecting of every soul, nor to that of the anni-hilation of the hardened unrighteous, if any such there will be. The possibility of endless warfare against spiritual wickedness in the world to come presents no greater difficulty to theism than does the forthcomingness of moral evil in this present world.

Indeed some theists have gone to the other extreme and have argued that the divine love must ever involve sacrifice and victory, and that the presence of evil is necessary for the continued exercise of the highest love. Just as God is not God without His world, so, it is said, divine love is not divine love without sinning recipients for Him to seek and to save. According to this view there is no rest remaining for all the people of God, and no tranquil blessedness for God Himself: evil will for ever be in process of being overcome. It is implied that a statically perfect world would be less noble than process towards it, or that progress is not necessarily approach to a realisable goal. Just as we may find satisfaction in conflict and tension, so God may ever rejoice in His own sorrows and find peace in the victory over evil: "the eternal world contains Gethsemane". So some have speculated: but in recoil from the old ideas of impassibility and static perfection they have retained somewhat of the rigidity which belonged to ancient thought. It is not necessary to believe that, because the highest kind of good that we know is only realisable in our world through the possibility, if not the actuality, of evil, therefore the continuous presence of evil is essential to the conservation of goodness. Human experience suggests the contrary. There is such a thing as has been called 'the saint's rest'—the relative freedom from moral conflict and from temptation, earned by self-discipline and struggle; and it may have a joy of its own and an interest which does not need the zest of militancy for its maintenance. All morality is not the same morality: there is one goodness of the happy warrior, and another goodness of him who has fought the good fight. And all these kinds of moral state, or of goodness and blessedness, cannot be fully actualised potentialities at once, because some are incompatible with others. It is therefore forbidden to us to postulate that the divine love must ever manifest itself in every specific type; and it is unnecessary to suppose that ethical life is precluded to the Supreme Spirit unless there be for Him the possibility of ever sorrowing and striving with sinful souls, or that the existence of evil is an essential condition of the continuing love of God. But, apart from the baselessness of both the kinds of *a priori* speculation that have been considered, the question of the continuance or the self-extinction of moral evil is irrelevant to theodicy.

The problem of evil has thus far been discussed with almost exclusive reference to evil of the moral kind. And the solution that has been presented consists in shewing the tenability of the belief that in our developing world all things work together, as a whole, for the highest conceivable good. The possibility of moral evil and the actuality of its consequences are inevitable concomitants of the 'best possible' evolutionary world. It is not maintained that everything is good, or that "whatever is, is right", or that partial evil is not evil because it is a condition of universal good. Nor is it implied that every particular evil is directly essential to the emergence of some particular good, or that it has its necessary place, like a dissonance in music, in the harmony of the world-process. When it is asserted that all things work together for good, by 'all things' is not meant each and every single thing, but the sum of things regarded as one whole or complex, the universe as a coherent order.

It is by adhering to this general view that the theist can best face the problem presented by the existence of that form of evil for which human freedom is not necessarily, and generally not at all, responsible: the physical evil, or the pain and suffering occasioned by the course of Nature in sentient beings. Indeed any other position than that which has just been summarised seems obviously inadequate as a basis for the explanation of the forthcomingness of physical ills. In order to reconcile the suffering inflicted by the material world upon mankind and other sentient creatures with the goodness and power of the Creator it is both superfluous and insufficient to seek to shew that in every particular case pain is essential to some special end, or that in each single instance suffering may fulfil some particular providential purpose. To attempt a theodicy on these lines is as hopeless as it would be to-day to develope a teleological argument from particular instances of adaptedness, after the manner of Paley. But, as there is a wider teleology than Paley's so is there a wider theodicy than that which consists in pleading that human and animal pain are sometimes prophylactic—a warning against danger, or that human suffering is sometimes punitive or purgatorial, and thus subservient to benign ends. These assertions are undoubtedly true, and there is no need to belittle their import. But by themselves they will not carry us far towards a theodicy. They but touch the fringe of the problem: or, to change the metaphor, they do not go to the root of the matter. It is useless, again, to minimise the pain of the sentient world, or even to reduce our possibly extravagant and unscientific estimate of its intensity, except for the purpose of arguing that, in spite of pain, animal life is probably happy on the whole: otherwise a single pang of useless or super-fluous pain is enough to raise our problem. It involves faulty psychology to assert that pain is the necessary background to pleasure; for a lesser pleasure would seem to yield a sufficient contrast to render the enjoyment of intenser pleasure possible. And if pain be sometimes stimulating, educational, preventitive, or remedial, as well as sometimes stunting, crushing, and provo-cative of moral evil, this fact is only significant for an estimation of the worth-whileness of sentient life. The knife may be necessary to cure the disease, but why the necessity of the disease? The escape from mortal danger may require the painful warning, but why the mortal danger? Or, speaking generally, what are we to make of the remoter evil which renders the nearer evil necessary or salutary? The real problem obviously lies further back than these particular and partial solutions reach. It must be shewn that pain is either a necessary by-product of an order of things requisite for the emergence of the higher goods, or an essential instrument to organic evolution, or both. Short of this, we cannot refute the charge that the world is a clumsy arrangement or an imperfectly adjusted mechanism.

It can be argued, however, that the former of the foregoing alternatives is applicable in the case of human suffering, while the latter of them can be invoked to meet especially the case of animal pain. The suffering of the lower animals is not merely an accidental superfluity emerging out of the evolutionary process, but is essentially instrumental to organic progress. It renders unnecessary a large amount of inheritance of specialised structure and function, and so prevents the suppression of plasticity; and, as the 'sensitive edge' turned towards danger, or as prophylactic, it is of value for organic progressiveness. Although evil, it is also good for something. Much of human suffering, and many of the outrages of this present life upon our rational prudences and our most sacred affections, on the other hand, seem to be good for nothing, or to be non-essential for the realisation of goodness. If a man already has it in him to meet pain with fortitude and patience, he is not necessarily one whit the better man after actually enduring excruciating tortures; and if an all-powerful being 'appointed' him such tortures, merely in order that his fortitude might pass from potentiality to actuality, such a being would be but a superbrute. However, it can be argued that the forthcomingness of our suffering is inevitably incidental to a moral order in a developing world. It issues ultimately out of what is inappropriately called metaphysical evil, or is a necessary outcome of a determinate cosmos of the particular kind that can sustain rational and moral life. The problem which it raises will therefore be solved if it can be maintained that no suffering such as we experience is superfluous to the cosmos as a coherent system and a moral order, however excessive pain often may be as a means to the accomplishment of specific ends such as are attainable by discipline and chastening.

It cannot be too strongly insisted that a world which is to be a moral order must be a physical order characterised by law or regularity. The routine of Nature may be differently described by the spiritualist, the dualist, etc.; but the diversity of these ultimate explanations of law does not affect the present problem. The theist is only concerned to invoke the fact that law-abidingness, on the scale which science is able to assert its subsistence in Nature as already *naturata*, is an essential condition of the world being a theatre of moral life. Without such regularity in physical phenomena there could be no probability to guide us: no prediction, no prudence, no accumulation of ordered experience, no pursuit of premeditated ends, no formation of habit, no possibility of character or of culture. Our intellectual faculties could not have developed. And, had they been innate, they would have wasted themselves, as Comte observed, in wild extravagances and sunk rapidly into incurable sloth; while our nobler feelings would have been unable to prevent the ascendancy of the lower instincts, and our active powers would have abandoned themselves to purposeless agitation. All this is obvious; but it has often been ignored in discussion of the problem of physical evil. Nevertheless, Nature's regularity is the key to this problem. Once let it be admitted that, in order to be a theatre for moral life, the world must be largely characterised by uniformity or constancy, and most significant consequences will be seen to follow. It becomes idle to complain, as some writers have done, that the orderliness of the world is too dear at the cost of the suffering and hardship which it entails, and might more or less be dispensed with for the benefit of the sentient and rational beings which people the world. As Hume admitted, if the "conducting of the world by general laws" were superseded by particular volitions, no man could employ his reason in the conduct of his life. And without rationality, morality is impossible: so, if the moral status of man be the goal of the evolutionary process, the reign of law is a *sine quâ non*. It is a condition of the forthcomingness of the highest good, in spite of the fact that it is not an unmixed good but a source of suffering. We cannot have the advantages of a determinate order of things without its logically or its causally necessary disadvantages. Nor can we be evaluating subjects without capacity to feel. The disadvantages, viz. particular ills, need not be regarded, however, as directly willed by God as ends in themselves or as particular means, among other equally possible but painless means, to particular ends. To make use of an ancient distinction, we may say that God wills them consequently, not antecedently. That is to say, they are not desired as such, or in themselves, but are only willed because the moral order, which is willed absolutely or antecedently by God, cannot be had without them. Now to will a moral order is to will the best possible world; and it also involves adoption of what we necessarily, if somewhat anthropomorphically, must call a determinate world-plan. Such a determinate method of procedure to realise a definite end in an evolutionary world, however, rules out once and for all any other possible goals and methods. As

Dr Martineau has put it, the cosmical equation being defined, only such results as are compatible with the values of its roots can be worked out, and these must be worked out. All determination is negation. If two consequences follow from a system of propositions, or two physical properties are involved in a configuration of particles, we cannot have the one without the other, though the one may be pleasing or beneficial to man and the other may be painful, or in its immediate effects hurtful. And such a result by no means implies lack of benevolence or of power on the part of the Creator, so long as power does not include inconsistency or indeterminateness. It simply bespeaks the inexorableness of logic, the compatibility of things, and the self-consistency of the Supreme Being. That painful events occur in the causal chain is a fact; but, that there could be a determinate evolutionary world of unalloyed comfort, yet adapted by its law-abidingness to the developement of rationality and morality, is a proposition the burden of proving which must be allotted to the opponent of theism. One can only add that, in so far as experience in this world enables us to judge, such proof seems impossible. To illustrate what is here meant: if water is to have the various properties in virtue of which it plays its beneficial part in the economy of the physical world and the life of mankind, it cannot at the same time lack its obnoxious capacity to drown us. The specific gravity of water is as much a necessary outcome of its ultimate constitution as its freezing-point, or its thirst-quenching and cleansing functions. There cannot be assigned to any substance an arbitrarily selected group of qualities, from which all that ever may prove unfortunate to any sentient organism can be eliminated, especially if one organism's meat is to be another's poison, and yet the world, of which that substance forms a part, be a calculable cosmos. Mere determinateness and fixity of nature involve such and such concatenations of qualities, and rule out others. Thus physical ills follow with the same necessity as physical goods from the determinate 'world-plan' which secures that the world be a suitable stage for intelligent and ethical life.

And if this be so, the disadvantages which accrue from the determinateness and regularity of the physical world cannot be regarded either as absolute or as superfluous evils. They are not absolute evils because they are parts of an order which subserves

the highest good in providing opportunity for moral developement. And they are not superfluous ills because they are the
necessary outcome of that order. They are collateral effects of
what, in itself or as a whole, is good because instrumental to the
highest good. They are not good, when good is hedonically
defined; but they are good for good, when good is otherwise
defined, rather than good for nothing.

As in the case of moral evil, so also in the case of physical evil,
appeal has sometimes been made from necessary linkages and
conditionings to a supposed possibility of their being over-ridden
by divine omnipotence. And as it was found absurd to suppose
that God could make developing beings at the same time morally
free and temptationless, so it involves absurdity to suppose that the
world could be a moral order without being a physical cosmos.
To save mankind from the painful consequences which flow from
a determinate world-order, such as the earthquake and the
pestilence, would involve renunciation of a world-order, and therefore of a moral order, and the substitution of a chaos of incalculable
miracle. Doubtless some directive agency, or the introduction of
new streams of causation into the course of Nature, is conceivable
without subversion of such regularity as is requisite for human
prudence and without the stultification of our science. But the
general suspension of painful events, requisite on the vast scale
presupposed in the elimination of physical ills, would abolish
order and convert a cosmos into an unintelligible chaos in which
anything might succeed upon anything. We should have to
"renounce reason" if we would thus be "saved from tears", as
Martineau says.

Physical evil, then, must necessarily be. And the goodness of
God is vindicated if there be no reason to believe that the world-
process involves more misery than Nature's uniformity entails.
It is not incumbent on the theist to prove that particular evils are
never greater than we judge to be necessary for the production
of particular salutary effects: that difficult task confronts only the
particular kind of theism which is concerned to dispense with
proximate causes and a more or less autonomous world, and
regards God as the sole and immediate cause of every natural
event, and of every incident in a personal life. According to the
theodicy which has here been sketched, it is not necessary to

suppose that every specific form of suffering that man undergoes
—*e.g.* the agony of tetanus or of cancer—is antecedently willed
by God as a means to some particular end. It can be admitted that
excruciating pains are more severe than they need be for evoking
virtues such as patience and fortitude, and that to assign them to
God's antecedent will would be to attribute devilishness to the
Deity. Moreover, the fact that some human beings are born as
abortions, as imbecile or insane, seems to be inexplicable on the
view that every form of suffering is a particular providence, or an
antecedently willed dispensation for educating and spiritually
perfecting the person on whom the affliction falls; while to suppose
that suffering is inflicted on one person for the spiritual edification
of another is again to conceive of God as immoral. But the hardest
fact of all for human equanimity, in presence of physical and
mental evil, is that the apportionment of suffering among individuals is entirely irreconcilable by us with any divine plan of
adjustment of particular afflictions to the particular needs, circumstances, and stages of moral developement, of individual
sufferers. Even more distressing to human thought than the
goading intensity of some kinds of pain is the seemingly chaotic
distribution of human ills. If we could trace the utility of particular sufferings with their varying degrees of endurableness, or
discern any adaptation of pain to the person's sensibility, moral
state, and need of awakening or chastening, then philosophy
might be able to agree with the simple-minded piety which assigns
a special purpose to every instance of suffering, and finds therein
the visitation or appointment of an all-wise and all-good God. But
the wind is not tempered to the shorn lamb; the fieriest trials often
overtake those who least need torments to inspire fear, to evoke
repentance, or to perfect patience, and also those who, through
no fault of their own, lack the mature religious faith and moral
experience by which alone they could understand how affliction
may be endured for their souls' good. "All things come alike to
all: there is one event to the righteous and to the wicked"—to
those who may be enabled, and to those who are unable, to profit
by severe trial.

Disastrous as these facts are to the extremer forms of the
doctrine of divine immanence in Nature, they are compatible with
theism such as allows to the created world somewhat of delegated

autonomy. According to the wider theodicy which has here been presented, the human afflictions arising from our relations with the physical world are not willed as such by God at all, or for any purpose. They are rather inevitable, if incidental, accompaniments or by-products of the world-order which, as a whole, and by means of its uniformity, is a pre-requisite of the actualisation of the highest good that we can conceive a world as embodying. The world is none the less God's world for its callousness to man; but its autonomy, not the particular incidence of each single ill, is what the religious should attribute to His "appointment".

Further, man himself does not deem his suffering to be an excessive price to pay for the dignity of his ethical status, once he recognises physical evil to be inevitable in a moral world. He is then not compelled to see in his suffering self a mere means either to the perfecting of the race, or to the realisation of a divine purpose, or to the manifestation of the 'glory' of God. And this is an important consideration for any theodicy. For man is an end for himself, whatever else he may be. *My* ills can only be justified to *me* if the remoter advantage of there being ills at all be *mine*: not humanity's, or even God's, alone. But in that the remoter advantage is the enjoyment of rational and ethical dignity, the individual man can acquiesce in God's purpose for the world: God's ideal may be his also. It is the assurance that God is fulfilling us individually as well as Himself, and fulfilling us for ourselves as well as for Himself, that makes human life in this bitter-sweet world endurable by the sensitively and delicately minded, the tender-hearted, believer. It is because a being of the earth, yet so God-like as man, could not be moulded into the image of God *save from within himself*, as a person or a free agent, that man can account the payment of the sometimes exorbitant price of the chance of learning love inevitable.

If the doctrine of a future life be a corollary of theism, or an implication of the moral purposiveness and meaning which may reasonably be read into the cosmos, it can be invoked to throw further light on the problem of evil. The balance of felicity and unhappiness in an individual life cannot be struck so long as we confine our thought to experience of the present world alone, if we have reason to believe that the earth is "no goal, but starting-point for man". We may then venture to add to our knowledge the faith that "the sufferings of this present time are not worthy to be compared with the glory that shall be revealed". Pain is indeed none the less pain, nor any kind of evil the less evil, for that it shall be done away, or compensated, or because it is a necessary means or by-product. But its hideousness is somewhat transfigured if, besides being involved in the 'best possible' world, it can be seen to have been "but for a moment" in the time-span of just men made perfect. It is not the reality of evil that is here under consideration, but simply the worth-whileness of this life in which evil has a temporary and necessary place. That should not be estimated by looking only at what may now be seen; but for the idea of compensation hereafter theodicy and theistic religion have no further use. They do not ask us to tolerate the evils of the present world, and to abstain from blaming the Creator for them, because of a compensation stored up for us in another world: they rather insist that in this life, with all its evils, we may already discern the world-purpose of God to be a reign of love.

This life acquires, indeed, a new aspect if death be but translation to another mansion in the Father's house, and exchange of one kind of service for another. And it is a question whether theism, in asserting the world-ground to be a Spirit and the Father of spirits, and in ascribing to the world the rôle of ministering to rational and moral life, can stop short of adding the doctrine of a future life to its fundamental articles of belief, without stultifying its previously reached interpretation of the world and man. For it would not be a perfectly reasonable world which produced free beings, with Godward aspirations and illimitable ideals, only to cut them off in everlasting death, mocking their hopes and frustrating their purposes. Such spirits, even with their moral status, would after all be pawns, not children of God. Certainly a God who can be worshipped by moral beings must be a respecter of the persons whom He has moulded into His own image. Hence theists generally regard the Supreme Being as a God, not of the dead, but of the living.[1]

There is one particular problem within the larger problem of evil, to which the doctrine of a future life has a special relevance:

[1] A discussion of the grounds of the belief in immortality will be found in the Appendix, Note E.

a problem of the kind indicated by the remark, made at the beginning of this chapter, that explanatory theories are apt to bear within themselves, or to set up, fresh difficulties. If the theistic gospel be the only sufficient interpretation of the intelligibility, orderliness, and progressiveness of the world as a whole, it is not unique in respect of explaining without creating new *explicanda*. It does not forthwith brightly illumine every dark recess of the mind of him who would use it as a lantern to his feet. Its very acceptance creates at least one perplexity, not forthcoming for those who reject the theistic interpretation, and necessitates a special theodicy to resolve that perplexity. For it is a difficulty besetting theistic faith that faith itself can be tried; and perhaps many will find here the sharpest edge of the wider problem of evil. God may seem to them to allow so little insight into His dealings with persons, and so little of intelligent—as distinct from purely moral—co-operation with Him in working out their individual destiny, that they scarcely dare call Him 'Father', though ethical theism requires that they should do so. Their cosmic philosophy appears to collapse in that some of its deduced consequences do not seem to be verified in experience. Moreover, an unwavering faith, a steady and unfaltering sense of the reality of things unseen, is a condition of the peace which alone enables the believer to serve God with a quiet mind, and also of the spiritual zeal and effectiveness of his life. It is the feeling with which the believer regards that life, his alone and his for once alone, that should most strongly evidence his kinship with the Deity; and he should be able to deem the efficacy of his little life-work not indifferent to his God. Should God then try his very faith, and so render all that he might build with it precarious? Should the very spring of religious love, the source of the unique beauty and sublimity of character moulded by pure religious sentiment, be capable of being lost, though a man may yearn to retain possession of it above all things else? Duty, service, and blamelessness of life are not always easy even when faith is unclouded; but that the one bond which links the soul with God should be imperilled by the probationary influences of this life seems at first sight hard to reconcile with the relations which theism asserts to subsist between the soul, the world, and God.

We can see that it is of the very nature of faith to provide from within itself for its own trial; for faith is not sight, and whatever truth may be apprehended by faith must be "deadened of its absolute blaze". We can also see that a trial of faith is necessitated from without, in that advance in knowledge and in ethical appreciation render beliefs, which in earlier times were (ψ) reasonable, no longer tenable. So the difficulty before us narrows down to the old and recurrent question, why, if there is a God whose world-purpose is communion between finite spirits and Himself, is faith rather than knowledge vouchsafed to us, or why is not revelation readable by him who runs, with infallible certainty and (ps) immediacy?

The conditions of revelation and its apprehension will be discussed later; but, in so far as they are involved in the outgrowth from the problem of evil that is now before us, there are two considerations of which theism may avail itself in meeting its difficulty.

Firstly, it may be suggested that if our wills be ours to make harmonious with the divine will, and the quest for the highest is to be veritably *our* quest and adventure, God must not be too certainly knowable to us, as well as not too active upon us. Otherwise, just as excess of motivation would defeat ethical freedom, so over-abundance of light would preclude that 'groping after God' which is the obverse of revelation to a developing and free agent such as man. The formation (as contrasted with the fruition) of character, and the winning of truth by truth-seeking (as contrasted with the passive imbibing of ready-made infallibilities), require an invisible rather than a visible or demonstrable God, a partial revelation rather than a beatific vision, a divine co-operation rather than a divine overwhelming, the possibility of failure to find rather than the security of essentially non-moral and non-personal success. There must "needs provision be For keeping the soul's prowess possible". In other words, the confinement of cognition, as to God and His dealings, or as to our whence and whither, to the form of faith, which is the free soul's venture and cannot be, as ecclesiastical theology has generally taught, an arbitrary gift of God; the consequent possibility of reasonable doubt; the necessity of each soul to fight its way to reasonable belief or conviction compatible with knowledge: these appear to be implications of the purpose of God, and conditions of religious life for creaturely and developing moral personalities. It is from religion, rather than from cosmic philosophy, that we must seek any more light on this matter. And perhaps it begins to appear that these are not discontinuous.

Further, the difficulty presented to theistic faith by the fact that faith is dangerously liable to trial, so long as it does not degenerate into supine credulity, is removed if the belief that this present life is not the whole of life be not faithlessly treated. The momentousness of failure here to achieve our life's ends then becomes relatively insignificant: especially if God cares more for what we are than for what we do. There is such a thing as success in failure. We can attach exaggerated importance, in one sense, to the actual filling of this life with finished products, just as too much importance used to be attached to the particular moral state and the particular contents of an individual's faith at the hour of his passing. It is in harmony with the world-view presented by theism to regard growth towards perfection, whether of character or of faith, rather than attainment of perfectness, as the divine purpose for our earthly life. All aspiration that is here unrealised, all tasks remaining unaccomplished when death cuts us off, all baffled search, honest doubt, and faith that has been shipwrecked while men of goodwill and pure heart have worked in half-light or shadow, may be fulfilled in the life beyond. Bereavement of faith, therefore, like bereavement of friends, is not endless separation, but rather a phase in a process which knows vicissitudes.

Thus the special problem of the temptability of personal faith is to be met in the same way as the larger problem of evil in general. It remains no less a trial to faith that faith necessarily must be tried, just as evil is none the less evil for that it is necessary or that it shall be done away. But if this life is not *all*-important, and if the world-purpose is not consistently ethical unless there is a hereafter for moral persons, the question why faith that is vital for the fullest life is not immune from trial no longer constitutes a formidable difficulty. The facts which suggest a theistic interpretation of the world also suggest that in this life our seeking rather than our finding is God's purpose for us: question and counter-question, intercourse and dialogue, rather than full light and certain knowledge. The risks attending faith are not fatal, while they are conditions of the ethico-religious status in the life that now is.

CHAPTER VIII

Divine Immanence and Revelation

The relation of God to the world has been but incidentally and fragmentarily discussed in the preceding chapters, save in so far as it consists in creation. Consequently it has not as yet been necessary to indicate in what respects the theism which has been reached by a teleological argument resembles and differs from the theory as to the relation of God to His world which philosophers technically call deism. This latter theory dispenses not only with occasional interventions of the Deity in the cosmic course, but also with the notion of divine immanence in any form. It is a view that has seldom, if ever, been explicitly held by natural theologians: it was even repudiated as equivalent to atheism by the more representative of the writers known as the deists of the seventeenth and eighteenth centuries. But, whether or not it has found actual supporters, this more rigorous deism is of theoretical interest in that it represents one of the extreme limits—pantheism or absolute monism being the other—between which theism holds a middle place and, by distinguishing itself from each of which, theism finds its own definition.

It has already been observed that the *modus operandi* of divine creativity is inevitably unintelligible, or inexplicable in terms of our empirically derived concepts such as time and causation, while, unless this creativity be fact, the apparent conspiration of the many mutually interacting world-elements, or of an ontological plurality, to constitute one intelligible and value-realising whole, or a cosmological unity, is left altogether inexplicable. The world, it has been argued, is God's utterance. Its nature depends on His nature and will, not His nature on that of a self-subsistent universe. And this is what is chiefly to be meant by the phrase 'divine transcendence', which also implies that the world, as posited, created, or planted out, is other than God, though God is ever its 'ground', in a sense previously defined. Further, all that has been said before implies that the world, as thus determined, exists not merely in the sense in which ideas exist for a mind, but as Actual. Phenomenal interactions involve ontal determinants and *rapport*,

H

else there is no use in speaking either of phenomena or of things *per se*. This delegated activity, the ontal counterpart to proximate causation, may be of varying degrees of spontaneity culminating in human freewill; but all along the line it bespeaks a relative independence of God, a devolved autonomy, an origination of causal nexus other than, though derived from, the direct creativity of the Deity, in whatever other respects and senses the world and its course may be dependent on God, either as transcendent or as immanent.

These assertions are not made as so many arbitrary assumptions desirable for the elaboration of a specific variety of theism. They will indeed be recognised as an outcome of the inquiry pursued in vol. I, which is a quest for a philosophy dictated by experience and facts, with indifference to theological issues. They are also implied in the theism which has been reached and expounded in preceding chapters of the present volume. In view of the foregoing discussion of the world's evil and the problems thereby raised, the tenability of ethical theism will be seen to be dependent on the truth of these statements; for, if there be no real causation other than God's, every evil must be His direct act. Hence for every reason they must be determinative, in so far as they have relevance, of such further doctrine concerning the relation of God to the world and man as can reasonably be superimposed on what has been set forth before.

The question thus arises whether there is any such relation of God to the world as may be called divine immanence in a world which must be regarded as *natura naturans* (as distinct from *Deus naturans*) as well as a relatively settled order describable as *natura naturata*. This will involve inquiry as to what specific relations immanence may then embrace.

Certain conceptions of immanence that have been current in theology can be at once dismissed. Thus 'immanence' cannot mean identity, such as is indicated by Spinoza's phrase *Deus sive Natura*, or that God is the one underlying substance of which the world and all that is therein are the appearance to us, or that He is the sole cause of all becoming in the world which depends upon Him for its forthcomingness. Such conceptions are rather pantheistic than theistic, and imply a metaphysic other than that which is suggested and controlled by the facts which are the primary data for all philosophising. On the other hand, 'immanence' cannot mean mere inactive ubiquity or omnipresence, such as might be predicated of a passive spectator of the world's course, or of a God whose creative and purposive agency is confined to decreeing the world's primary collocations. This is not disputed; for although theists have often so stated their doctrine of immanence that it is indistinguishable from one or other of the pantheistic conceptions mentioned above, they have unanimously repudiated this latter identification as a denial of immanence. And indeed, the rigorously deistic doctrine of a God withdrawn from the world so as not even to act upon it is inconceivable. In the first place it involves the notion of creation as an event in time, else it becomes atheism. And, further, it is inconsistent with God's being the ground, and the sole ground, of the world. For the world and its actual ground cannot be conceived as separable, in the sense that the Creator stands wholly apart from what is *ex hypothesi* dependent upon Him and, throughout its evolutionary changes, embodies His unchanging purpose.

Our first approximation to a definite and theistically satisfactory conception of immanence, then, is to have established that immanence must be an active, and not a contemplative, relation of God to the world.[1] The next step is to find more precise ideas, in terms of which to construe this active relation, than the vague and scarcely determinate notion of immanence, which is a spatial and physical metaphor needing translation into non-spatial terms current in scientific philosophy, or than the equally vague synonyms, that God inhabits, pervades, or informs the universe. None of these well-sounding words conveys definite meaning to those who would think things out as clearly as is possible and would drive back the outposts of mystery to its irreducible stronghold, the ultimate.

---

[1] Sometimes the assertion that God is immanent in the world seems to mean simply that the world is God's utterance or self-manifestation, or that He is 'in' it in the sense in which an artist is said to be, or to live, in his painting. But this is true of the artist's relation to his picture though he may never touch or see it again after executing it; and the same would be true of God's relation to the world even if that were conceived in the rigorously deistic sense. Such immanence is identical with transcendence, and involves no further divine action than that which we call creation. In the present context immanence is discussed on the assumption that it is activity other than creation or 'primary collocation', and is to be contrasted with transcendence.

A somewhat less vague substitute for the notion of immanence is that of continuous maintenance, in which the divine indwelling is usually regarded as wholly or partly consisting, and which admits of a little further clarification. One definite form of maintenance is that which S. Augustine imagined and Descartes, with a mathematician's love for discrete instants, formulated in the doctrine of the continuous re-creation of the world at each successive moment. But this fancy is as baseless and as non-explanatory as it is inconsistent with either theism or fact-controlled metaphysics. It implies that there are no souls or substances, no causes but God, no meaning in the world save for its Creator. Dismissing this conception of maintenance on the ground that there are substance-causes, and souls for whom also the world has meaning, we may go on to question whether, if maintenance next be construed merely as keeping created existents in existence, the supposition of such maintenance is necessary. It seems superfluous to suppose that the beings which God creates or plants out, with existence-for-self, needs must be evanescent according to their own natures, as if createdness implied fleetingness, and that they can only be rendered perduring by continuous new outputs of divine creativity. Not this, again, but something other must be meant by maintenance if the conception is to be valuable or indispensable to theism. The conserving activities of the "strength and stay upholding all creation" will need to be conceived as sustaining the order of the world as a whole by *rapport* with, or action upon, its more or less perduring constituent elements: through God's immanence all things *con*sist, and continue to consist as a purpose-realising cosmos instead of disrupting, in virtue of their delegated spontaneity and independence, into a purpose-foiling aggregate. Here, at last, is a conception which theism needs, and one to which the name of 'immanence' can appropriately be given. For theism does attribute to God's creatures delegated spontaneity such as conceivably might develope into erratic tendencies. And it is only with the qualification which this attribution involves that the theist can use such expressions as that in God "we live and move and have our being": to take these words more literally would be to identify the world-ground with the world instead of to insist on the inseparableness and distinctness of God and His world. But if all, or even any, of the world-constituents have this relative independence as sub-stance-causes, their conspiration to produce our cosmos, with its particular trend and purpose, can be the better accounted for if we suppose their possible waywardness to be compensated by a continual directive or creative activity of God, for Whom the world, with all its differentiated detail and its ever new emergent products, is always one whole. When, in an earlier chapter, the empirical approach to theism was made, it may perhaps have seemed to be suggested that the orderedness or increasing purpose-fulfilment of the evolving world could be sufficiently accounted for by the original natures and the resulting interactions of the world-constituents, or if God's activity were confined to creation and collocation; but although an immanent activity of God was not then explicitly invoked it may now be seen to have been implicitly involved. In other words, theism has a use for the conception of divine immanence, if not a need of it, in the precise form in which it has just been defined.[1]

Any further step toward the elucidation of the notion of im-manence in so far as immanence in what, at the phenomenal level, we call the physical or material world is concerned, can only be taken when we make a choice between the two alternative meta-physical theories of matter. (Neutral monism is here ignored, as having no explanatory value.) Immanence will need to be conceived differently, if matter be regarded as inert and disparate from spirit, from the way in which it may be conceived if matter be the appearance of what has some measure of awareness and conation.

It has been observed before that, previously to the establishment of theism, there is no means of crucially deciding between dualism and spiritualistic pluralism; and now it may be added that when we look back upon the world from the theistic point of view which has been reached, relative (as distinct from absolute) dualism scarcely becomes untenable. But it becomes a more obviously dispensable theory. For theism is constrained to regard inert matter, if such a thing there be, as but a medium for the inter-action of spirits, apart from which the immensities of the material

[1] Compensation of tendencies in virtue of which the developing world might cease to be the cosmos described in ch. IV must not be taken to include suppression of 'inerrancies' which constitute physical evils. As argued in ch. VII, divine correction of all the latter inerrancies would involve sacrifice of the uniformity which renders the cosmos a theatre of moral life.

universe are meaningless and valueless. Theism, again, cannot regard this material medium as necessary to God, as if the Creator needed means or stages to His ends; at most it would be needful to created spiritual beings. And it would not be something prior to them, an environment indispensable in itself, which must be got ready by an evolution from the 'primary collocations' for their reception, and to which they have to be fitted. Still less is it thinkable that this lifeless medium is the matrix out of which spirits have emerged—a *generatio aequivoca*. If this medium be regarded as indispensable for the interaction and inter-communication of spiritual beings, two alternative ways of describing its origination are *prima facie* open to theism.

The one of these is to regard the medium as in no degree comparable to the independent 'mechanism' contemplated by deism, but rather as the continuous mediation of the Creator, the outcome of His unceasing creativity within the world of spirits. Theism would then involve occasionalism, or the theory of divine 'assistance'. On this view laws of Nature would be expressions of God's orderly maintaining and compensating acts, not statements as to the settled behaviour of relatively independent or, as it were, partly God-abandoned things. Material Nature would be wholly the product of God's immanent activity, and every event in the course of Nature would be a direct outcome of His antecedent will. God would be 'everywhere' and mechanism, even in the less rigid sense of delegated autonomy and proximate causation, 'nowhere'. The theist who so conceived of immanence might as well then go to the whole length of dispensing with the medium altogether, as did Berkeley, and resolve it into sense-symbolism or mediation: for if the medium were Real it would be inoperative, because inert. Yet, satisfying in some respects as this theory would be to theism, it involves insuperable difficulties. It entirely destroys the theodicy expounded in chap. VII, and indeed removes *all* possibility of coping with the problem of evil. For if every physical happening is directly caused by God and reveals His nature, that nature cannot be benevolent. So long as we regard the ills and indignities which Nature inflicts upon us embodied souls as inevitable consequences of interactions between continuants or substance-causes whose natures were 'originally' posited so as to produce an orderly world and to work together for the realisation of the highest good, their forthcomingness presents no insuperable obstacle to ethical theism: but if such evils be not by-products of proximate causation they would seem to be superfluous and to bespeak malignancy. This disastrous consequence of what may be called the thoroughgoing doctrine of divine immanence in the physical world seems to have been overlooked, or at least not to have been reckoned with, by writers who have favoured it on account of its more attractive aspects. The doctrine is here repudiated, not only as incompatible with ethical theism, but also because it conflicts with the fundamental assumptions on which all scientific induction has been found to be based, and so involves the stultification of human reason. If there is no *Natura, naturata* or *naturans*, with devolved autonomy and relative independence; if the apparent nexus between apparent things is mere appearance, and the only real nexus is that between God's volitional fiats, which to us should be unpredictable if not incomprehensible: then a theology is postulated at the same time that all grounds for reasonably establishing any theology are demolished.

The second alternative open to theism, when it retains a dualistic metaphysic, is to drop the wholesale occasionalism involved in the conception of immanence previously criticised, to adopt so much of deistic tendency as to enable itself to attribute relative independence or free play to the ontal beings of which physical Nature is a phenomenal revelation, and to recognise an order in which causation is not wholly or mainly immediate divine creation. Immanence will then be conceived as divine action upon the world-elements, whether continuous or occasional. It may find expression either in unceasing providential guidance or in the sporadic creative activity which miracle involves when it is conceived as the production of effects such as could not emerge out of the unassisted potencies of the world-elements themselves. Whether such supernatural *miracula*, as distinct from natural *mirabilia*, have ever been forthcoming is a question which does not admit of a certain answer, because our knowledge of the intrinsic potencies of Nature is not exhaustive; consequently alleged miracles can never have the evidential value that theology used to ascribe to them, or be coercive proofs of the exercise of immediate divine activity. But general providential control is an activity which, as we have seen, theism has good reason to ascribe

216 DIVINE IMMANENCE AND REVELATION

to the Deity: partly because separation of the world-ground from the world, which non-intervention would bespeak, is unthinkable; and partly because the emergence of the cosmos, with its marvellously intricate adaptations and continuous stabilisation, is hardly explicable, or is less than a reasonable probability, without it. And the immanence or activity involved in providential control of the already created, however inscrutable be its *modus operandi*, is no more open to objection than is creation. Indeed there is no call to draw a hard distinction between transcendent, or creative, and immanent, activity, other than that between 'original' positing—to speak in terms of temporality—and action upon what has been posited. The possibility of such immanent activity, in so far as the Creator is concerned, goes without saying; and, in so far as Nature is concerned, immanent activity, or action upon the physical world, could only be ruled out as impossible if laws of Nature were a self-subsistent *prius*, which they cannot be, or if Nature were the closed system which we have no reason to assert it to be.

Assuming, then, the abstract possibility of divine intervention in the realm which we may call the natural, or that of proximate causation, and of supernatural or divine guidance thereof, we may further inquire whether such supernatural agency may be conceived or imagined in terms of any analogy with what lies within the sphere of our experience. "It has often been assimilated to what is commonly called human interference with the course of Nature, which is an observable actuality. When, by using a pump, we make water flow upwards, we violate no law of Nature; but, combining forces each of which is purely natural, and which Nature herself does not combine, we produce an effect which Nature herself does not produce. If 'Nature' be defined so as to exclude man, then in such human volitional acts we already see the supernatural. If in 'Nature' we include man, we are still confronted only with the natural; but in divine activity of similar type we should be presented with the supernatural, for it would serve no purpose to include God in Nature or to call any of His acts secondary causes. As in the case of analogous human procedure, there need be no violation or suspension of law, and nothing to put science to confusion, in so far as causation is concerned. Supernatural intervention would be a combining, regulating, or subordinating of natural forces, transcending the capacities or intrinsic potentialities of Nature; but the objectionable terms, 'interference', 'violation', 'suspension', etc., all of which bespeak the unduly rigorous conception of law that has already been stigmatised as pseudo-scientific, become gratuitous".[1] Such activity *ab extra*—to use a spatial metaphor—and *upon* physical Nature would seem to be all that can be meant by the poetic phrase 'immanence *in*' (inert matter), which, taken literally, is meaningless.

Within certain limits which it is perhaps impossible to specify, there is no incompatibility between this alleged immanent activity of God and the established probabilities which we call laws of Nature, and which presuppose a settled order of Nature with its relative independence and its routine. Physicists such as the late Prof. Poynting have pictured the possibility of providential control of the physical cosmos, in terms of physical conceptions, by attributing to the Deity the same kind of action on material particles as Clerk Maxwell attributed to his imaginary demon. That is to say, Poynting supposed that God might bring about events, such as could not issue from unaided Nature, by altering the paths of molecules. A force at right angles to the direction of molecules would accomplish this alteration without changing their masses or the total energy of the system involved; it would do no work yet would effect a transformation of energy. That spirit cannot thus act, after the manner of an 'impressed' force, on 'matter' is an unproved dogma, and one which within the domain of psychophysics seems inadequate to the explanation of observable facts; while it involves no new assumption to say that the supreme Spirit is not limited to operations lying within the capacity of our souls. And, inasmuch as a scientific observer of macroscopic phenomena does not watch individual molecules or microscopic movements on a cosmic scale, he would detect nothing abnormal in the case of such supernatural intervention, however far-reaching were its effects. This particular way of picturing the divine modification of Nature's course is only mentioned by way of indicating that guidance within the realm of the physical is no scientific impossibility, or even inconsistent with scientific probabilities in respect of conflicting with a reign of law

[1] Quoted, with slight verbal alteration, from the author's *Miracle and its philosophical presuppositions*, pp. 51 ff.

of which science is entitled to speak. But it should follow that, if we are inclined to object to prayer for divine intervention in the material world, it is vain to base our objection on purely scientific grounds. With philosophical and ethico-religious grounds, which are another matter, we here have no concern. Thus to point out the limitations of science in its bearing upon theism or religious faith is perhaps to court the charge of disparaging science and encouraging superstition; but this charge can be cheerfully borne so long as the foregoing representations are not refuted.

Hitherto the immanence of God in the physical world has been discussed on the presupposition of a dualistic metaphysics, involving the theist in the assertion of an inert medium, and in an occasionalistic interpretation of the relation of God to His spiritual creatures. But dualism is not a proven theory: indeed it presents several difficulties from which the alternative theory, viz. pluralistic spiritualism, is free. Provisionally adopting now this latter theory as our metaphysical presupposition, we no longer have a medium to be taken into account: there remains no inert matter, and no attempt to conceive of divine immanence in lifeless stuff is called for from theism. Matter is ultimately spirit; natural laws are statements as to the routine into which spiritual monads have settled, or the channels hollowed out by agents whose deeds flow along them as streams of fact; contingency is "at the heart of things". All causal interaction becomes spiritual *rapport*, involving no medium other than what the monads themselves provide for one another. Any divine operation that is to be called immanent will likewise be direct *rapport* with spiritual agents, from the barest monad up to the souls of men and perhaps spirits of higher order. It matters nothing whether we assert such operation to be upon, or to be within, the spiritual beings; for the meanings of the two prepositions are the same, provided that 'within' insinuates no obliteration of the finite subjecthood of the monads by pantheistic absorption, no reduction of them to the absolutist's 'finite centres' or 'organisations of content', and no cancelling of the conative activity or delegated spontaneity which created spiritual beings must possess in order to be, on the one hand, not the dualist's inert matter over again, and, on the other hand, distinct from God. Assuming that the monads, or the things *per se* behind physical phenomena, have "windows" such as

Leibniz arbitrarily denied them and for which he made the Deity the substitute, direct *rapport* between them is the necessary metaphysical presupposition of the fact that things happen and deeds get done. This interaction is no more explicable than that between God and the monads: it is one of the ultimate mysteries. And inasmuch as God is not to be likened, as a mere magnification, to any member in the hierarchy of His creatures, but, as unique and as the ground of all, may possess powers totally inconceivable by His highest creatures, there well may be communication between Him and the monads more intimate and immediate than that which subsists between human souls, not to say than that which subsists between our souls and humbler monads. Indeed there may be some further relation subsisting between the monads and God, their one ground, which is neither identity nor such disconnectedness as may be involved in interaction (if it be comparable to action at a distance) between monad and monad, and is suggested by the phrase 'planting out', which has been used to indicate somewhat of the meaning of 'creation'. Such a supposed relation or connexion would seem to be what is asserted when theistic writers have spoken of our 'inclusion'—in some unwonted sense—in the God "in Whom" we live and have our being. Assuming that there is any such relation, it may be remarked that 'inclusion' is an inapt and also a misleading name for it, because suggesting our absorption into the One, or suppression of the relative independence that is involved in our subjecthood, freewill, etc., and implying that our acts are God's acts. A more appropriate name is 'inherence', which does not threaten obliteration of the relatively independent monads, while bespeaking connectedness of the kind contemplated. If monads and human souls 'inhere' in their ground, divine immanence will still consist in action upon them, but also in something more. The 'planted out', so to say, will have its roots in the planter: and this would as fittingly be called immanence of the world and man in God as immanence of God in the world and man. But this notion of inherence is not needed by theism. It is not implied by the idea of a world-ground, nor by dependence, maintenance, or immanence —in the sense of action upon, or interaction with, created things. It is suggested by no facts, and would perhaps be difficult to reconcile with some facts. And it is not required for philosophical or metaphysical interpretation of the facts. The conception is but admissible within the sphere of conjecture as to the unknowable: conjecture which can neither be verified nor refuted because there is no touchstone in Actuality wherewith to test it. Arising without any solicitation from within the realm of the Objective, this idea must issue from subjectivity or predilection, or else from adoption of a metaphysical system akin to absolute monism, in which it is implicated. Empirically derived theism cannot include it within the class of reasonably grounded beliefs.

It has been said before that the immanence of God in Nature, construed as action upon the world-elements, is established by the same reasoning as leads to belief in God and His transcendent or creative activity. Theism is the outcome of a more comprehensive survey of the interrelations of things than the sciences severally undertake; and so long as secondary causes, accepted without philosophical scrutiny of their nexus as a totality, are deemed sufficient for proximate or secondary explanation, the idea of an immanent God is a superfluity. But theism itself requires the interpolation, into the causal nexus studied by the sciences in so far as it is observable, of causal agencies that are not observable, and yet would offer no violence to scientific truth. The immanent activity of the world-ground upon physical Nature is a needful supplement to transcendent activity; for, without it, the course of this value-realising world is hardly explicable.

The question whether theism can assert a divine indwelling in man involves considerations of quite another kind than those pertaining to the immanence of God in the physical world. For any immediate touch or influence of God upon human souls or personalities needs to be conceived consistently with the theistic belief that the *purpose* of the world is ethical, or includes the ethical. Limitations are thus imposed on the scope of God's immanent action, if any such there be, upon self-determining and moral persons. The divine indwelling cannot be regarded as 'possession', as if God used human minds as His passive vehicles or instruments. It cannot be a kind of *afflatus* involving either complete or partial supersession of the human subject's personal activities. Such beliefs, implying that omnipotence may treat persons, for their personal good, as impersonal stocks and stones, are survivals of imperfectly moralised religion, evincing inadequate discernment of the essence of morality and personality. It would be unduly dogmatical, however, to deny on ethical grounds the possibility of *any* divine contact with persons that is of the sub-personal, or of the subconscious, order. For "the whole man" is more than the rational and ethical agent to which the austerely puritanical moralist would reduce it; and it may in all reverence be the hope of anyone, who in the loveableness of human persons has found a foretaste of 'the infinities', that in God Himself there is yet more than righteousness for which the finite soul may be athirst. Moreover the status of developed personality has not been possessed by all mankind throughout the duration of the race's existence: *if* there has been an indwelling of God in man that may be called 'as old as the creation', divine immanence must once have been confined to impersonal influences. Nevertheless, in moralised man immanence is not to be postulated as divine influence on moral conduct.

Provisionally leaving open, then, the theoretical possibility of some kind of divine immanence in man, we may continue to narrow down its actual scope by further application of restrictive ethical and psychological considerations, with a view to ascertaining whether any room is left for operations that may be called immanent, and whether there are any grounds for believing these supposable operations to be actual. It scarcely needs stating, after the epistemological discussions pursued in the former volume of this work, that God's immanence in man must be something less than what is implied when human reason is spoken of as an innate divine light, or an energising of the Logos, and when conscience is described as the voice of God within us. It is incompatible with established knowledge, as well as with the implications of theistic belief, that the human mind is thus the passive mouthpiece of God.

Similarly the kind of immanence that is involved in the religious notion of a prevenient grace, without which a man "can do no good thing", is incompatible with philosophical theism. Taken literally, rather than as an emotional expression of self-abasement before the All-Holy, the words quoted are untrue. The statement that man's natural or unaided 'instincts' and volitions tend only in the direction of moral evil, while any tendency in the direction of goodness is due to supernatural or non-human initiation, implies no less than that human psychology should be struck off the list of natural sciences. And ethics would insist that in so far as our virtuous behaviour is due to divine causation, and not to our freewill, it is not ours, nor is it, therefore—in the strict sense —(humanly) moral, but only correct. Indeed so long as God's immanence in man is identified with grace, and grace in turn is conceived as a quasi-physical, non-moral, or impersonal force, an occult and coercive influence upon the soul, a sporadic intervention of omnipotence "taking by assault our personal defences" (to borrow Dr Oman's phrase), ethical theism can be but hostile to the doctrine, as inconsistent with its own fundamental principles. Grace, in this sense, is often commended as God's gracious condescension to human frailty; but it would rather bespeak God's overriding of moral personality. Moreover if such grace were given and received at all without violation of the sanctities of moral personality, it would be inexcusable for not removing *en bloc* the moral infirmities of men: moral restrictions once set aside, there remain no impediments to an omnipotent Creator. Thus, while we may fully bear in mind the psychological fact that attention, which is so large a factor in volition, may be solicited by impersonal influences beyond the reach of introspection, and though we may allow that, while there cannot be less in the unfathomed mental life of man than psychology has discovered there may well be more, so that it is *possible* to imagine divine operations upon the inmost springs of human conduct, we are nevertheless precluded by the theistic conception of the world-purpose from allowing the actuality of any of the alleged instances of divine immanence in man that have as yet been mentioned. They all involve an essentially non-moral estimation of the inviolable personality and the ethical freedom of the 'image of God'.

Again, it is no longer necessary to invoke new inrushes of divine creativity[1] in order to explain the origination of mankind's rationality, conscience, religious beliefs, or theology; these, we have already seen, can be naturally accounted for in terms of unaided evolution from what is due to the transcendent activity, as distinct from the immanent activity, of God. And if the sciences offer no

---

[1] I have been asked "what are *new* inrushes of creative activity, if creativeness is not subject to the category of time?" The wider question of the conceivability of immanence in Nature is thus raised. The answer is to be found in the discussion of temporality and eternity, ch. v (iii); see especially pp. 133–135.

impediment to the religious supposition that mankind's effort to read aright what is written upon the created world has been divinely assisted, it is doubtful, for more than one reason, whether that supposition is true. The groping of the race after God, for the most part misdirected and ineffectual, scarcely bespeaks the co-operation of a Light enlightening every man, any supernatural touch upon the springs of human conduct, or any guidance of man's native faculties. And as in the case of grace, so also in the case of truth, the question arises why, if assistance can be given in any measure without violating freedom, has it been given in measures so stinted? If the answer be 'to allow scope for freedom', it is overlooked that the smallest assistance, of impersonal kind, violates freedom. If divine assistance of this sort be invoked, it must be regarded, it would seem, as imparted to selected individuals. And this view raises in turn a similar difficulty: it bespeaks divine parsimony when there appears to be no conceivable reason why the gift should not be bestowed universally. Divine immanence in physical Nature, or continuous 'impersonal' action upon impersonal world-elements, which is ethically unobjectionable, has been asserted to be a postulate needful to account for those elements ever continuing to consist as a cosmos: a general providence, concerned with individual things because concerned with all things as one totality, is implied in empirically established theism. But what are sometimes called particular providences, unconcerned with the consistency of the order as a whole, while their possibility is unquestionable, are a much more precarious supposition; and when concerned with persons in place of things they may be non-compossible with the conditions of an ethical purpose for ethical agents. It may be concluded, then, that divine immanence in man, in any form in which it must invade, and impersonally influence, man's personality as involved in appropriation of truth and formation of moral character, is a doctrine which ethical theism cannot countenance: immanence in human subjects, in any other form, or of any other kind, perhaps no theologian is concerned to maintain. The fact that human history, shewing the emergence of new values, reveals, at least as much as does the course of physical Nature, the world-purpose of God, does not necessarily bespeak immanent guidance (of mankind) as distinct from transcendent activity and delegation of autonomy. If it may appear to do so, so long as we do not ask precisely what we mean by 'immanence' in Nature and in man respectively, it becomes obvious that it cannot do so when we bethink ourselves of the disparity between physical Objects and moral agents.

REVELATION.

A special case of the distinction between transcendent and immanent divine activity is the distinction between natural and revealed religion or theology, when drawn with the maximum of mutual exclusiveness. And the different views held by theologians as to what revelation consists in, and how it is mediated, are largely determined by inclination towards the deistic and the pantheistic bound of theism respectively, and by emphasis upon the transcendent or upon the immanent action of God, as the case may be.

(i) *Revelation in the sphere of natural theology*

All theists, including deists, agree that the created world, man, and his native faculties are an utterance of God which, when interpreted as such by man, constitutes a revelation of the existence, and to some extent of the attributes, of the Deity. Whereas God is by nature invisible, man can at any rate know Him by His works. And this utterance involves only the transcendent activity of God—at least in so far as man is concerned. Conceiving the human reception, whereby utterance becomes revelation, as involving no divine immanence in man, the English deists, with all their disparagement or denial of 'revealed' religion, were nevertheless able to speak, as natural theologians, of a divine revelation. This revelation they called internal, meaning that it is intrinsic to the created world as a rational and moral cosmos.[1] And the theist of to-day, while repudiating the deistic or rationalistic conception of human reason as a static and infallible faculty possessed by mankind from the first, may be so deistically inclined as to dispense with the invocation of divine inspiration or guidance of human minds, such as would be distinguished as immanent activity, and to regard the internal revelation, with which natural theology is concerned, as involving none but transcendent action.

[1] 'Internal revelation' has been more commonly used, as by Coleridge, in a sense almost antithetic to this, connoting God's direct imparting of truth to faculties intrinsic to man.

He too may speak of a revelation "as old as creation", and perhaps may recognise no other. But, unlike the deists, he would only regard the divine factor in it—the creative utterance—as static, or written once and for all. Man's reception and interpretation of this utterance he would regard as gradual, and as conditioned by the natural developement of mankind's native and unassisted faculties. In other words, such a theist would speak of progressive revelation, meaning thereby progressive discovery of the import of the divine utterance. The process of revelation, thus conceived as human advance in religious knowledge, has been aptly compared with the climbing of a mountain, when the landscape which already lies around is more and more brought into view.

When natural theology denies divine immanence in man and doubts the forthcomingness of revelation other than such is inscribed upon the world and man, its doctrine may be summed up in the formula, 'God utters, man discovers or reveals'. 'Reveal' will then bear the sense in which we use the word when we speak of revealing a picture, or of a picture being revealed, by our unveiling it. But when natural theologians assert that even the kind of revelation which the deists called internal involves also the immanent action of God upon human minds, their formula is 'God inspires, man discovers'. And this doctrine cannot be accepted by empirically established natural theology, for two reasons which may once more be stated. There is no more need to invoke immanent inspiration, over and above transcendent utterance, in order to account for mankind's progressive discovery of the nature of God than to explain man's acquisition of any other kind of knowledge: the venture of faith involved in natural theology is akin to that involved in inductive science, and does not presuppose a *donum superadditum* of grace. Again, ethical theism, taking human personality as the determinative consideration in connexion with the present issue, must reject immanent inspiration because it can only be conceived as an impersonal or non-ethical invasion of ethical freedom and personality, incompatible with the theistic conception of either God or moralised man. What Coleridge meant in saying that he believed the Bible because it "found him" might have been expressed more accurately by saying he believed the Bible because he found its truth by his own personal insight and response, rather than as vouched for by authoritative declarations as to biblical inspiration: and unless theological and religious truth is thus found, personally discerned, and appropriated, it scarcely is truth *for us*, *i.e.* of spiritual value to us. So the Reformation and the Enlightenment taught us for all time; and had the discovery been made and assimilated in the early days of dogmatic theology, the history, and much of the structure, of ecclesiastical doctrine, as also the institutional embodiment of doctrine, would doubtless have been different. A church's doctrine of God and His dealings with men must inevitably be debased, here and there, by association with an anthropology deficient in its appreciation of the ethical dignity of human personality and in its recognition of the essential nature of what is strictly to be called moral: superstitions and trivialities are then apt to usurp the place of the sublimities, and to be commended as condescensions of God to the needs of man.[1]

(ii) *Revelation in the sphere of revealed religion*

'Revealed religion' is a technical phrase, used to distinguish religion and theology based on alleged divine operations occurring within the span of human history from the natural theology which is concerned only with the revelation vouchsafed in God's 'original' creative utterance. The phrase involves no denial that there is revelation of this latter kind, but it denotes revelation imparted in other ways: revelation surpassing, in fulness of content, that which is inscribed on the created world, and putting man in possession of some knowledge that is 'above reason', in the senses that it is not attainable by reason and that it is not comprehensible or assimilable by the human understanding. Occasionally the divine activity involved in this kind of revealing has been conceived as what would more aptly be called inspiration. For instance, William Law, when opposing the deists, maintained that revelation (revealing) is a spiritual influence, apparently an immediate touch of God upon the human soul, inscrutable to reason and received without any exercise of the reason. But much

---

[1] On the subject of moral personality and its significance for theology, especially in connexion with the conceptions of grace and revelation, the reader is referred to Dr J. Oman's work, *Grace and Personality*. As a presentation of the Christian view of the relations between God, the world, and man, in its ethical majesty unclouded by tradition of doubtful morality, this little book, if one may take the liberty to say so, is one of the more valuable treasures in theological literature.

more usually the revealing has been conceived as dictation or imparting, in propositional form, of ready-made truth or information, "at sundry times" or "in divers portions" through individuals. Utterances introduced, in the Old Testament, by a formula such as "Thus saith the Lord" have been believed to be delivered by the Deity; and the disclosure of truth concerning God and His relations with mankind is believed by Christians to have been made by One who is very God as well as very man, not only through His life and works, but also in words, the purport at least of which is preserved in the gospels.

The former of these views as to the nature of revelation within the sphere of 'revealed' religion is in essence the same as that which is adopted when the revelation contemplated by natural theology is construed as involving divine immanence in man. This has been discussed to some extent already. But some indication may here be given as to how the progressiveness of human discovery is to be accounted for when progressive revelation, in the sense of inspiration, is abandoned as a superfluous or an untenable hypothesis.

It may be said that science, philosophy, and theology alike arose out of the mythology which was mankind's attempt to explain things and their origins before the requisite knowledge was forthcoming. Myths, in the broader sense in which the word is used, are 'instinctive' analogies or humanisations, usually abounding in crude anthropomorphism. Religion could at first find expression only in metaphorical language of this kind, as no other mode of interpreting the mysterious, or the Beyond, was possible. In the ages when man's imagination was necessarily more fully developed than was his reason, mythology was an inevitable phase in the growth of thought. And in this humanising of Nature by means of the relatively few ideas common to men we may perhaps see a sufficient explanation of the likeness which subsists between the mythological explanations of different peoples, due allowance being made for differences of environment and national genius. Primitive theologising, in the times of the ignorance which "God winked at", may well have been due to all men having been "made of one blood...that they should seek the Lord, if haply they might feel after him and find him"; but it is not easy to reconcile with the facts of history, or with the

conditions of human freedom, the supposition that man's groping
was prompted or directed by influxes of divine activity into human
mentality, and that in this sense God has in every age stooped to
man as he was in order to make him what he was not. God may
be conceived as the creator of souls with limited capacities, but
hardly as the implanter or the inspirer of notions destined to be
found ethically and otherwise defective by man himself. Mythology
would seem to be the lisping of infantile humanity to the unknown
God rather than God's talk, so to speak, with mankind in its
childhood. And the surmise as to a Beyond, which found various
expressions in the ages when morality was undeveloped, bespeaks
no *ad hoc* intervention of the Deity. For instance, if totemism
embodies the early recognition that survival depends on other
things than manipulation of matter, viz. sympathy and solidarity
or being in touch with forces that are rather moral than physical,
its emergence can be accounted for by natural causes, and it is
unnecessary, if it be not unseemly, to attribute totemism, with its
apparently bizarre aspects, to divine suggestion.

The transition from mythology and kindred modes of imagination to reason was gradual; and the mythopœic method survived
after reason had become expert, being used, *e.g.* by Pythagoras
and Empedocles, and by Plotinus. Indeed history inclines us to
believe that probably it will not cease to be pursued so long as the
demands of emotion for ideal objects shall exceed the supply of
grounds in fact and reason. But wherever morality has become
determinative of what may be called mankind's theological search,
mythology has tended to become obsolete. The Old Testament is
indeed the classic history of the developement of religion from
trust in local and tribal *numina* to monotheism; but its value
consists pre-eminently in its portrayal of the part played by ethical
considerations in the refinement of theological beliefs. The Hebrew
prophets sought after God mainly in order to secure a moral
victory over the world: hence their unique contribution to ethical,
as distinct from merely metaphysical, theism. Whereas before
morality intervened progress was scarcely more than stagnation,
the moralising of religion, once begun, led to rapid and impressive
advances in the discovery of the nature of God and His purpose
for the world and man. Nothing succeeds like success, especially
if the first success be to have struck the one road which leads to the

goal. Moralisation of religion was a possibility open to any nation; and it is not necessary to suppose that a special illumination was imparted in time to the Hebrew race to start it on its singular progressiveness, or that a special favour was bestowed, reserving to it alone the promise of achievement. Indeed we have been told that, centuries before Amos and later Hebrew prophets had completed the advance from henotheism to monotheism, a Pharaoh had transfigured an Egyptian sun-god into the All-Father in heaven, sole God and creator, whose chief attribute is love, and who is not to be worshipped in the form of any image. The 'chosen' race having once conceived their covenant-relation with God as of a moral nature, and thereby having become a peculiar people, progress in social morality, widening of interests beyond the bounds of the national, acquisition by outstanding personalities of moral insight deepened by reflection, and suchlike natural developements, account for Israel's growing sense of the absoluteness and holiness of its God and of the brotherhood of mankind.

The supernatural inspiration that has been invoked as the sole or the main cause of this unique religious progress has hitherto generally been said to be vouched for, in the case of the prophets, by the psychological accompaniments of prophetic utterance, *i.e.* the experiences which led the prophets to regard themselves as deliverers of a divinely communicated message. But such belief, again, has become superfluous in these latter days. The visions, auditions, etc., with which some prophecies are associated are now explicable in terms of hypnotic trance, auto-suggestion, and so forth; and we know that what has been subconsciously elaborated may emerge above the threshold suddenly or spasmodically, and be suggestive of a power superior to any of which we are aware as functioning in the processes of normal or supraliminal mental life. What is interpreted as inspiration would seem to mark the end of subconscious elaboration and the beginning of supraliminal experience. Again, the experiences of more normal kind which the prophets have described, such as unusual exaltation or strong emotion, the sense of power (momentary or abiding) and of compulsion to utter, are paralleled in the case of the discoverer and the genius in fields in which divine influence is not wont to be invoked. Such facts as these do not rule out the possibility of divine co-operation, but they destroy the evidential value of the prophet's experience itself. That, as was represented in vol. i, chap. xii, is 'immediate' apprehension of supernatural influence only in the 'psychic' and not in the 'psychological' sense. The prophetic functions of the literary prophets, involving moral reason and intuition, are very different from those ascribed by antiquity to the demented, the frenzied, the oracle, or the clair-voyant wizard, and from everything with which the name 'mantic' is associated; and the primitive view of inspiration may be said to have given place to that of divine illumination or influence such as leaves the natural faculties of the prophet unimpaired while exciting them to supranormal activity: but so long as inspiration, grace, and revelation are conceived as anything other than personal transactions with free persons, involving reception such as is more or less a rational and moral response, those theological conceptions can never wholly exclude from their connotations the notion of impersonal coercion, which, save in its crudest forms, has been retained in the theology of Christian churches. So long, con-sequently, those conceptions can find no place within the ethical theism that has here been described. It is not that theism of this kind would deny God's initiative, or replace grace by human merit; but it would repudiate any conception of the divine condescension, or of the gracious relations of God to man, which involves the supposition that He treats persons as impersonal.

The other view as to the nature of revelation within the sphere of revealed religion, viz. that revelation is communication of ready-made truth or information, final and infallible, is the one that has been most generally accepted and applied. If we may assume that what might be called the oracular theory of prophetic inspiration is now generally abandoned, the only instance of alleged revela-tion, in the sense now in question, which need be considered is that which is believed to have been mediated by Christ, as God incarnate in man: or at least so much of it as is contained in His verbal utterances, apart from his life or his personality, inter-dependent as these are.

The idea of revelation as a verbal communication of truth is not so obviously incompatible with the ethical implications of theism as the ideas of revelation which have hitherto been con-sidered; for it allows, at least to some extent, of the functioning

of man's rational and moral faculties being involved in the
reception of what purports to be divine utterance. Yet, on closer
examination, this conception of revelation also seems liable, if
in a lesser degree, to the objections that have been urged against
the cruder conceptions. It bespeaks somewhat of 'impersonal'
dealing, if in a more subtle sense of the word, with man by God.
Information such as is called religious truth, the primary function
of which should be to promote a personal and spiritual relationship
rather than to resolve metaphysical or other mysteries, cannot
simply be conveyed or delivered by divine omnipotence, because
human receptivity and assimilation are involved in its imparting.
It cannot be coercively thrust upon us ready-made, so to speak,
nor received otherwise than through our personal conviction,
individual insight, and free response. The Objectivity of the truth,
in this instance, is not the sole consideration. The spiritual and
practical value of a truth is as important as its trueness; and that
value, for a given individual, is conditioned by his insight, its
truth 'for him', its 'finding' him—*i.e.* his 'finding' it. And if
an infallible and final revelation, in the form of supplementary
authoritative information as to things divine, has thus been
vouchsafed to one generation of men, we know by experience that
instead of ever steadily shining by its own light it has entailed
upon later generations considerable perplexity as to what, in its
pristine purity, it may have been. The question as to what is "the
essence of Christianity" has been dividing theologians into
diverse schools since criticism emerged to produce confusion.
History shews that an infallible revelation would require an
infallible recipient and interpreter as well as an omniscient utterer.
And the added supposition of an infallible church, or of an infallible pope, necessitates recourse to the notion of 'impersonal'
coercion or overriding, which is offensive to the theism for which
the ethical dignity of free human personality is as fundamental a
truth as is the self-revealing nature of God. To the former of these
truths ecclesiastical theology, or the traditional exposition of
'revealed' religion, has not done adequate justice. And less than
justice is done to the essential requirement, that the dealings of a
personal God with personal beings must be personal, by the
conception of revelation as a communication of doctrine, involving the removal of mysteries by a fractional imparting of

omniscience, comparable to a bestowal of irresistible grace. Revelation is more satisfactorily conceived, from the ethical point of view, as an enabling of man to get his own insight than as providing him with a substitute for it; as a seeking of free response rather than as a dictation of dogma; and as analogous to teaching a person to think for himself rather than to filling a pitcher with water.[1]

Thus far revelation, of the kind which is presupposed by 'revealed' religion, has been discussed as if it were a communication of truth assimilable, though not attainable, by the natural reason of man. As a matter of fact, however, those of the truths believed to have been revealed by Christ which are the most fundamental and important from the point of view of traditional Christian dogmatics are not of that nature. For instance, the doctrine of the Incarnation, in which the Christological utterances attributed in the gospels to Christ find concise explication, is 'above reason', as will presently be shewn, in the sense that it cannot be formulated in terms of the knowledge and the concepts provided by human psychology—the only concepts by means of which natural reason can synthesise or analyse the idea of incarnation. And this doctrine, on which others are dependent, is implied in the assertion that sayings of Christ are utterances of God, and is generally presupposed when Christ's life and personality are affirmed to be a manifestation of the nature or the attributes of God. It is consequently involved in the conception of revelation which 'revealed' religion uses. The name of knowledge, or of knowable truth, however, must not be bestowed upon propositions which cannot be assimilated by thought and co-ordinated with knowledge, or which assert what reason is unable to comprehend. There may be truth above reason if 'truth' be here a synonym for 'fact', but if 'truth' means known or knowable correspondence of judgements with facts there can be no truth above reason, because all knowing involves something contained within the meaning of the comprehensive word 'reason'. When Locke, who was a typical representative of the view that revelation consists in imparting knowledge, distinguished 'revealed' religion from the theology which Bacon had pronounced to be "divine in respect of its

[1] For a fuller presentation of the idea of revelation as conditioned by considerations as to moral personality see Dr Oman, *op. cit.*, part II, chap. VII, and *passim*.

object" but "natural in respect of the light" by which it is received, he insisted, as against the deists, that revelation can convey knowledge that is undiscoverable by reason. He was careful to stipulate that alleged revelation cannot be accepted if it be "against reason": reason, he would say, is the sole test of truth but not its sole source. Locke also recognised that the 'knowledge' afforded by revelation is less certain—we should now substitute 'less probable'—than that afforded by reason. But he did not so plainly discern that reason, besides being one source, and the only test, of truth, is also involved in constituting and establishing the *knowable* trueness of any proposition, from whatever source it may emanate. And in this oversight he has been generally followed, as he was also preceded, by exponents of dogmatic theology. Kant's theory of knowledge, on the other hand, insisted on the essential contribution of the human mind to all knowledge or belief, and indeed to the constitution of their very objects as known or knowable. He may thus be said to have prepared the way for a more accurate and adequate interpretation of what revelation must needs be. The faith, we may further conclude, which is involved in acceptance of dogma that is not only undiscoverable and unprovable, but also unassimilable, by natural reason, is in some respects essentially different from that which is required for what in this work has been technically called reasonable belief—that is, belief grounded in 'knowledge' and congruent therewith.

It was asserted above that the doctrine of a divine incarnation in man, implied in the conception of revelation which is now being discussed, is above reason: not only in the senses in which it is generally confessed so to be, but also in the further sense of unintelligible, or unassimilable with forthcoming knowledge and inexpressible in the concepts which such knowledge presupposes or dictates. This statement should not be left without justification, and a justification of it will now be submitted.

The simplest possible conception of the Incarnation which is asserted by ecclesiastical theology is that which would be presented in the statement that, in Christ, God Himself replaced the human soul which is the dominant monad in an ordinary human self, and the perduring subject and synthesising agent in a man's mental life. Christ, that is to say, was God functioning in and through a human body. This supposition would account for the supernatural works and experiences attributed to Christ; but it does not explain those that are indistinguishable in character from the works and experiences of human persons. It does not seem to have been adequately realised, in the age which produced formulae such as 'two natures in one person' and 'an impersonal human nature', that a human nature (properly so called) must owe its specifically human characteristics not only to the kind of body, but also to the kind (or order) of soul, which constitutes a human person. The souls of men are presumably one order, and of one rank in respect of range of varying faculty and capacity, within a hierarchy of souls—"families in heaven and earth"—and certainly are of different rank from that of God, the creator of spirits. We should therefore expect the experiences determined by interrelations between the supreme Spirit and a human body to be of a different type from experiences determined by interrelations between a human soul and a human body. The seemingly human experiences of Christ cannot, on this interpretation, be properly called human at all, however much likeness to the experiences of an embodied human soul they may evince. And that they should be, from the point of view of the external observer, similar to those of ordinary men, as if their subject were a human soul, is a mystery calling for explanation. Indeed suggestions have been provided by theologians, such as the ancient doctrine known as docetism and the modern hypothesis of a divine *kenosis*, because requisite to supplement the primary dogma that God was the soul of Christ, and particularly to account for the knowledge, with its limitations, of Christ 'as man'. Other difficulties are indeed presented to thought by the supposition that the world-ground substituted itself for the human soul in what, but for that substitution, would have been a man: it is not easy, *e.g.* to conceive of God as at the same time the 'omniscient' upholder of the universe and a spirit restricted to such knowledge and experience as a body mediates to a human soul. But without inquiry into these difficulties it seems plain that this version of the doctrine of a divine incarnation is a statement of what is above reason, in the sense of unassimilable with forthcoming knowledge.

Another way of conceiving the Incarnation is to suppose that, properly and strictly speaking, Christ possessed a human nature, in that his body was associated with a human soul, as well as a divine nature, in that God functioned as an additional subject associated with that body. From the point of view of modern knowledge there could not be two natures unless there were two persons, or rather two subjects: an 'impersonal' human nature, or a human nature without a human soul, is but a human body and not a human nature, or else is but an abstraction and a non-actuality. So far, then, this second interpretation is preferable to the first. There is, indeed, nothing 'above reason', *i.e.* either inconceivable or 'against knowledge', in the supposition that the personality of Christ was due to the combined synthetic activities of two separate subjects. There is merely something to which empirical knowledge can supply no actual analogy. The phenomena of dual personality and of co-consciousness, described in the preceding volume of this work, are irrelevant because they do not necessarily, or even probably, bespeak the activity of more than one soul in one body, whereas in the present case two subjects are involved; moreover those phenomena are of abnormal and pathological nature. Nevertheless this second hypothesis, though conceivable in the abstract, affords no explanation of the normality and the coherence of the mind and the life of the historical Christ, or of the lack, in his mentality as a whole, of abruptness in the transitions, backwards and forwards, between experiences suggestive of a divine subject and experiences suggestive of a human subject. Again, then, a new mystery is set up by what should be an explanatory theory.

Between these two extremes other interpretations of incarnation are conceivable, and such have been forthcoming. But they all involve somewhat of that 'fusion' of the two natures or two subjects asserted in the second interpretation, which was repugnant to the mind of antiquity and is inconceivable to modern mental science. In some of them the notion of incarnation tends to approximate to that of what is now called divine immanence. And recently resort has been deliberately made to the doctrine of divine immanence in order to find an interpretation of divine incarnation such as is free from the difficulties besetting the interpretations which have just been set forth. But to introduce immanence is to abandon incarnation. By saying that God was in a unique degree immanent in Christ, what should be meant is that there was but one subject of all Christ's experiences, viz. a human soul; that there was no 'divine nature' in his 'person'; and that God acted inspirationally *upon* that soul, or upon Christ's human personality, but did not *erleben*, or was not the subject of, any of Christ's mental states and acts. On the other hand, if 'incarnation' is to have any meaning *sui generis* it must signify that God was either one of two subjects, or else the sole subject, involved in Christ's experience, and not merely that God exerted influence upon another subject belonging to the class called human souls. Immanence may be a substitute for incarnation: it cannot be one amongst other interpretations of incarnation.

Some liberal theologians to-day renounce both of the notions, incarnation and immanence, in their exposition of the personality of Christ. They reject the latter supposition because it does not seem to them to satisfy the demands of ethical theism, and the former because it cannot be conceived in terms of ideas derived from facts or thrust upon us by knowledge, and because it sets up mystery which is unassimilable with knowledge. They some-times also urge that historically it has engendered other doctrines, mysterious as itself, unethical in character, and burdensome to belief that would fain be such as has here been called reasonable: that it has encouraged obscurantism and fostered subsidiary superstitions such as have come to count, in doctrine and institu-tional religion, for far more than the ethical and religious teaching of Christ. And they emphasise that the type of Christianity which is rather based upon the Christological utterances attributed in the gospels to Christ than derived from his utterances concerning the conduct of human life in God's world, the transvaluation of secular valuations, and so forth, rests ultimately on a precarious historical foundation. It rests, that is to say, not on bare facts, as has hitherto been generally assumed, but on a particular inter-pretation of the facts, which, natural enough to the age in which Christ lived and which we cannot subject to cross-examination, is rendered suspect by latter-day critical inquiries. Modernism is radical enough to call in question the primitive interpretation of the impression produced by Christ, and to remind us that an impression presupposes interpreting recipients as well as an im-pressive personality. The theologians who uphold these views are indeed accused of arriving at them by a subjective method of dealing with the historical records, straining out of all the gospels alike, as unauthentic, every saying in which divine or superhuman claims are made by the founder of Christianity, despite the absence of objective canons of criticism requiring them in all cases to do so. But, assuming that those liberal theologians who have approached the problem from the side of literary and historical criticism are thus guilty of arbitrariness, or are guided by a foregone conclusion instead of investigating the documents disinterestedly, some would ask whether their foregone conclusion is not grounded upon considerations more relevant than the conclusions of disinterested study of ancient records.

Liberal theologians who approach the problem rather from the side of philosophy, and consider the conceivability and the probability of the metaphysical presuppositions involved in the traditional or catholic interpretation of Christ's person, may refuse to allow that it lies within the power of history to utter the last word upon this issue. As to the relevance of conclusions reached by literary and historical criticism, it must be observed that oral tradition may conceivably undergo modification before it is committed to writing; and that, if history can prove that a given interpretation was primitive, it is unable to prove that that interpretation is the only possible or the true one. Moreover we know that into practically every kind of observation of 'fact' more or less of interpretation enters—fact is received *ad modum recipientis* —and that into observation of the acts and utterances of an impressive personality interpretation may enter in a large measure. It is unlikely that the author of the fourth gospel had no predecessors in the sincere blending of perceptions with interpretative ideas. At any rate history leaves room for reasonable doubt as to creative imagination having had no share in producing the supernatural element in the primitive extant portrait of Christ, and as to Christ's fostering the contemporary Christological interpretation of himself.

If history could rigidly preclude these doubts, and if the conception of Christ as incarnate God were easily assimilable, both the historical facts as a whole and also with established psychological knowledge and the concepts which such knowledge involves or presupposes, the philosopher would be constrained to bow to the traditional interpretation of historical facts. Facts should be his data; and historical facts are no less worthy of his respect and reverence than facts of any other kind. And the historical method is the scientific method. The tendency to decry historical facts as too parochial and insignificant to be accepted as sources of universal truth bespeaks an emotional attitude rather than a philosophically reasoned conviction, and is due to the erroneous belief that there are 'truths of reason' valid of Actuality, yet independent of the 'contingent facts of history'. Again, contempt for the 'merely historical', entertained by those who would ground their beliefs on their own present experience alone, to the exclusion of all connexion with the implications of past Objective fact, is no philosophical habit of mind: it evinces the mistaken view that nascent emotion in present experience is a securer foundation of knowledge than facts experienced in the past, and that "reality in the making" is more 'real' than 'reality' which has been made. If, then, historical facts demanded belief that God appeared in the body of Christ upon the stage of human life and uttered pronouncements that have been faithfully recorded in documents, that fact and those utterances ought to be allowed by the philosopher to enter into all else of truth that philosophy has gained, and to be used for the reconstruction or transformation of all ideas failing to be adequate through not taking such a revelation into account. But when all this is said it remains true that the metaphysical interpretation of a personality of long ago, and an explanation (in terms of it) of the experiences of contemporary observers, are not problems of historical science, or soluble by use of the historical method alone. It is not history, then, that theologians of the liberal school need to challenge; nor do they need to disparage either historical facts or the method of historical and literary criticism. But they believe themselves to have reason to question, on grounds other than historical, an interpretation of historical events, etc., which history is unable to pronounce either true or false. They reject this interpretation on account of the incomprehensibility of its implications and the difficulty of assimilating them with the implications of ethical theism, which they regard as a philosophically reasoned world-view. And empirically established theism is unable to find a place in its theology for alleged truth that is 'above reason'. It must leave alleged truth of that kind to dogmatic theology, which takes more for granted, presupposes a different kind of faith, and rests upon other foundations. Hence natural theology does not find itself inhibited from discarding the conception of revelation as communication of dogma by being compelled to accept, as *demonstrably* actual, the outstanding alleged instance of revelation in that sense.

If this conception of revelation be abandoned, there remains only that to which we are directed when relevant considerations as to moral personality are allowed their full weight. Revelation is then described as the manifestation of God, in and through His world and mankind, to man, who is thereby enabled to discover by his own rational insight and moral experience the purpose and the nature of God. So conceived, revelation is not merely an exercise of that divine 'omnipotence', the unsifted notion of which is presupposed throughout ecclesiastically moulded religious thought, and the sifted notion of which is scarcely distinguishable from that of indeterminate being; it is conditioned by human receptivity. For instance, an ultimate or inexplicable conception, such as that of creation, does not admit of elucidation to man by an omnipotent God, because it is humanly incogitable. Indeed no truth that is above reason can properly be said to be revealable. For to be revealed implies being assimilated by reason: not merely to have received unintelligent assent, but to be seen by human insight to be true. A secret is not revealed to a man if it be uttered in a foreign language with which he is unacquainted, or even in his native tongue if in words whose meaning he cannot understand. A mystery cannot be revealed save by being made plain and ceasing to be a mystery. So, if God communicated incomprehensible information to man, men might describe their situation in the words which S. Paul used about 'speaking in tongues': "if I know not the meaning of the voice, I shall be unto him that speaketh a barbarian, and he that speaketh shall be a barbarian unto me". Conversely, if God and man be not "barbarians" to one another, revelation must necessarily consist in rational 'give and take' between a Person and persons. And, further, if God be a Person it will follow that in revealing Himself He will respect the moral personality of the persons whom He would enlighten. This ethical condition of revelation is overlooked when there is a predilection for the non-ethical categories of ancient Greek theology rather than for the conception of God and

His dealings with men which was taught by the Hebrew prophets and by Jesus Christ. Wherever the type of mysticism which prizes the ineffable and deems absorption into the One to be the highest good is regarded as religiousness *par excellence*; or the essence of religion is identified with a yearning after metaphysical or quasi-physical infinities; or personality is decried as 'unreal' and unworthy of survival, and selfhood is accounted selfishness on the part of an evanescent fragment or phase of The Absolute; or where it can be thought to be honouring God theologically to defame, or ascetically to mutilate, or otherwise to violate, human personality: there, of course, the combination of rationality and morality will not be looked upon as the essential condition of divine revelation or of human knowledge of God. Here, however, it is assumed, as previously established, that such revelation as has been accorded to man is a manifestation of ethical purpose in the world, and that no revelation of God could transcend the ethical.

The significance of Christ for theism of this type is now discernible. Theism may disown knowledge as to his being of one substance with the Father, or God manifest in the flesh. But it may regard him as a manifestation of God in the flesh, and as the unique revealer of God. Christ possessed in the fullest measure insight into the divine purpose in the world and for man, and consequently into the divine nature, which God would have mankind acquire. He taught and also lived the truth as to God, man, the world, and the relations in which they stand to one another, thus disclosing and making explicit what is implicit in the ethical theism which can claim to be a philosophically reasoned view of the world, based on knowledge in all its breadth. If acceptance of Christ's teaching concerning life in God's world, together with reverence for him and all for which he thus stood, may claim the name of Christianity with as much right as does the traditional interpretation of his personality, then Christianity may be said to be the climax of the historical developement of natural religion, and the crown of natural theology. 'Revealed' religion, in other words, becomes the final phase of natural religion; and revelation, instead of being a bestowal—or even a removal— of mysteries by a non-ethical or impersonal communication of infallible dogma, is God's causing Himself to be understood. Christ revealed God in that he understood Him and has enabled us, not to see *what* he saw without using the same means, but to see *as* he saw by our own 'personally' aided insight and assimilation. Acceptance of truth otherwise than thus—*e.g.* by taking refuge under authority and in infallibilities—involves a shirking of God's purpose for us and a renunciation of the God-given dignity of our souls.

It will perhaps already have become obvious that there is no discontinuity between religion and philosophical theology. Religion is but the practice of belief formulated in theology: no further demand on faith and no additional kind of faith are involved in it. Ever since mankind possessed a presentiment of a Beyond, or the vaguest theology, religion has been organic to human nature; it is the inevitable affective and volitional response to the ideal objects of theological belief. It is therefore not a morbid excrescence, or something dissociable from such belief as has seemed, at each stage of human progress, reasonable to its believers. Science has never stifled religion save when science has been temporarily thought to have proved that there is no Beyond. Religion has never been regarded as one of the childish things which riper experience should put away, with the same general consensus as assigns magic, *e.g.* to that class. This is due to the fact that theology, in its groping after God, has increasingly refined, under the guidance of morality especially, the conception of its ideal Object—God—until it has become such as can be believed by scientifically educated reason to have a Real counterpart. If theism be a reasonable theoretical belief, theistic religion is a reasonable attitude of mind. And if philosophy tells us that we cannot attain to knowledge of God save through knowledge about the world and man, religion assures us that we cannot understand this world and the meaning of life, nor find life much else than vanity and vexation of spirit, apart from interpreting all in terms of our knowledge of God. Then, indeed, we can possess our souls in a peace which passes understanding.

Theistic religion, to repeat, is the adoption in practical life, by way of emotional response and as determinative of volitional conduct, of the theistic world-view. And it is in this connexion that Christ, the religious genius of theism, is uniquely significant. Underlying his teaching, as embodied in the Lord's prayer and the beatitudes, etc., is a world-view, or a doctrine of God and His relation to the world and man, continuous as to its historical developement with that of the Hebrew prophets, and therefore otherwise grounded than upon inductive teleology, yet identical with the world-view which is reached from considerations of that kind. The world, that is to say, is God's world, and the purpose displayed in it and in human history is moral. But it is the implications of this theistic belief for the conduct of life, rather than its philosophical grounding and its relations to theoretical knowledge, which Christ expounds. Perhaps his attitude toward the problem of evil was that of naïve piety, which regards the ills of an individual life as of God's 'appointment' rather than as incidental to a world-order which as a whole, but not in all its details, expresses the divine purpose.[1] But however that may be, Christ shewed us how the knowledge that the world is God's may inspire faith, hope, and love. The world-ground is righteous: ethical goodness occupies the throne of the universe. The world may be indifferent to our moral aspirations, but the world-ground is not. Christ's religion is not identical with morality, or with reverence for moral ideals as such, but is an identification of those ideals with the meaning of the world. Like the Hebrew prophets, Christ ventures beyond the limits of theistic belief such as is reached by study of the world, in assigning to God the attributes of forbearance, pity, etc.; but like the philosophical theist, he conceived of God's love as pre-eminently moral: not as mere beneficence, nor as a reciprocation of the mystical yearning for inclusion. Hence his insistence on the inwardness of true morality, and the personalness of God's dealings with men. To "inherit the earth", as God's, is, on the one hand, not to deify it, as is involved in worldliness; on the other hand, it is not ascetically to renounce it, as is involved in other-worldliness. It is, however, to transmute all mundane

---

[1] Simple piety does not profess to have thought out the implications of its reverently cherished convictions; else it would discern that God's appointment of the events of any individual's life involves the appointment of the events of all lives connected with that one, and so on until every event in the history of mankind, and in the physical world also, needs to be ascribed to divine causation alone. The inconsistency of such a consequence with the cherished convictions that the self is free, the world has some autonomy, and God is loving, is perhaps prevented from manifesting itself by another belief whose implications are not drawn out, viz. in the divine 'omnipotence' which is really indeterminateness.

valuations, hedonic, personal, and social, under the guidance of the truth that this world is God's world, and this secular life is our only present and immediate concern. Such is the victory over the world which brings blessedness even if there be little of happiness, and which it is in the power of religion, and of nothing but religion, to give.

Although scant justice has been done in the foregoing observations to the sublimity of the religion and ethics of theism, as presented by Christ, this is not the place for a fuller exposition of them. A few words may be added, by way of bringing to a conclusion the brief consideration that has here been accorded to theistic religion, concerning religious faith and its relation to what has been called reasonable belief—*i.e.* belief based on inductive study of Nature and man—in a personal and moral world-ground.

Arguments from value to existence have been discussed before, and among them the plea that the idea of a world without God is intolerable to us, not because the world would then be left without a causal explanation but because our highest values would be driven from their seat, and the world would be stripped of all meaning. If this plea were intended for a theistic argument it would be paralleled by reasoning such as that, whereas it is intolerable that human beings should be burned to death for their religious convictions, it follows that human bodies are incombustible. Accordingly, it is sometimes confessed, by those who would base theism upon value-judgements alone, that the conclusion that the world has meaning, in the sense just indicated, is not one as to which there can be logical certainty, and that logical reasoning could at best establish its probability; while at the same time it is maintained that religious faith is certain as to the truth of theism, and that its certainty is not measured by the cogency of arguments but by the intensity of the believer's "feeling for the good". And the reliance which some would put upon Butler's principle, that probability is the guide of life, is said to be an adjustment which involves missing or misunderstanding the nerve of faith: religion lives in its own right.[1] Now, so long as faith remains to the end but faith, in the sense of convincedness without reasonable grounds for conviction, and so long as 'certainty' only means the mental state of certitude, these

---

[1] See, *e.g. The Nature and Right of Religion*, by Dr W. Morgan, p. 75.

representations may pass: save for the remark that Butler's principle is concerned with Objective grounds of common or communicable belief, whereas the faith whose nerve is said to be missed is something to which Butler's principle is irrelevant, viz. an individual or private attitude of mind, determined by subjective motivation rather than by Objective grounds. Certitude may be measured by 'feeling for the good' or by hope that what ought to be is the ground of what is; but probability, in Butler's sense, is measurable by strength of arguments, etc. Butler's saying is often disparaged in consequence of his critics failing to distinguish between logical certainty or probability and psychological certitude. No sanguine believer regards his *credenda* as merely probable: but what many a believer holds for certain, or has certitude about, may not only not be certain from the point of view of common knowledge or belief, but may have little or no probability. Faith, aloof from common grounds, may be the guide of an individual's inner life; but probability is the guide of life in so far as private convictions are related with what is common to all, with the Objective or (in one sense of the word) the Real, and with reasonableness.

But faith, in the sense of private certitude, is seldom content to remain to the end faith. The faith which professes to be trust in the Reality, the ontological primacy, or the conservation, of the valuable often takes a flying leap over probabilities and considers itself to have landed on the platform of certain knowledge.[1] However, it is more to the point to observe that faith usually derives some satisfaction from finding its affirmations supported by coherence with knowledge derived from other sources, and seldom is sanguine enough to persist in retaining those affirmations when they are discovered to be 'against knowledge'. One recalls here the remark of Locke: "I find every sect, so far as reason will help them, make use of it gladly; and when it fails them, they cry out, It is matter of faith and above reason". And it is with a view to shewing that there is a kind of religious faith

---

[1] One commonly assigned justification of this leap is the observation that valuation is rooted as deeply, and in the self-same nature, as is rational thought. But this no more implies that valuations of the ideal are assertions of the Reality of the ideal than that discernment of implication between propositions is identical with aesthetic or moral appreciation. Different faculties are not made identical by being lodged in the same subject.

which not only would welcome, but may actually enjoy, support from the organised body of probable belief which we call knowledge, that some of the foregoing pages have been written. Such religious faith is but the affective and volitional attitude evoked by theological beliefs which, in turn, claim to be a reasonable interpretation of the whole body of scientific knowledge. There is no incongruity or incompatibility between religious faith of this kind and the dry light and the 'disinterestedness' of science and philosophy, when the nature of these is properly understood. And there is no discontinuity between science, philosophical theology, and this kind of religion. Scientific minds—which, by the way, are not coextensive with minds trained by special study of the sciences—have no need to think that Christianity, in the sense which was just now claimed for that name, is an attitude toward the world and human life which cannot be reasonably justified. Religion is no more a surrender to emotional yearning, or to something akin to Nature's aesthetic appeal to our senses and imaginative fancy, than it is necessarily a blind trust in what is 'above reason' and vouched for only by external authority. Private certitude, trust in what reason cannot comprehend, and other such attitudes as have received the name of religious belief or religious faith, may be left to speak for themselves.[1] Their insecurity is irrelevant to the question whether or not there is a theistic world-view commending itself as more reasonable than other interpretations or than the refusal to interpret, and congruent with the knowledge—i.e. the probability—which is the guide of life and of science. The demonstration of this reasonableness is the primary task of the philosophical theology which would dissociate itself from philosophy of religion, if the latter pursuit be exposition of the implications of a non-reasonably grounded conviction.

[1] What many people regard as their religion is really of a composite nature, including other loyalties and sentiments than such as are distinguishable as purely religious: e.g. the aesthetic, whether sensuous or puritanical; romanticism, or reverence for past ages and for picturesque institutions; historical and even political associations; and so on to indefinitely remote ramifications. Sometimes there has been little room left in such 'religion' for reverence for God and moral duty: the subsidiary loyalties, so easily entertained that they readily pass into fanaticisms, have then usurped its place and name.

CHAPTER IX

God, the Self, and the World

In the interests of the serious student the greater part of this work has been devoted to subjects, knowledge about which is indispensable for the study of natural theology. In its final chapter attention may therefore be called to the connectedness of the problems which have severally been investigated—a conn ctedness in virtue of which this and the preceding volume are constituted an organic whole—and the conclusions to which numerous interrelated inquiries point may be collected. The provision of such a summary will leave the reader less ground for complaining that he has not been enabled to gain a view of the wood because he has been allowed only to examine the trees and to explore pathways through them.

One way of comparing and classifying the outstanding systems of philosophy, with which the student of philosophical theology needs to become acquainted, is according to how many, and which, of the three primary alleged entities, God, the self, and the world, are affirmed by the framers of these systems respectively; the kind or quality of the knowledge pertaining to each of these entities which is deemed to be obtainable; and the order in which they are asserted to come to be known. Indeed those who study the history of philosophy mainly with a view to becoming natural theologians may be recommended to read the relevant works of Descartes, Spinoza, Leibniz, Locke, Berkeley, Hume, Kant, etc., with especial intent to ascertain and compare the treatments which these philosophers have severally given to those particular epistemological and ontological questions. And the conclusions which have been reached in the foregoing chapters can partly be stated in the form of answers to those same questions.

The reader has not been allowed to forget that the method of seeking knowledge used throughout this work is empirical. But he may be reminded at the close that reasons were adduced at the outset for the adoption of that method as the only one which can lead to knowledge, whatever knowledge may prove to be and however limited be its range in philosophy and theology, rather than to speculative thought such as may have little or no relevance to Actuality. It may be hoped that by now he finds himself in a somewhat better position to judge as to the soundness of those reasons. And he may perhaps have come also to realise that this issue is the most important of all the many that have been submitted to his judgement, because decision of it is determinative and far-reaching in respect of consequences: not less so within the particular sphere of theology than in other departments of philosophy of which theology makes instrumental use. Such unity as this treatise possesses is mainly due to its being an exposition of an empirical approach to the science of knowledge, ontology, and theology. Neither its constructive nor its polemical argumentation will carry conviction to anyone who rejects the type of empiricism described in vol. 1 and applied throughout both volumes. But those who have been confirmed in the belief that to begin 'from above', in philosophy and theology, is but to give an exposition of the consequences which flow from a foregone conclusion of an individual thinker rather than to treat philosophy as a quest for conclusions such as may be reasonably reached from universally accepted data and under the constant control of facts and sciences, will perhaps have found some interest in watching a sustained application of the empirical method, even if they have not found themselves able to accept, as sufficiently established, all the numerous linkages and connexions by which a philosophy of the soul, the world, and God has thereby been constructed. The *a priori* method has had abundant representatives throughout the centuries; the empirical, inductive, and explanatory method, adopted in varying degrees of fragmentariness and completeness by Locke and Butler, Lotze and James Ward, has been so much less common that somewhat of distinctiveness attaches to the least distinguished of attempts to use and to commend it. It may be recalled that at the outset a caution was given to the beginner that anything wont to be called empiricism is generally accounted heresy; but by now he will probably have become aware that the Lockean empiricism, which Kant rightly deemed to constitute an *impasse* for epistemology, has been transcended by the discovery and use of an empirical psychology of common, or so-called 'universal', Experience, which has enabled us to see that Kant's resort to a kind of rationalism, in order to get beyond the limitations of such empirical epistemology as was within Locke's reach, is as mistaken as it is superfluous.

The effects of standing committed to an empirical theory of knowledge, and the influence of the adoption of that theory upon the structure and contents of this treatise are so plain that the most summary recapitulation of them will here be sufficient. Defence of the assertion that all our ideas are ultimately derived from percepts, and that their relevance and validity is only assured within the contexts from which they have been abstracted, accounts for frequent animadversion upon the treatment of ideas as if they were things, or upon hypostatisation of abstractions, and for the lengthy examination of the extremer kinds of rationalism and of theology based upon them. The empirical theory of validity involves the illegitimacy of the usual identification of common or Objective ideas, etc., with universal and absolute ideas, etc.: hence the rejection of the doctrine of absolute values, and of theories of value and ethical arguments for theism based upon it. The empirical and genetic inquiry as to what knowledge, or knowing, consists in revealed that there is actually no such thing as the knowledge, the logical presuppositions of which have often been the great search of rationalistic epistemologists: no such thing, for instance, as the kind of knowledge of Nature which Kant thought was forthcoming, and on the strength of belief in which he was unable to find a place within knowledge for biology, aesthetics, ethics, and theology. Use of empirical methods leads to the discovery that all that is called knowledge of Actuality is partly human interpretation, in that it involves 'real' categories derived from the soul itself, and imposed upon data, thereby rendered knowable, by no logical right whatever. It was by appeal to facts that decision was made in favour of phenomenalism, with its distinction between the phenomenal and the ontal, as the only one of the group of theories of knowledge which are at the same time theories as to ultimate Reality (the ontal) that is tenable. And induction, of one kind or another, having been shewn to be the sole means by which all generalised statements about the Actual world have been obtained, it was by examination of problematic induction that the alogical character of the 'probability' on which it rests was claimed to have been proved. Lastly, in so far as the contents of vol. 1 are concerned, it was by use of empirical criteria

that the epistemology of mysticism was tested and its claims—
prior to the establishment of theism by other means than mystical
experience—were refused; and that the limitations of the scientific
method in the physical sciences were assigned. And now let it
be observed that the inquiry, from first to last, pursued in the
former volume of this work, an inquiry which may be described
as almost wholly concerned with a psychological and genetic theory
of knowledge, no more had a theistic motivation affecting the
selection of its conclusions than it presupposed any theological
postulates. Philosophical prolegomena to philosophical theology
are what they are, whether the theology to which they may ultimately be found to point be theistic or atheistic. And it is a
misunderstanding, on the part of one or two of the writers who
have honoured the already published volume with a review, which
has led them to describe that volume as an exposition of such a
psychology and epistemology as its author deems theism to
require. The truth is that the psychological and epistemological
theories which were selected, after due examination of their
alternatives, were concluded to be dictated by nothing but the
relevant facts. That these empirically reached conclusions admit
of being turned to account for the construction of an argument
for theism; that they imply certain consequences determinative of
our knowledge about the world and man, and that such knowledge
finds its most natural and reasonable explanation in the idea of
God: these are posterior disclosures or inferences.

   And it follows from the same conclusions within the sphere of
epistemology that not only theism, but any metaphysical theory
or world-view whatsoever, can at best claim to be a reasonable
belief ultimately grounded on the alogical probability which is the
guide of life and of science, and verifiable only in the sense that
it renders the known explicable. No *a priori*, rational, logically
coercive, or deductive proof is possible. The conclusions established in vol. I, in fact, rule out various types of theistic argument
and also various types of theism. That this is so is made explicit
in foregoing chapters of the present volume. Procedure 'from
above', the antithesis of the method pursued throughout this work,
has been convicted of issuing in 'explanations' such as only
increase our perplexities by creating puzzles and problems more
intractable than those involved in the *explicanda*. But procedure

from the fact-data of presumptive knowledge, and critical regress such as tests itself by accord with facts while endeavouring to discover what knowing exactly is and what are its actual pre-conditions, can now be seen to be capable of yielding a chain of successive conclusions reaching from the primary data of per-ception and introspection to particular assertions about the world-ground: a chain of many links, indeed, but unbroken anywhere by discontinuity. If discontinuity be said to be involved in transition from known facts and generalisations to their invisible explanation-ground, it must be borne in mind that discontinuity essentially similar lurks in all inductive knowledge and in all causal explanation, and that therefore there is at any rate no discontinuity between theistic belief and scientific knowledge. That, of course, is all that was meant in speaking of an unbroken chain. And it is in shewing the unbrokenness of the chain that demonstration of the reasonableness of theistic faith consists. That demonstration constitutes one of the main purposes of the second volume of this treatise. With the sanguineness of individual certitude, with the rights of personal faith, and with tenacious hold upon alleged truths above reason, common or public philo-sophy has no concern; but if philosophy can shew that theistic belief, such as some take to be the essence of Christianity, is reasonable in the sense that it is continuous with the faith of science and is on a par, in respect of its intellectual status, with the probabilities which are involved in all explanation and in all other knowledge concerning Actuality, it will have provided an answer to a question which will never fail to be of vital interest to human beings.

Perhaps it scarcely needs to be re-emphasised that almost the whole of this treatise, in so far as it may be regarded as an exposition of knowledge about man, the world, and God, and of the means whereby such knowledge or reasonable belief is obtainable, is concerned with the proving of a *demonstrandum*. Its procedure may be compared with an ascent from the plains to a hill-top. And until towards the end of the work there is nothing comparable to a return from the height climbed: no interpretation of the facts in the light of knowledge such as only becomes possible after reaching the summit. The landscape, so to speak, is de-scribed as seen from below or from each new point of view gained;

it gradually increases both in area and in clearness of discernibility. Such procedure is of course requisite so long as proving or climbing is in process. No appeal can be made, for instance, to the deliverances of religious experience, which assume the truth or certainty of what as yet stands in need of proof; nor to valuations which owe their specific nature to definitely theistic presuppositions. How commonly theistic arguments have been vitiated by tacitly assuming in their premisses what ought first to emerge in their conclusions has been already illustrated. And, to avoid misunderstanding, it may here be explicitly observed that, when a misuse of religious experience or of value-considerations, in theistic arguments, has been criticised, it is not in every case that the truth of certain statements has been called in question, but only their invocation while proof of them is still in process. It is in this respect that, *e.g.* the Ritschlian theology has been repudiated. Every theist would accept many of its value-judgements as true; but as a basis for theistic proof they are worthless because they implicitly beg the question to be answered: and it is in that respect alone that they have here been discarded. On the other hand, when theism has been reasonably established we may reasonably revalue the world and human life in the light of its implications. So we pass from natural theology to religion redeemed from subjectivity. Private certitude is able to support itself, not indeed upon demonstrable certainties, but on probabilities coextensive with all our knowing, which in part is believing. What is commonly called faith, and even what is commonly called knowledge, is largely hope. Religious faith is a hope for the best in respect of the world being man's home and household; scientific knowledge is based on a hope for the best in respect of the world being structurally intelligible and calculable. By revaluing the world, as science departmentally studies and describes it, in terms of its purpose, as suggested to sympathetic interpretativeness rather than presented to analytic intelligence, transition is made to the intellectual presupposition of theistic religious sentiment, and we get our victory over the world. Theism, such as would be reasonable, however, must adapt itself to the fact that God's world abounds in evil: a fact which of itself renders all the ancient search for metaphysical perfection, or an infinity of infinite attributes, hopeless. But the fact of evil is not incompatible with the idea of a determinate Being, personal and ethical, as the ground of a cosmos whose purpose is primarily the realisation of moral values. And that idea being suggested by a conspection of the world, as comprehensive as our human faculties can obtain, we may reasonably use it as determinative of our reasonable reaction to our inevitable sufferings. For instance the indignity to which we rational beings are subjected in that our bodies, which mediate to our souls their knowledge of the world, of themselves, and of God, and to the empirical self its personality, are at the same time breeding-nurseries for an untold number of species of organisms which are loathsome as fellow-lodgers, becomes tolerable if we are persuaded that the cosmic order which provides for God-like finite personalities, just because of its determinate 'thusness', must also provide parasitic microbes or cease to be a cosmos. Theistic belief may afford equanimity in the presence of such circumstances; and the equanimity is religious.

The conclusions which have thus far been recapitulated are of a general nature, and are determined mainly by adhesion to empirical principles. It is now time to turn to the more particular conclusions concerning the soul, the world, God, and the relations between them, to which the application of this method to specific data has led.

As to the order in which these entities come to be known, it will have been made plain that God is known last, in that knowledge as to the world-ground is only attainable by way of explaining the world and man. Of the latter two of them, neither is known with superior completeness before the other. The permanent ego, or the soul, is not intuited, in the sense of being immediately apprehended, as is a sense-datum, but reflectively: self-consciousness is mediated partly by cognition of external objects, and not by introspection alone. On the other hand, the data of sensory individual experience only yield knowledge of the World when overlaid by categories which are ultimately derived from the soul itself, and which owe their conceptual elaboration to communication with other selves. Knowledge of the self and knowledge of the world are interdependent from the first stages which we can trace, and grow *pari passu*.

The world, as described by common sense and science, the soul, as conceived by psychologists, and God, as postulated by the theologian, are all on a par in respect of knownness, in that, previously to such verification as may be in each case forthcoming, all three are hypothetical beings which are *thought* to have existence independent of our thinking, and are thought of in order to systematise and to account for data which are simply posited and read off, or at least for such data when elaborated by further 'knowledge'-processes. Realism, of a certain kind, and positivism, such as once flourished, would accept this statement in the case of the soul and God, but would regard the world as known with certainty, if not with immediacy. But these theories of knowledge have been found not to bear examination. It is to be concluded, then, that all of the three cardinal entities with which philosophy is employed are, in the first instance, ideal Objects or concepts, and that it is a further question whether there are existents, Real and not ideal, which these concepts are 'concepts of'. The ontological argument being fallacious, the Real existence of God enjoys no certainty superior to that of the existence of the world or of the soul. The knowledge of God is not demonstrable, nor is knowledge of the soul intuitively or immediately certain, as Locke held: God, the soul, and the world (as distinct from unordered sensa) are all Objects of probable belief. And the probability in question is in each case ultimately alogical. The world of physical Objects is a system of concepts (with a core of percepts) which has proved to be pragmatically convenient, and which must therefore bear *some relation to* Reality, but it cannot be identical with the ontal; and science, in its microscopic theories, has been found to take us no nearer to the ontal. The soul is believed to be Real, and not merely an ideal construction, because if it is not Actual the psychology of an individual's mental life becomes but a mass of inexplicable mysteries; and it is for a similar reason, in another context of facts, that God has been asserted to be Real. In both these cases belief is a question of whether we will reasonably explain or we will forgo reasonable explanation. He who would forgo such explanations is logically unimpugnable as to his agnosticism. But he generally finds no difficulty in renouncing the purely logical and agnostic attitude when the Object inviting him to a venture of faith is the world. He then freely makes use, for the conduct of his life, of postulatory categories and probabilities to which he has no logical right: he is content to abide by interpretative explanatoriness where, if he is a philosopher, he knows that neither formal nor 'constitutive' knowledge is forthcoming. Why appeal to metaphysical entities should without demur be made in order to account for the forthcomingness of our sensations, and yet be withheld when it is a question of the equally Objective relations and orderings of those sensations, or of the ordering of psychical happenings which are for present purposes on a par with them, would seem to be an affair of personal biography rather than a question of either logicality or reasonableness. Wheresoever we walk, we walk by faith and not by sight alone: by reasonableness and not by rationality. And, as has been observed before, to persist in Humean scepticism or agnosticism in one's psychology and theology, while betaking oneself to realism or to Kantianism in physics and cosmology, is an epistemological inconsistency. No more in cosmology than in theology should certitude pose as certainty, can any other guide than probability be invoked, or can anything other than fruitfulness in explanation-potency be adopted as the criterion of such 'truth' as it lies within the power of philosophy to attain.

Explanation, in fact, acquires in the present volume an importance similar to that which in the former volume was assigned to reasonableness and probability. Hence a chapter has been devoted to inquiry into the rôles of the various kinds of explanation pursued in diverse fields of thought and knowledge. Belief in God becomes reasonable if the idea of God be found as indispensable for explanation of the totality of our scientific knowledge about the world and man as is the idea of the soul for explanation of the totality of our knowledge about the individual mind. And that the idea of God is thus indispensable was maintained in chap. IV. Two general conclusions inferrible from our knowledge of the world, rendering the argument of chap. IV possible, had already been drawn in the first two chapters of this volume; so the argument for theism may be said to have been begun in chap. I. If, as Kant taught, all the order in the world, or all the regularity of Nature, as formulated in scientific laws, were imposed by man's mind and had no Real counterpart, the world would, of course, offer no testimony to its origination in divine creativeness; but Kant's theory, and views similar to it in effect, were found to be untenable. Again, if science could be identified with metaphysics of Nature and could also be shewn to imply a rigidly mechanical theory of the physical world, the world's regularity might be conceived as due to fortuitous causes or to behaviour intrinsic to a self-subsistent aggregate of things; but in chap. ii it was submitted that natural science points to neither of these conclusions. That chapter, therefore, also establishes preconditions of a teleological argument by shewing that the world is not self-explanatory, and supplies a necessary link in the reasoning from the world to God. But it was in chap. iv that our hill-top was reached. And, to use a similar figure of speech, the succeeding chapters are a description of the view which then presented itself, as seen otherwise than through the gathered and earth-born mist. The existence of evil in the world, however, was found to be as deter-minative of reasonable theism as is the teleological ordering of the cosmos. Any theory which is compelled to ignore evil, or which can offer no explanation of its forthcomingness, may be ignored. Likewise, any doctrine of divine immanence which abolishes the relative independence and autonomy ascribed to created things, with their delegated causal activities, since it implies that God antecedently wills evil or does evil in order that good may come, is inconsistent with ethical theism. So also is any conception of divine immanence, or of divine revelation, which involves deroga-tion from the moral freedom and personality of humanity. God *and* the world *and* man is the theistic formula for the totality of what is known to exist—if knowledge is but reasonable explana-tion: and no relaxing of the disjunctiveness of the conjunction 'and', in that formula, can be tolerated by theism in the way of compromise with absolutism or monism.

The few metaphysical statements, suggested by empirical knowledge, which can be made as to these three orders of existents may now be set forth.

The world is known interpretatively, or partly through anthro-pic assimilation; and phenomenally, because our first acquaintance with it is in sensory perception. What its constituent elements are *per se* we have no means of knowing. They may be spiritual. But we know the ontal, if through the phenomenal, because pheno-menal knowledge is *relevant to* the ontal. The ontal world must be such as, in its *rapport* with us, to excite our perceptions and to evoke our affective responses to it and our valuations of its appearances. It must have structural detail corresponding to, and at least coextensive with, the structural detail of the phenomenal world. As structure involves relations, and our minds no more create subsistent relations than they posit Real terms, the reign of law in so much of the phenomenal world as we know must have its counterpart in the ontal world. But the portion of the universe which we know is not isolable, as if regularity could obtain in it without obtaining elsewhere: it is what it is because the whole universe is what it is. And the world appears to be an organic whole rather than an aggregate: its stabilisation and its evolutionary progressiveness, which are facts, bespeak interadaptation on a vast scale and of indefinitely pervasive reach. The world has no wisdom, yet it suggests wisdom and art. Only on the supposition that it is designed does its actual nature receive any explanation. The world can have no meaning for itself, but man can discern meaning in it as much as in human behaviour and inventions. If Nature be the utterance of a supreme Spirit, its beauty and sublimity may be the expression of that Spirit's joyful activity. Certainly Nature conveys to us more than it can be in and for itself: a "sense" of something deeply interfused. This "sense" may be mistaken, and Nature's potency to evoke it may conceivably be a meaningless by-product. But as other large facts also suggest a Beyond which is within—an inscrutable background of mystery in which science's facts have their setting, and at the same time an intelligent ordering without which those facts would be a colossal accumulation of undesigned coincidences, the view that the world's meaning, of every kind, is a revelation of God to man is reasonable. These last observations, however, have carried us on to the relations in which, from the point of view of theism, the world stands to God and man.

Man himself is part of the world-problem that is presented to man to solve. As empirical selves we are organic to the world, and the world cannot be adequately discussed apart from man, in so far as he is a part of Nature. Nature is the mother of this wondrous child; and he, in Gregory of Nyssa's phrase, is "the consecrator of the universe". We are not impersonal spectroscopes: it is we who make, out of the potencies of the ontal world, its values as well as its phenomena. It is only in thinking and valuing beings, which 'man' typically denotes, that what Nature 'is equal to' comes to be revealed; and it is only in man that the purpose, as distinct from the art, impressed upon the world discloses itself. The world, apart from man, does not supply grounds from which the God of ethical theism can be interpretatively inferred. It is the moral—or, speaking more comprehensively and truly—the personal status of man that provides one of the essential grounds for that inference.

On the other hand, it is not as 'noümenal man', in Kant's sense, or as a pure ego, that man yields the clue to the world-purpose: for personality and morality are mediated through embodiment and can only be predicated, according to knowledge, of the empirical self which, unlike the soul (so far as we know) is organic to the world. If God "holds the soul attached to Him by its roots" it is not by descending to its depths that we can there find Him; and if by the self is only meant the soul we cannot apply the saying of Clement of Alexandria, "if one knows himself he will know God". There is good reason to believe that the soul or dominant monad in man is not organic to Nature, and that it is known as ontal, and not phenomenally; but it is our knowledge of man in so far as he is organic to the world, together with our knowledge of the world-process in which man is as yet the highest known product, rather than our knowledge as to the human soul, which lends itself for use in the construction of a theistic argument. As to the origin, the process of embodiment, and the continued life of the soul after death, we can gain no light from empirical knowledge. Psychology cannot adopt traducianism, and theism cannot take kindly to Lotze's occasionalistic creationism. There remains the view that embodiment of pre-existent souls is part and parcel of the world's autonomy. But whichever way we turn for an explanatory theory in this connexion we are baffled by difficulties: if the last of the suppositions that have been mentioned be adopted we become puzzled as to what sort of life the souls of men yet to be born are now living, and how it is that they in no wise manifest themselves, as do other and humbler monads, while they pass their sheol-like pre-existence.

Theism, however, has a theodicy, as we have seen, wherewith to meet carpings as to man's being left unable to acquire knowledge about matters concerning which he cannot but be curious: and there we may leave the problem of ignorance. But by way of concluding this brief recapitulation of the knowledge of the self, or of man, in which previous inquiries have resulted, it may be repeated that ethical theism, which takes the realisation of personality and of moral values to be the *raison d'être* of the world, must stand aloof from all philosophical and theological tendencies to belittle the dignity and the rights of human personality, or to disparage man's place in the cosmos. Such a tendency appears in the behaviouristic psychology which would reduce human mentality to physical events; and again in religion moulded by metaphysical rather than by ethical ideas, which has sought to magnify the glory of God by defaming His "image", debasing it to the level of the impersonal stock or stone. The world, inclusive of man, has sometimes been regarded as existing solely for the glory of God and the display of His omnipotence and omniscience. Even S. Paul, who speaks eloquently of "the glorious liberty of the children of God", was capable of likening God's dealings with men to those of a potter making vessels unto honour and unto dishonour out of the lump of clay, and could entertain the notions of election and predestination. And in much of what has passed for Christian theology there has been a blending of Christ's ethical theism with non-ethical anthropology, implying in turn the conception of God as a physical force or an arbitrary will rather than as a father of spirits who respects the rights and privacies of other and humbler persons. All the theological doctrine that may be deducible from the latter conception of God and His relationship to man can be accepted by ethical theism: all that is associated with an idea of God and an idea of man belonging to the former of these types must be anathematised as incongruent with science and ethics.

How knowledge or reasonable belief as to the existence and nature of God is reached from previous knowledge of the world and man has been too recently and uninterruptedly set forth to require recapitulation. But this chapter shall end on the key-note of the key in which it opened. It opened by indicating the connectedness of study of the world (with a view to inferring the nature of its ground) with study of the faculties of the human soul. The former study, in isolation from the latter, may lead to science; but it will not lead to natural philosophy or conduct to metaphysics. It is idle to raise metaphysical questions before studying what knowledge is, or to proceed as if the intelligibility of the ontal world to man did not depend upon anthropic interpretativeness. The study of the human faculties, in other words, is as essential for philosophical knowledge about the world as is attention to the presented data. The pregnant saying of Comte, to the effect that between the self and [knowledge of] the world stands mankind, is one into the form of which a multitude of philosophically important truths might be cast, expressive of the interdependence which exists not only between philosophical studies and issues but also between the processes studied and the actualities involved in them. Thus, between the soul and the world stands the body, which mediates to the soul its phenomenal knowledge of the ontal, its primary categories, its personality; mankind, or intersubjective intercourse, stands between the individual and his morality and personality as well as between him and his objective knowledge of the world, and between him and his rationality; between the world and its values stands man's interest: and so on, indefinitely. And it is precisely this interconnectedness of things that urges the reasonable 'whole man', as contrasted with the unreasonable 'rational man', to seek an explanation, and to find it in the supposition that the world and man constitute an organic whole whose ground is God, and whose *raison d'être* is realisation of the good, or love. None of these three existents is comprehensible without the others, and none of them is knowable by rationality that is not eked out with reasonableness.[1] Some musicians tell us that melody presupposes harmony, or that the chord is the musical unit. I do not profess to understand these statements, but they suggest a concise expression for the theological conclusion to which the lengthy discussion pursued through these two volumes seems to point. God, man, and the world constitute a chord, and none of its three notes has the ring of truth without the accompaniment of the other two. To say the same in terms of another metaphor: the cosmos is no logico-geometrical scheme, but an adventure of divine love.

[1] It would thus seem that a philosophical reason can be assigned for the Gilbertian coupling of "in for a penny in for a pound" with "'tis love that makes the world go round"!

APPENDIX

Note A. *Hypothesis, theory, fictions, etc.*

Any lines that have been drawn between hypothesis and theory, and between the hypothetical and the fictional, are conventional and vary according to taste. 'Hypothesis' has been used sometimes so elastically as to include the indispensable postulates or first principles of a science, the conventional definitions, etc., which distinguish one metric geometry from another, the provisional working-hypothesis as to a particular group of phenomena, and fictitious entities such as caloric fluid and lines of force. Theory has sometimes been distinguished from hypothesis in respect of its greater generality and wider range; or as denoting what is accepted and *de fide*, while hypothesis is tentative and supersedible, perhaps heresy such as is incidental to groping orthodoxy; or as verified, whereas hypothesis is unverifiable or as yet unverified, in one or other of the senses of 'verification' respectively appropriate, *e.g.* to the missing link, to Uranus before it was seen, and to the electron or the ether. The question of word-usage is not important; but distinction, in respect of epistemological status, between propositions and entities ranging from the fictions of professed opportunism to the generalisations of stabilised and comprehensive theory, may prove useful in dealing with questions involving physical science.

When Newton disclaimed the framing of hypotheses he was neither indulging in irony nor misconceiving the nature of his dynamics. In the language of to-day, he intended to be descriptive, not explanatory; scientific, not metaphysical. Newton expressly denied that, by his "mathematical conception" of force, he meant to rehabilitate anything such as we might call the occult quality. From this kind of hypothesis he would refrain; and that is, perhaps, what was chiefly in the mind of his followers who regarded hypotheses as "the poison of the reason and the bane of philosophy".

The most useless kind of occult quality is that of which the *vis dormitiva* may be cited as an instance. Proffered as explanatory, it but restates what is to be explained. The undesigned purposiveness, of which the adaptedness of Nature is sometimes said to be an outcome, but which seems to be the same adaptedness under a new name, is another specimen of this sub-species. Not very different is the entelechy of vitalists; it is certainly occult, and if it subserves explanation, it is explanation of the obscure by the more obscure. There are other species of fiction, however, that have some practical value. One of such is the partial fiction that retains imaginally an element of the perceptual, but is ideal; a simplification that is never actually encountered but, in spite of purposive incorrectness, has utility: *e.g.* the frictionless pulley, the perfect fluid, the isolated magnet-pole, the fictitious experiment such as is used to commend Newton's first law of motion. More completely fictitious are the caloric fluid, which at one time nevertheless served to colligate facts; working-models, such as the various imaginal mechanisms representing the structure of the ether, which do not minister to simplification but to another kind of explanation, viz. reduction to the familiar, however complex or obscure. Science has made use of fictions such as valency-bonds, lines of force, etc., avowedly symbolical and never treated realistically but, like the working-model, facilitating comprehension in quasi-intuitional form. It is impossible to draw hard lines, but perhaps Faraday's lines of force may be said to have been raised from fictional to hypothetical rank when they were mathematically treated by Maxwell. Again the ether would seem to have completed the cycle from fiction, through hypothesis, to theory of vast generality and usefulness, and back to out-worn mythology; although light, etc., can never admit of *mechanical* explanation without the invoking of a medium. The electron is, at the present stage of science, a universally accepted imaginal construct, and in *that* sense a fiction. It is a fiction which is pragmatically and macroscopically verified, in that theory of wide range rests securely upon it: but this is no guarantee that in the future it will not be superseded on account of inconsistency or inadequacy. No one doubts the scientific usefulness of any of the non-perceptual entities, ether, electrons, quanta, space-time; presumably no one holds that all these entities, useful and indispensable as each may be in a certain scientific sphere or universe of discourse, are transparently compatible with one another. Science consequently needs to be somewhat opportunistic; and those of its exponents who conceive its rôle to be but description, *as if* its fictions were facts, and its fictions to be *Hülfsmittel* or provisional scaffolding, need not shrink from confessing that this is so. On the other hand, the scientific realist, who takes the theoretical physics of the day to be ontology, and objects to the word 'fiction' in all its senses, from the most polite to the most offensive, must adopt the heroic attitude of ignoring all lessons from past history, of hoping that all present troubles will be smoothed away, and, as shall be elsewhere submitted, of shutting his eyes to the inevitable issue of at once ontologising the imaginal and kinematicising the physical.

One other type of fictional entity remains to be mentioned, viz. the conceptual, as distinguished from the sensorily imaginal, thus far considered. Of this, again, there are distinct kinds, such as potential energy and entropy in physics, and conceptions such as the *Urthier* of Goethe in biology. The latter of these, called the schematic fiction, is a type, according to analogy with which, all animals were anatomically 'explained' as modifications of it; though it was never supposed to be an extinct creature from which all animals are descended and derived by actual metamorphosis. This particular fancy was not without its scientific usefulness, as it is said to have suggested improved classification, and to have prepared the way for the Darwinian theory.

It will have been observed that the non-Actuality of some fictions is no hindrance to their usefulness; and, this being so in some cases, it well may be so in all. The descriptionist's 'how' may sometimes stand for, or include, 'as if': and correspondence with Actuality, or with some aspect of it, is not necessarily identity therewith. The fiction being non-perceptual, and therefore not admitting of direct or sensible verification, it is selected and adopted solely because it is serviceable; and its services are like those rendered by the hypothesis.

Using 'fiction' to denote entities derived by constructive imagination, abstraction, etc., and 'hypothesis' for hypothetical or suppositional propositions, we may observe that hypotheses often, but not always, involve fictions. In some hypotheses the supposed or interpolated term may be an Actual or spatio-temporal thing, homogeneous with the data, and a completion of them —as in the case of the missing link, or of Uranus before the telescope was focussed on it. In other hypotheses the interpolated term may be non-homogeneous with the data, a substitution rather than a completion, and unverifiable by way of becoming a percept: then we have what may politely be called a fictional hypothesis, whether it have the prestige of the atomic theory, whether it be discarded—as was the corpuscular theory of light, or whether it even be professedly fictional, as in the case of the hypothesis of electric fluids. Hypotheses often are 'verifiable': only that word will now mean something different from perceptual presentableness, viz. co-ordination of facts, as observed up to date. Hypotheses may be selected as more serviceable, as are fictions, or as more probable guesses at truth.

The indispensableness of hypothesis to science has already been indicated, in connexion with the method and logic of induction. Like the spider's self-spun web or the builder's scaffolding, the hypothesis of the physicist enables him to poise, while on the way to what may prove firm standing-ground. And, more than this, mere observation and classification of facts, or the method that Bacon asserted to leave little room to acuteness and strength of genius, is incapable of yielding what we now regard as science. The happy guess is essential. "Seek and ye shall find" is the principle on which scientific discovery is based. But the seeking is not mere rummaging. To approach Nature with a blank mind, or with a mind approximating to the *tabula rasa*, is to find nothing worth finding. Kepler tells how he worked for years, refuting conjecture after conjecture, before arriving at the discovery that the orbits are ellipses. On the other hand, happy guesses may remain but guesses. Some few of the guesses of the ancient Greeks have proved happy, and they have sometimes been regarded as discoveries and anticipations of great generalisations of modern science. But "he only discovers who proves". Not untested fancy, for which sometimes the honourable name of 'philosophy' is arrogated, but shrewdness based on experience, constitutes the imagination that produces genuine and scientific hypotheses.

In the middle part of last century Rankine complained that hypothesis was then being taken by men of science to be as authoritative as fact, and that hypothesising was being confounded with deduction. The latter mistake led, in the rationalistic school of physics founded by Descartes, to the decrying of hypothesis and the exaltation of what passed for deductiveness. It still persists, in some measure, though the situation has greatly changed since Rankine initiated the modern tendency, really as old as Hobbes though in the meantime suppressed by realism, that has here been called descriptionism. The lesser authoritativeness of hypothesis, as compared with fact that is never wholly devoid of theory, and, at the same time, its indispensableness can best be appreciated after noting the several rôles which the framing of hypotheses serves.

Hypotheses, even some that are avowedly fictional and not only unverified but also unverifiable, have heuristic value. As possible anticipations of possible experience, they lead an observer to look, and sometimes to see or find. They are suggestive and directive of experiment. Again, they may serve to colligate phenomenal facts and render comprehension of them possible, while destitute of ontological virtue: they may describe in terms of 'as if'. They may even enable us to predict phenomena, and so reveal themselves to have some relation to ontal truth, without implying the Reality of their conceptual entities. That bodies behave as if they were constituted as the physical theory of the period regards them as constituted is by no means logically equivalent to the assertion that they are, or must be, so constituted. We err when we expect more enlightenment of that sort from the hypotheses than from the facts themselves. The equations arrived at by use of the ether-theory survive; the ether itself is a hypothesis with which many physicists now dispense, as scaffolding for which there is no further use. Nevertheless, hypotheses form the premisses of deduction, the consequences of which may be experimentally tested. So they stimulate research and lead to verification or to rejection of theory. As for the more theoretical, as contrasted with these practical, uses, it need not be pointed out that hypotheses minister to classification and subsumption of facts under laws; nor that they promote simplification in the sense that they may reduce the number of *explicanda*. But simplicity or economy, heuristic value, and verity as to the ontal, are by no means necessarily coincident.

Lastly, the conceptual entities of pure mathematics are fictions, in the sense that they owe their existence as ideas to the abstracting and idealising activities of minds. The word 'fiction' originally denotes what is thus fashioned or made; and retention of it, in that sense, need not give offence, so long as the derived meaning of falsity, *i.e.* antithesis with truth rather than with 'position', is not irrelevantly insinuated. The eternal truths or laws of the pure sciences, again, are not necessarily valid of facts.

Note B. *The ontological argument*

The ontological argument is once or twice referred to in these pages as possessing a unique importance if it were valid. It is the only argument, derived from existential or theoretical considerations as distinct from concepts of value, which attempts to prove the existence of an infinite or perfect being. Hence it is important to distinguish it from other arguments, in close conjunction with which it has been placed by some philosophers who have made use of it; and also from expressions of religious faith, to the effect that the best that we can conceive and hope for must be. The argument has nothing in common with an expression of faith, save that faith may assert the same proposition that the argument would demonstrate: it purports to be a logically rigorous proof, if not the only theistic proof that is of that nature. And it has nothing in common, save again as to its conclusion, with arguments which turn on the origination or causation of our idea of a perfect being. The ontological argument, properly so called, is that the idea of the most perfect being, and that idea alone, involves the Real existence of its ideal content. And this alone is what is in mind whenever the phrase 'the ontological argument' is here used.

What have been professed to be restatements of this argument, in a form to which Kant's criticisms are innocuous or irrelevant, are really substitutes for it which are irrelevant both to the old argument and to the Kantian criticism thereof. For instance, it is not the Hegelian's Absolute that is in question in the historical argument, but the rationalistic theist's God: so it is no reply to Kant to point out that he does not demolish the grounds on which the 'God' of Hegel, or the 'God' of Spinoza either, is asserted to exist. And the recently expressed comment that the Kantian epistemology is only applicable to knowledge concerning what is given in sensation, and consequently cannot invalidate the *a priori*, is only pertinent if, among humanly conceived ideas, there are any which are not ultimately derived from sensory objects. Until instances of such ideas are adduced, the criticisms passed by Hume and Kant upon the ontological argument will not have been refuted.

Note C. *The 'proper' infinite and its importation into speculative theology*

The new infinite—to adopt its popular name—is primarily a property of classes. A class is an aggregate of terms or members, to all of which some common predicate attaches, called the class-concept. Thus men form a class, denoted by the class-concept Man or humanity, of which George V is a member. The relation of a member to its class is not identical with that of a part to a whole. There are wholes that are not aggregates, and aggregates that are not classes. The new infinite also applies to series, which are classes whose members have some order. Infinite classes are constituted or given at once by definition of the class-concept, so that successive synthesis, such as is involved in the older conception of infinity, is superfluous, and endlessness is irrelevant. Of non-serial collections it cannot be said that they have or have not ends. Some infinite series have ends while others have not. The series of instants between the beginning of time and a given moment is infinite though it has one end; that between any two instants of time has two ends. The positive characteristic of the new infinite is thus described by Dedekind: a collection is infinite if it can be put in a one-to-one correspondence with, or is equal (in number of terms) to, one of its own parts. What is meant may be explained by the following instance. If we write in a row the series of natural numbers, 1, 2, 3, 4, etc., and underneath it the series of even numbers, 2, 4, 6, 8, etc., there is always a number in the lower series to correspond to one in the upper series, and neither series includes the same number twice. These two infinite series have the same number of terms, though the lower differs from the upper series in being non-inclusive of the whole and infinite series of odd numbers. The number of numbers in the natural series is not greater than, but equal to, its part, the even series. And it is this equality in respect of number of terms, between part and whole, that constitutes the infinity of the whole. Each member of the part corresponds to a member in the whole, so that an infinite collection can be defined as one that can be represented, or (in the language of Leibniz's monadology) 'mirrored', as to complexity of structure or number of terms, by one of its parts. Not negative endlessness but positive self-representativeness is the characteristic of the new infinity; and self-representation can be illustrated by the ideal example of a picture containing a picture of itself, which in turn must contain a picture of itself, and so on. Again, the infinity of a collection is not altered by subtraction of the finite, or even of the infinite, from it.

The new notion is based on a new definition of number. So long as a number was defined in terms of $n + 1$, all numbers could but be finite, for trans-finite numbers would be excluded by the definition. And some authorities think that the new theory only seems to escape the apparent contradiction involved in infinite number by incorporating the contradiction into its definition, violating the concepts of whole, part, and equality, in the act of introducing them. But as other philosophers and mathematicians discern no contradictoriness here, it becomes the non-mathematician to refrain from passing an opinion. On another and a more important issue, however, he may pronounce without presumption. Actuality contains numerable things, but not numbers; and if the 'proper' infinite has significance for pure mathematics, it does not follow that it has applicability to anything Actual. The illustration of the self-representative picture or map is obviously but 'possible', not Actual; and that in infinite time Tristram

Shandy, taking two years to write the history of two days, could complete his biography, seems to preclude application of the new mathematics to existent things. There may be formal validity in its principles; but nothing existent can be infinite in the new sense.

Theology professes to be concerned with the existent or Actual; and the Actualities with which it deals are not classes or series whose members are factitiously correlatable with numbers. It is therefore antecedently impossible for the new infinity to have relevance within its sphere. Nevertheless attempts have been made to find it useful. And if the procedure were legitimate, the results would doubtless be of interest.

The earliest and simplest suggestion of this kind was offered by one of the chief pioneers of the new mathematics. Bolzano, in his *Paradoxien des Unendlichen*, p. 9, says: "We call God infinite, because we must attribute to Him powers of more than one kind which possess an infinite magnitude (*Grösse*)". But though magnitude, or capacity for the relations of greater and less, is predicable of divine attributes, it does not seem possible to conceive of any one of them as a whole which has a part equal to itself. Infinity is therefore inapplicable to them.

More recently the new idea of infinity has been turned to account for elucidation of the incomprehensible mystery involved in the doctrine of the Trinity. There can be three, or any number, of infinite manifolds in one, as has been already observed: so infinite manifolds can form an infinite triune system. And Prof. Keyser (*The New Infinite and the Old Theology*, p. 88) regards it as plain that, in the doctrine of three Persons in one God, "we have to do with the structure of infinite manifolds". But whatever view be adopted as to the ontological status of the divine hypostases, from modalism to tritheism, it would seem impossible to regard them as manifolds of discrete terms. A Person in the Sabellian sense is not a collection of separable states, and a Person, if analogous to a human person, is not a series or an aggregate of mutually exclusive experiences.

Prof. Royce has approached the problem of the two natures in the Person of Christ from the point of view of the newer infinity (*The World and the Individual*, vol. 1, Supplementary Essay; *The Hibbert Journal*, 1, 1). He submits that Christ may be infinitely less than God, and one of an infinite number of 'parts' within the divine whole, yet able not "to count it robbery to be equal with God", provided that He has received an infinite expression in the universe by immortal life of perfect (infinite) self-attainment. But to speak of infinite expression or infinite self-attainment as if 'infinite' then meant what it does in the new mathematics is no more than a play upon words. The 'infinity' of Cantor and Dedekind is a definite and highly specialised technical term applicable only within the restricted sphere of classes; whereas Royce invests it with a vague or analogical signification. Similarly the 'self-representation' of trans-finite mathematics is a technical conception of precise range; it has nothing in common, save its name, with self-representation in the ordinary sense. God may be self-representative, but may hardly be conceived as a class in a one-to-one correspondence with another class which is a part of Him. It is overlooked by this philosopher, as also by the mathematician whose theological speculation on the Trinity has been cited, that the wholes, parts, and members of which mathematicians speak are not comparable with the existents contemplated by theology. So long as technical terms are not abused the newer mathematical doctrine does not lend itself for describing the self-limited Deity as in a definite sense infinite; and it is a mistake to suppose that theology may rest content if only it may somehow cling to the *word* 'infinite'.

One further instance of application of the new infinity to theology may be adduced. Prof. Keyser has dealt with the problem of the relation of divine fore-knowledge to human freedom. As we have already seen, complete knowledge of the past, including no knowledge of the future, if identifiable with knowledge of an infinite series, might be called infinite knowledge though falling short of omniscience. And such knowledge, it is observed by Prof. Keyser, would admit of reconciliation with our freewill, because not including fore-knowledge, round which the old difficulty centres. It may be remarked that it is precisely omniscience, as including foreknowledge of human volitions, that theologians have been anxious to ascribe to God; and if this be not assured, they would care little for being allowed to call the divine knowledge of the past 'infinite'. But it is more to the point to observe that when Prof. Keyser argues that, since infinite knowledge of the past is of the same 'dignity' as knowledge of both past and future, therefore freedom is compatible with the 'dignity' of omniscience, though not with omniscience, he seems to glide from the technical sense of 'dignity' (Cantor's *Mächtigkeit*) as it figures in trans-finite mathematics to the sense which the word bears in common discourse. And that tendency vitiates all the forthcoming attempts to import the 'proper' or 'new' infinity into the sphere of theology.

Note D. *The doctrine of the Trinity*

The developement of the doctrine of the Trinity by the Christian Church was a consequence of the interpretation of Christ's personality in terms of the idea of incarnation. The doctrine of the Incarnation asserts that the One God was the sole subject of the mental life of Christ. The doctrine of the Trinity was fashioned in order to explain how this incarnate subject, and also the non-incarnate Father and the Holy Spirit, could be embraced in the one undivided Godhead. On the one hand it was necessary to avoid a separation of several subjects within the Godhead; for that would be tritheism. On the other hand it was necessary to assert distinctions, intrinsic to the Deity, in virtue of which there should be an eternal difference, in some respect, between God as Father and fount of all being, God as the subject or soul of the God-man, and God as the Holy Spirit. Yet these differences were not to consist merely in various modes of energising, or to pertain to economic rôles, attributes, or aspects, or to be adjectival. In the language of modern logic, the Church would fain conceive of them as characterised rather than as characterising, or as substantival rather than as predicates.

Indeed it may be said that from Tertullian to Aquinas the expounders of the doctrine of the Trinity were seeking to find a notion of a kind of entity, denoted by the technical term 'Person', which is neither an individual nor an attribute of an individual, but is intermediate between the substantival and the adjectival; or which is the ground or basis of a special function rather than a special function, and yet stops short of being an individual subject. In the *res substantivae*, so called, of Tertullian; in the Cappadocian fathers' *hypostases*, sometimes spoken of as being, and sometimes as having, the respective ἰδιότητες of aseity, begottenness, and procession; in their τρόποι τῆς ὑπάρξεως, which are neither subjects nor subjective states nor modes of action; and in the 'relations' of Aquinas, which are not accidents, nor distinctions set up by our knowledge-processes, but really subsistent *personae* though not really distinct in God: in all these and similar descriptions we see attempts to express a notion of an entity of this kind. It is but natural that in seeking for a notion of what is intermediate between easily imaginable or conceivable entities, but is not itself imaginable or conceivable, the same thinker should, on different occasions, use expressions and analogies suggestive of tritheism and modes of speech implicative of monarchianism; and it is not surprising to find, at the end of a treatise on the Trinity, a great doctor confessing that he has been discoursing about a mystery that is above reason, on which analogies drawn from human experience, and concepts furnished by logic and philosophy, throw no light. But one thing has been made clear by an age-long attempt definitely to conceive what we now see to be obviously inconceivable: and that is that the clearest and most assured statements of the doctors leave no doubt but that tritheism is repugnant to the Church and that orthodoxy, whenever it is not vacillating or vague, is as monarchian as Sabellianism. If the Persons of the Trinity be not Gods, and if any 'mode of being' intermediate between the substantival existent and the adjectival subsistent be inconceivable, then nothing but rigid monotheism or monarchianism is left, and academic orthodoxy is at least logical in being modalistic. The doctrine of the Trinity, however, when thus interpreted, offers no fresh contribution to theism. It possesses no unique philosophical import, and it can scarcely have any religious or devotional significance. This it only acquires when it is subconsciously interpreted, as probably it is by the religious user, tritheistically. If God is triune only in a sense in which any human being can be called a trinity, the fact seems insignificant both for theology and for practical religion. On the other hand, the recent tendency of orthodox theologians to speak of God as 'a social being', and to appropriate such philosophical advantages as the conception of a plural Deity would offer, involves an unconscious desertion of the catholic faith.

Note E. *Immortality*

Arguments for and against human immortality, or life after death, may be classified thus:

I. Arguments not presupposing theism.
  (1) Empirical.
  (2) Metaphysical—*i.e.* ontological.
  (3) Ethical.

II. Arguments presupposing theism, to the effect that immortality is, or is not, a corollary of theism.

I. (1) The form in which the question as to human immortality is usually propounded, viz. has man an immortal soul? tacitly assumes that the man is primarily his body. And there are doubtless reasons why this assumption should be ingrained in common thought leavened with science. Matter seems, to those who have not pursued philosophical inquiries, so much better known than mind or spirit, and mind seems to be so much more dependent upon body than changes in the body are dependent upon mental activities. But while science shews the close connexion between brain and thought it does not warrant the conclusion that the soul and its activities are products of the brain, and that they must vanish when the physical organism dies. The sensation with which we are acquainted is mediated by the body; but it is not a scientifically established fact that the kind of body which we now possess is essential for the soul's life and possession of personality. And there is no scientific reason for believing that the soul shares the change and decay of material things. Their dissolution is generally describable as resolution into parts; but the soul cannot be supposed to consist of separable parts, or to be an aggregate of mind-dust. For all that physiology knows, the soul may at death enter into connexion with another kind of body, about which, however, it is futile to speculate. It is possible that while the body that now is determines the nature of the soul's activities, sensations, etc., as we know them, it at the same time imposes limitations upon the potentialities of the soul; and that though the death of the body may put an end to sensation it may be the beginning of a non-sensible experience, or of an experience in which another kind of *rapport* than that which constitutes sensation is substituted for it. Empirical science, therefore, cannot infer, from the fact that the present life of the self is dependent on that of the present body, the impossibility of a future life of the soul. Science here leaves room for faith.

On the other hand, psychical research cannot be said as yet to have established the soul's survival of bodily death. The proofs which have been alleged are based chiefly on facts concerning what is called cross-reference: *i.e.* two independent mediums may write fragments, both series of which are meaningless by themselves but yield sense when pieced together. But communication from a disembodied spirit is not to be taken to be the only and the certain explanation of the facts until, *e.g.*, telepathy of the living has been shewn to be inadmissible.

(2) Metaphysical arguments for the immortality of the soul, of several kinds, were put forth by Plato. One of these was based on the fancy that knowledge is reminiscence; others rest on the mistaken notion that knowledge is pure thought about pure essences, or is eternal and implies eternal knowers. Perhaps the most influential of them is that (in the *Phaedo*) which sets out from the assertion that the essence of the soul is life, whence it is concluded that the soul is essentially living. Of course, if the soul be defined as the reified abstraction, life, to speak of a mortal soul involves self-contradiction; but, like all *a priori* proofs, this one assumes that the definition from which the desired consequent is deducible has application to anything that is actual.

Kant brought the same charge, amongst others, against the rational psychology of his day. This, proceeding on lines laid down by Descartes, deduced a *res cogitans* from the empirically given *cogito*, identified this *res* with substance, in the most abstract sense of the term, and asserted it to be imperishable because simple or indiscerptible. Plainly this reasoning is only a linkage of abstract ideas; that the soul, the actuality of which is demanded by the facts of observable human mentality, is a substance as thus conceived, and is consequently imperishable or self-subsistent as well as indiscerptible, is a question of fact, not of ideas, and one which the forthcoming facts do not enable us to answer in the positive.

It may be observed that if the arguments based on definitions of substance, etc., were valid, they would not serve to establish personal immortality: survival of soul-substance is not necessarily continuity of personality. Yet it is immortality in the latter sense that alone is of human interest, of religious worth, and of significance for theistic theology. Some philosophers assert that memory of the previous life, or lives, is essential to personal immortality; others, deeming memory to be conditioned by the body, credit the soul with a power to retain the effects of experiences of the embodied life, *e.g.* wisdom and love, even if memory be lost. This, however, is dogma concerning the unknowable. And whenever immortality is asserted on metaphysical grounds that are independent of theistic belief or exclusive of such belief, as when souls are identified with self-subsistent differentiations of The Absolute, it would seem that the limits of knowledge are transcended and that definitions of concepts are confounded with matters of fact or actualities.

(3) Moral arguments belonging to class I all rest on ethical postulates which, apart from theism, are uncertain or improbable. Thus, one of Plato's arguments assumes that the soul is made for virtue, *i.e.* for freeing itself from

bodily passions, and concludes that the soul is destined to be separated from the body. Another, resembling Kant's argument which is confessed to rest upon a postulate, assumes the final harmonisation of virtue and happiness: immortality is a condition of the realisation of the highest good. But, apart from theism, there is no ground for reasonable belief as to the realisation of the highest good.

The outcome of the foregoing review of arguments which do not presuppose theism is that a future life is not impossible or inconceivable, but, on the other hand, is not demonstrable.

II. With the presupposition of theism we pass into the sphere of probability and faith. Immortality becomes a matter of more or less reasonable belief, as distinct from deducibility from assured metaphysical principles or from more or less arbitrary postulations concerning the harmonising of moral experience. It is no matter, however, of subjective or personal desires, e.g. for the continuance of life or of love, but rather a demand for coherence in what is, as a matter of fact, a moral universe. The world would not be irrational, in the logical sense, were the present life the only life; but it is a further question whether the world would be reasonable, or rational in the teleological sense: in other words, whether theism does not imply human immortality.

Theists are not altogether agreed on this point. Those who incline toward absolute monism are sometimes disposed to disparage human personality, to regard it as unworthy of survival, and to speak of the conservation of personal values, universalised, in abstraction from the personal bearers of them. But in so far as monism is approached, theism is deserted: wherefore, strictly speaking, these views are irrelevant to the present inquiry. Some theists, however, consider that, before we can assert immortality to be an implication of theism, it is necessary to know more than is known concerning God's purpose for the world. The facts and generalisations which receive an adequate explanation in the postulate of an intelligent and ethical world-ground, it is said, do not of themselves authorise belief in the *perfect* reasonableness of the world, but only in so much of reasonableness as we actually find. It may be the divine purpose in the world to produce moral personalities; but it is a further venture of faith, and a venture which transcends reasonable belief, to assert that the divine purpose includes the perfecting of finite moral persons, or provision for the fulfilment of their aspirations toward holiness and harmony with the will of God.

At first sight this representation, that empirically established theism does not imply immortality, may seem to be more congruent with the inferences reached in this volume than is the opposite view. But, on further examination, the conclusion appears doubtful. The facts, of which theism is the interpretation, may of themselves indicate no more than that the world is a moral order to the extent of producing moral persons and the conditions of rational and moral life. But, just because moral personality is what it is, this interpretation seems to involve more than do the facts themselves. If the *raison d'être* of the world were merely to produce moralised persons and not to provide for their perduringness, the world-purpose could be described as moral, but not in the sense of seeking the highest conceivable good: a Devil might cause moral beings to emerge, in order to tantalise them. A moral order, in the latter sense, must not only produce moral beings: it must also respect moral persons and satisfy moral demands. God cannot be an ethically perfect Being and not respect the moral aspirations of the personalities which He has called into existence:

> Thou madest man, he knows not why,
> He thinks he was not made to die ;
> And Thou hast made him: Thou art just.

The world, in short, cannot safely be regarded as realising a *divine* purpose unless man's life continues after death If the world is inexplicable without God, its purpose is immoral without divine righteousness. But righteousness is not merely compensating justice. Just distribution of rewards and punishments is no function of the present dispensation; and, if the only reward of virtue be virtue, it is no function of the future dispensation. The righteousness which theism must ascribe to God consists rather in provision of adequate opportunities for the developement of all that is potential in God-given personality, conservation of the valuable, and love such as precludes the mockery of scheming that a rational creature's guiding light through life shall be a Will o' the wisp.

INDEX